The
CARDINALS WAY

ALSO BY HOWARD MEGDAL

The Baseball Talmud

Taking the Field

Wilpon's Folly

The CARDINALS WAY

How One Team Embraced Tradition and Moneyball at the Same Time

HOWARD MEGDAL

THOMAS DUNNE BOOKS
St. Martin's Press
New York

THOMAS DUNNE BOOKS.
An imprint of St. Martin's Press.

THE CARDINALS WAY. Copyright © 2016 by Howard Megdal. All rights reserved.
For information, address
St. Martin's Press, 175 Fifth Avenue, New York, N.Y. 10010.

www.thomasdunnebooks.com
www.stmartins.com

Designed by Kathryn Parise

The Library of Congress Cataloging-in-Publication Data is available upon request.

ISBN 978-1-250-05831-7 (hardcover) ISBN 978-1-250-90045-6 (paperback)
ISBN 978-1-4668-6239-5 (e-book)

Our books may be purchased in bulk for promotional, educational, or business use. Please contact your local bookseller or the Macmillan Corporate and Premium Sales Department at (800) 221-7945, extension 5442, or by e-mail at MacmillanSpecialMarkets@macmillan.com.

First Edition: February 2016

*To Rachel, the Branch Rickey of wives, and Mirabelle and Juliet,
my favorite prospects with limitless ceilings*

Contents

Prologue		1
1	The Cardinal Idea	11
2	The Language of George Kissell	18
3	Bill DeWitt Jr.	41
4	Luhnow Enters	55
5	Happy Days Are Here Again	124
6	After He's Gone	164
Epilogue: Transition and the		
Irreplaceable Cardinal		256
Acknowledgments		275
Notes		279
Index		283

The CARDINALS WAY

Prologue

For years everyone had been telling Mike Matheny how great the Cardinals were, and in April 2014, sitting in the visiting manager's office at Great American Ball Park in Cincinnati, Matheny finally had enough. It was Matheny at peak Midwestern modesty.

If somebody told you Mike Matheny was the newest star in Hollywood, you'd buy it. But really, he belongs to a different Hollywood era physically and in manner, with intense blue eyes and the countenance of the guy you'd bet your money on in a western blockbuster's climactic gunfight.

He looks like a manager. He sounds like a manager. And when Cardinals general manager John Mozeliak started looking for the person to continue the franchise's success after the 2011 World Series championship, Matheny's presence and ties to the organization made him the easy choice. His game-management skills are oft discussed and still developing. His relationships with people are why he has the job.

With reporters, Matheny answers the questions he wants to answer. And he doesn't dodge others: he flat out tells you he doesn't wish to respond.

But it would be a mistake to think his focus implies he has taciturn interactions with his players. Nearly every Cardinal has a story about a conversation with Matheny at a key time in his career, almost always initiated by the skipper. Still just forty-three as the 2014 season began, Matheny's ability to come in and succeed Tony La Russa, a legendary manager, isn't talked about often, largely because of how seamlessly it happened.

Matheny took over in 2012 and led the Cardinals to the NLCS. In 2013, his Cardinals won the pennant before falling to the Boston Red Sox in the World Series. In 2014, they returned to the postseason, and lost in the NLCS once again. And as this book went to press in August 2015, the Cardinals were on a pace to win well over 100 games, with a Tom Verducci story about them in *Sports Illustrated* using both "beast" and "superteam" in the headline.

Coming on the heels of Tony La Russa's 2011 World Series championship in his final season, the Cardinals have put together the kind of sustained success that is rare in baseball, drawing all kinds of attention and a simple question.

How are they doing it?

Accordingly, there'd been a great deal of talk about "the Cardinals Way." It had come to represent many different things in the public eye and media discussions: a code of conduct, a particular outlook on baseball, a moral compass. It had been co-opted, used as shorthand, and Matheny was sick of all the praise.

"I don't even want to use the *Cardinals Way* term anymore," Matheny said. "But that whole idea is really something to be inside this clubhouse and inside more importantly the minor league clubhouse. About what it's supposed to look like and not really for commercialization or for promotion.

"I think it got out of hand to the point where it's ugly to people outside of this organization. No good comes from it. And I think it's put people on the offensive. And they have all the reason in the world [to want to beat the Cardinals].... You know, it's like we're out there running, carrying this big banner, and that's not necessarily—not at all—who we are."[1]

You can understand where Matheny's coming from. After all, who needs teams more motivated to play you? Other fans around baseball took similar

Prologue

exception to the consistent refrain about Cardinals fans being the "best fans in baseball," as if the way the Cardinals (and many, many other teams) choose to thank their fans for support had turned into a boast by those very fans.

A Twitter account even sprung up, @BestFansStLouis, highlighting awful things Cardinals fans would say on Twitter. What this proved, I couldn't tell you. Finding disgusting sentiments on the cesspool that is Twitter doesn't take long. And "best fans in baseball" is a fundamentally different concept from "perfect fanbase, purged of anything petty or nasty." In my experience, Cardinals fans do boo less and are more gracious when an opposing player makes a great play. They show up more, and more consistently. Their local television ratings in 2014 were the highest of any MLB team.

But this isn't a group of fans trying to maintain modesty—this is a key member of the Cardinals, trying to avoid entirely deserved praise. Let's take a step back and think about that. The Cardinals largely avoid publicizing the Cardinals Way as an idea, large or small. The name itself comes from a manual, written originally by George Kissell, a coach whom the Cardinals employed from 1940 until his death in 2008. Kissell was signed by Branch Rickey, meaning that the team's minor league player-development staff is either directly trained by a man Rickey hired or works from a manual created by that man. This is how directly the Cardinals connect to the creation of the farm system itself.

That isn't new, though. The attention to the Cardinals Way in recent years stems from the Cardinals' winning. The Cardinals made the postseason and advanced at least one round each season between 2011 and 2014. Notably, this was the first time the Cardinals had made the postseason four consecutive years.

And the Cardinals were not just winning but doing so while seeming to have a bottomless pit of talent to draw from, should anyone currently on their major league team falter. Also, the major league team was largely homegrown: seventeen of the twenty-five players on the 2014 postseason roster came through the Cardinals farm system.

Had the New York Yankees managed to build the kind of organizational strength the Cardinals have, can you imagine them trying to step back from the praise and, yes, the envy engendered by what the St. Louis Cardinals have created? Please—they'd have told Mariano Rivera to step aside, and named Rivera Avenue "The Yankee Way" instead.

But when I first started looking deep into what the St. Louis Cardinals were, how they'd created what has to be considered the model organization for Major League Baseball in the twenty-first century, I heard the same pleas from nearly everybody I spoke to—that the Cardinals weren't trying to prove they were smarter than everybody else, weren't trying to draw attention to themselves. I spent hundreds of hours with scores of people from the organization, and I can tell you, this was no pose of false modesty.

In working on this book, spending days, weeks, and months with everyone in this organization from owner Bill DeWitt Jr. to current and former Cardinals John Mozeliak, Dan Kantrovitz, Jeff Luhnow, Sig Mejdal, Gary LaRocque, and many others, I've learned those claims come from a deep sense that, while they take pride in what they've built, and what the Cardinals mean to the whole of baseball, they don't believe in relying purely on what has already worked as the road map to what will work now and in the future. Sure, there are traditions and practices—particularly through the rediscovery of statistical analysis, first pioneered by Branch Rickey, and reintroduced to the Cardinals by DeWitt's hiring of Luhnow, along with the on-field, dynamic work of Kissell—but they are the starting point for how the Cardinals determine what to do moving forward. And the upheaval caused by the hacking scandal—an effort by a member or members of the Cardinals' front office to break into the Houston Astros' computer database, where Jeff Luhnow is now the general manager, leading to an FBI investigation and the termination of Scouting Director Chris Correa by the Cardinals already—has only expedited the team's need to search for how to maintain that continuity, even as the team's succession plan gets challenged on multiple fronts.

But the challenge, from within and without, is not new. That need for in-

Prologue

novation not only drove the fundamental realignment of how the Cardinals operated over the past decade and powers everything Mozeliak and company are doing even now, but also simultaneously reflected and traced back to the work Branch Rickey himself did—Bill DeWitt Sr., father of the current owner, at his side—to take the Cardinals out of the poorhouse and into a position of royalty in the National League, a place they've held for a disproportionate amount of the one hundred years since.

How the Cardinals find themselves in this enviable position within the league, drawing so much attention for a phrase that does little more than describe how and why the Cardinals act, is not some secret formula or words scribbled by George Kissell many decades ago.

The Cardinals of today are very much a product of Kissell's work for many decades. They are also the Cardinals of today because of decisions DeWitt made, back in 2003, to completely change the business model of the team, from an old-school approach to a balancing between traditional methods and analytics. They are reformed in a vision put forward by Jeff Luhnow, who made the leap from business-turnaround expert to senior baseball executive in weeks, in the teeth of an often hostile working environment (more than we even knew at the time, it turns out) and skeptical press. And it is up to all of them, led by DeWitt and Mozeliak, to continue innovating, with the need to find consensus within a battle-scarred organization renewed by what DeWitt has described as "a rogueish act." In essence, this is the reverse of the original action that led to DeWitt hiring Luhnow in the first place back in 2003. As this book goes to press, the Cardinals, without any desire to change philosophies, are deciding just what the hacking scandal means to their future. No one will question a decision to change course, and future decisions by Major League Baseball or a court of law may force greater changes upon them.

But for the Cardinals of the last decade, the changed course was voluntary, enormous. And in the midst—from 2000 to 2006—of six play-off appearances, a pair of National League pennants, and the 2006 World Series championship, it appeared to many to be close to madness.

The Cardinals who ultimately emerged from this process begun by Luhnow and DeWitt were a collection of extremely bright people of utterly divergent backgrounds and personalities. You couldn't sit in a room with the understated brilliance of Dan Kantrovitz and masterful scout Charlie Gonzalez, as passionate as he is encyclopedic, and conclude that the Cardinals employ one specific personality type.

The results have been extraordinary, and the methods seemingly obvious, as with all great decisions in retrospect. Analytics helped the Cardinals take a leap forward as a baseball team. And that the Cardinals, in particular, incorporated statistical analysis helped analytics become the industry standard.

Incorporating analytics, through the hiring of Luhnow starting in September 2003, allowed the team to revamp the way they acquired players, particularly through the draft. Luhnow took a microscope to everything the Cardinals did, and from the draft to the study of their pitchers' mechanics, plenty of prototypical analytical practices became part of the Cardinals Way.

Interestingly, however, almost nothing changed about either the Kissell-inspired on-field practices or with the perhaps more significant ways Kissell preached for coaches and managers to emotionally connect with players.

As DeWitt put it, though, in our first interview in August 2013, "There were great people who were here when we got here. And so the Cardinals had that tradition of development that we were able to build on. But if you don't have the talent, all the development in the world won't get you good players."

DeWitt didn't purchase the Cardinals until 1996. But the foundation he described dates back a hundred years. Incredibly, the intellectual and personal through-line from the very start of major league teams entering the player-development business to the present-day Cardinals is clear, more practical than symbolic, and essentially guaranteed the flip side of DeWitt's point.

Once the Cardinals figured out how to input more talent into their system, a hundred-year tradition, complete with established practices dating back to Branch Rickey and Bill DeWitt, Sr., and refined by George Kissell, supercharged the results. An incredible tradition merged with a group of great baseball minds to maximize what baseball's new collective-bargaining agreements eventually forced other teams to try to emulate.

The St. Louis Cardinals, ahead of the curve on the very existence of the farm system that transformed twentieth-century baseball, have once again ridden a combination of foresight and attention to detail at every level to represent a particular moment in baseball history here in the twenty-first century.

False starts occurred along the way—a skeptical group within the organization itself, the ill-fated 2004 draft, among others. Realistically, what is astonishing about the St. Louis Cardinals over the past decade isn't their sometimes-contentious path to their current state. Finding baseball executives to argue strategy, or scouts to disagree over a particular player, might be the easiest task on earth. And it appears that the rancor that led to the hacking of Luhnow's new team's database came from personal, not philosophical differences—Chris Correa, for instance, was a Luhnow hire with full analytical buy-in.

The marvel is how completely the Cardinals of today are both the manifestation of a vision Branch Rickey had a hundred years ago, and how much of the team's current business model both fits what Rickey envisioned and is practiced by direct acolytes of Rickey himself.

There is no Cardinals Way without George Kissell, signed by Branch Rickey. There is no Cardinals Way without Red Schoendienst, signed by Branch Rickey.

There's no analytic revamp of the Cardinals without Bill DeWitt Jr., raised in and around baseball by Bill DeWitt Sr., whom Rickey hired at age thirteen and worked with for decades. There's no analytics revamp of the Cardinals without Luhnow, hired by DeWitt less than a month after they first met. And bringing in Luhnow, and the analytics team he assembled, wasn't some rejection of Cardinals tradition—the very concept of an analytics department dates back to Rickey, who hired Travis Hoke,[2] baseball's first team-employed statistician, in 1914 to chart every game "with base and out efficiency" in mind.

The hiring of Luhnow was characterized by some in the organization and many outsiders as a new direction for the Cardinals, a break with tradition. Really, it was nothing more than a restoration of a key component of Branch Rickey's tradition, dating back a hundred years. And the key to the Cardinals sustaining that success in the years to come will depend on maintaining that level of innovation, even as that talent finds homes all around the league.

It also represented something vital for the industry itself, in the post-*Moneyball* world. The extent to which that book created sides, a supposed war of ideas, is frequently cited by both those with primarily analytics background and the scouts. So for the Cardinals to incorporate both worldviews into a highly successful franchise—perhaps the most successful of the twenty-first century to date—signaled to everybody that not only would integrating the two approaches be possible, it would be the wisest possible course.

Accordingly, the St. Louis Cardinals, circa the 2010s, will mean something significant to baseball fans now and forever, just as the Oriole Way did under Paul Richards and Earl Weaver, or the Big Red Machine conjures up the best Cincinnati Reds teams of the 1970s, or the $100,000 Infield is Philadelphia A's baseball approximately a hundred years ago.

Here's how it happened—from Rickey and DeWitt to DeWitt and Mozeliak. Here's how it happened, from George Kissell's insight and training to Jeff Luhnow's, Sig Mejdal's and Michael Girsch's revolution to Dan Kantrovitz and Gary LaRocque's implementation. And here's how it works in practice, as seen through the eyes of players and coaches, scouts and analytics experts, operating the Cardinals Way at all levels of the farm system right now.

Mike Matheny may object, but he's only forty-five, and he's only been present for a small part of the history of the determining factors in the success of the St. Louis Cardinals. Even Branch Rickey himself was once fired as manager of the Cardinals, and if anything, it ultimately enhanced his building of the organization. The Cardinals Way is almost a hundred years old, both the deep connection with young players and reliance on new data, and it doesn't appear to be going anywhere.

So there's pride, but no belief from the Cardinals that this is somehow the best or only way to do things. The implicit idea that would come with such an attitude, that twenty-nine other teams ought to follow the Cardinals' example, wouldn't even make sense, though many will try, and the Astros, in particular, will be a fascinating test case of many of the ideas that once drove the Cardinals' success, with so many of those who drove the Cardinals' innovative engine now in Houston with, as Luhnow put it to me in August 2015, "a clean sheet of paper." Meanwhile, this Cardinals Way is a product of a hundred years of serendipity, a number of innovative baseball men creating a tradition that predates any efforts to duplicate it, and a group in place now who have the ability to both maximize and build on what the St. Louis Cardinals began a century ago.

1

THE CARDINAL IDEA

Want to know what will happen tomorrow? Read yesterday's paper.
—Mike Shannon

I love *Baseball Prospectus*. But I couldn't help noticing this paragraph by Russell Carleton, in his March 4, 2014, column on the Cardinals:

"Before we create too much of a mythology surrounding *The Cardinal Way*, let's be realistic for a minute. The Cardinals did not invent player development. They do not have a monopoly on smart guys who are good at molding young bats and young arms. They did not invent the idea of making sure that there was a coherent philosophy running through the player development system. Lots of teams make it a point to ensure that from the Sally League to the National League, the expectations that pitchers have are as uniform as they can be. It sets up a nice uniformity and eases the transitions that players might face as they move up in the minors. For all we know, they may not be the first team to write an internal book—or a series of memos which, if someone had bothered to collect them into a three-ring binder, would look like a book."[1]

Let me stop you right there, Russell. The Cardinals did, in fact, invent player development. They did invent the idea of making sure a coherent philosophy ran through the player-development system.

And they were the first team to write an internal book, too—but we'll get to George Kissell soon enough.

First, we need to talk about Branch Rickey, inventor of the farm system. Rickey was many things: an Ohio schoolboy. A catcher good enough to play in the major leagues, before an arm injury ended his career. An academic and a teacher, repeatedly offered jobs outside the confines of the game that ultimately employed him for six decades. The bringer of integration to Major League Baseball, and of Jackie Robinson to millions of people who will never forget seeing him play.

But Rickey spent twenty-five years of his life, from 1917 to 1942, with the St. Louis Cardinals. And the foundation for how the Cardinals, and ultimately, every major league team acquired and developed talent came from Rickey himself.

It is easy to assert, with benefit of hindsight, that the farm system was an eventuality, a claim that still allows Rickey to claim credit for getting there first. But both opinion at the time of Rickey's great innovation, and even the example of other leagues to this day, argue against this limited view.

The idea of a farm club predates Rickey. John T. Brush, owner of the Cincinnati Red Stockings,[2] also owned the Indianapolis Hoosiers of the Western League and shifted players between the teams. But pushback from other minor league teams limited this practice until the second decade of the twentieth century.

Around this time, Rickey was coaching baseball at the University of Michigan. And he was hired by Robert Lee Hedges, owner of the St. Louis... Browns.

It's startling to consider just how much fate could have shifted in St. Louis baseball if any number of things had happened slightly differently, or earlier, or later. This book could easily have been about the most successful franchise in baseball history—the Browns. Hedges believed in Rickey's idea of a farm system and hired Rickey originally in 1913, for $7,500, to create that

The Cardinal Idea

farm system.³ Hedges also hired Charlie Barrett, who went on to become one of Rickey's most successful scouts with the Cardinals.

During his time with the Browns, Rickey, in need of an administrative assistant, hired a thirteen-year-old peanut vendor at Sportsman's Park to be his new assistant: Bill DeWitt Sr.

The Browns, not the Cardinals, owned Sportsman's Park. The Browns drew bigger crowds than the Cardinals. The Cardinals were the money losers in town. Even after the Cardinals were sold by the Robison family, the debt the new ownership took on (the deal with the Robison family essentially mortgaged the Cardinals, with payments constantly due) meant constantly trying to meet debt obligations while maintaining, if not building, the team.

The Cardinals even opened up shares of the team to fans, hoping for a cash infusion. It was referred to publicly as "The Cardinal Idea." Incredible as it may seem, given the fan support the Cardinals enjoy today, response was tepid at best. No St. Louis child born since 1902 has reached age twenty-five without seeing a World Series championship parade in his town. But in 1917, the year Rickey started with the Cardinals, the oldest children that astonishing stat covers were only fifteen years old.

Hedges became a casualty of the settlement with the Federal League, a third major league built to challenge that NL and AL circuits. As part of the settlement, Hedges sold the Browns to Phil Ball, owner of the St. Louis Federal League team, a man temperamentally unsuited, and not particularly inclined, to work with Rickey. As for Rickey's farm system? "I don't want anything to do with it!" Ball reportedly said.⁴

So when an opportunity opened up with the Cardinals, under their new ownership group, to join their front office as president, Rickey made the move. DeWitt and Barrett soon followed, along with other scouts, who helped populate those first Cardinal farm system teams. That wouldn't have happened for the Cardinals had Rickey remained with the Browns.

Those early years were hardly representative of what the Cardinals would become. Rickey would bring expensive rugs that belonged to his wife's family into team offices in Sportsman's Park for the day to make the team look more respectable during meetings with the owners of potential minor league affiliates.[5]

But two circumstances changed for the Cardinals at the tail end of the 1910s. Sam Breadon, who'd had a small stake in the team, decided to get more involved, eventually buying enough to become president of the team, fully funding the expansion of Rickey's farm system for the Cardinals, while simultaneously retiring the last of the debt due to the Robison family. In exchange, Rickey willingly gave up his title of president to Breadon.

And the second thing: Breadon, now in charge, decided to give Branch Rickey an entirely free hand to run baseball operations.[6]

Now the farm system would become the true "Cardinal Idea."

The system, born in part of necessity, would quickly expand as was necessary. Bill DeWitt, Sr., ultimately, became the first "farm director" in Major League Baseball history.

"He was very close to Branch Rickey," Bill DeWitt Jr. recalled, in my September 2014 interview with him, about his father. "He used to travel with him. When they had all these farm teams, they would go visit them and sort out what was going on—check on the players. There were so few people in the front office, like eight to ten people. They really didn't have a farm director, but he was the de facto farm director."

Rickey, and the Cardinals scouts, such as Charlie Barrett, had been scouring the high minors for players for the last few years of the 1910s. But their eye for talent had become so respected, other owners, armed with the knowledge that Rickey wanted these players and nothing else, would swoop in and outbid the relatively penniless Cardinals for them. Rickey, fed up with this happening, wired Barrett in Texas, "Pack up and come home—we'll develop our own players."

Thus, the Cardinals acquired a controlling interest in a Class C team in Fort Smith, Arkansas. The youngest, rawest players with promise Rickey

The Cardinal Idea

could find would be sent there, preparing them to play with the Cardinals. However, no player could be expected to jump from Class C to the majors. Accordingly, when Charlie Barrett brought word of a possible ownership stake to be had in the Houston franchise of the Texas League, the steps that would become commonplace for all began to fall into place for the Cardinals.

There to implement it all was Rickey's farm director, DeWitt Sr. Or as DeWitt Sr. himself put it in a 1980 interview: "I think I knew more about Branch Rickey in the twenty years I was associated with him. I used to sleep at his house at night. I lunched there. I ate dinner at his house. And so I knew him better than anybody during that twenty-year period."[7]

Does the Rickey/DeWitt farm system, in retrospect, seem obvious, the only proper way to develop talent? Perhaps. But no one can claim it was inevitable. No less a man than John McGraw dismissed the idea of a farm system, and the New York Giants didn't begin to build one until after he died in 1934.[8] That echoed the feelings of many throughout the major leagues. The Yankees didn't speak to Commissioner Landis about doing so until 1928 and didn't buy their first farm team until 1931, in Newark, New Jersey.

Nor were many minor league teams happy about this new idea, either. As John B. Sheridan wrote in his February 5, 1920, column in *The Sporting News,* "Managers of minor league baseball want players. Grievously. Must have them. Are turning heaven and earth to get them. Players are hard to find. When a minor league manager does light upon a likely lad he offers him a contract. The lordly lad pushes the minor league contract aside with a wide wave of his hand and says:

"'I am very sorry, but Charley Barrett has offered me a contract with the St. Louis Nationals, which you are probably aware is a major league club, even if it is in a lowly position....'

"Barrett's specialty is signing untried, fledgling, amateur, semi-professional, any sort of platers to the St. Louis National League club contracts at figures which will permit of the players being sent to the minor leagues for development. Barrett goes about the country picking up boys at from $125 to $200 a month."

The Cardinals won the World Series, finally, in 1926. That first crop of astonishing young stars, developed through the nascent farm system, included Jim Bottomley, George Toporcer, Lester Bell, Chick Hafey, Taylor Douthit, Ray Blades, Wattie Holm, Heine Mueller, Tommy Thevenow, Flint Rehm, and Eddie Dyer.

For those keeping score at home, that's a pair of Hall of Famers in Bottomley and Hafey, a 20-game winner for those world champions in Rehm, two-thirds of the championship outfield in Douthit and Blades, and a number of other key contributors who powered the Cardinals for much of the decade.

And once the time came for the Cardinals to build that farm system, finding enough other minor league teams to go along with it still might have proved impossible if not for Rickey's vast network of contacts and personal relationships, and the ability of people such as Charlie Barrett to scout and Bill DeWitt Sr. to carry out that vision.

As he did so, DeWitt Sr., at the strong urging of Rickey, finished his education.

"I have a picture of my father and his brother with Branch Rickey," DeWitt Jr. told me. "It says, 'To William, a great friend.' The fact that he said 'to William.' I read someplace that he called everybody by their formal name. I mean—I wonder if, when he was eighteen, he called him William—he must've!

"But Charlie Barrett called him Orville, which was his middle name. So he was the young guy around the office, relied on to contribute, do a lot of stuff."

Then DeWitt Sr. went to college. Rickey sent him.

"My college work I did all at night, and I worked for the Cardinals in the daytime," DeWitt Sr. said.[9]

The Cardinal Idea

Then Rickey sent him to law school. DeWitt passed the bar. Eventually, he became treasurer for the Cardinals, working under Rickey.

Remarkably, the farm system Rickey, DeWitt, and Barrett put together is largely the one the Cardinals use even now. A man Rickey himself hired, George Kissell, spent many of the subsequent decades formulating its consistent approach to training players.

But the people who engineered it, and the animating principles behind player procurement that went with them, had another job to do before the Cardinals' restoration we see today. They had to go build out the rest of baseball. Bill DeWitt Sr., to the Browns (who won the AL pennant in 1944), the Yankees, the Tigers, then Cincinnati Reds, with the foundation that became the Big Red Machine. Larry MacPhail, then Rickey, to the Brooklyn Dodgers, who won NL pennants in 1941, 1947, 1949, 1952, 1953, 1955 and 1956.

All the while, a young man from upstate New York put together the animating principles, not to mention the hard work and personal relationships, that came to define the Cardinals minor league experience for scores of Hall of Famers, All-Stars, and those who never even made the big leagues.

2

THE LANGUAGE OF GEORGE KISSELL

He's legendary in this organization. And I would say about thirty to fifty percent of other organizations know George Kissell. And the reason they know him is because of how many managers and coaches he's sent to the big leagues.

—Mike Shannon

You meet George Kissell, and right away, in a day or two, you knew who he was.

—Red Schoendienst

If you didn't know better, you'd think George Kissell was an entirely fictional creation, a stand-in for the values most treasured by the game of baseball. His record is too impossibly broad, his reach ridiculous to behold and incalculable in scope. He lived eighty-eight years and not only stayed on with the Cardinals for sixty-eight years—from his signing in 1940 to his death in 2008—but combined the length of his tenure with the kind of tangible results, and correlating respect, that few achieve in this game.

For Kissell, it was a constant. You hear it in Hall of Fame speeches from some of the greats who played this game, and you hear it in letters written to Kissell by long-forgotten minor leaguers who crossed Kissell's path, briefly, decades ago.

The Language of George Kissell

The reason this matters to the Cardinals—the Cardinals of Lou Brock and Bob Gibson, of Willie McGee and Terry Pendleton, of Jim Edmonds and Scott Rolen, right through to the Cardinals of Michael Wacha and Matt Carpenter—is that so many of those people are still teaching the game the way George Kissell taught it to them in the organization. A man steeped in Rickey's lessons—signed by Rickey himself—directly mentored many of the managers in the Cardinals system here in 2015. Such continuity should be impossible for purely chronological reasons.

It isn't, because of George Kissell. Growing up on a farm in Evans Mills, New York, Kissell did not have a baseball-mad father. At first, his father didn't want to take him to a baseball tryout camp—there were chores to do. But a rainy night prior to the Cardinals' scheduled tryout camp—another Branch Rickey invention—meant no hay could be baled that day. So the two of them headed to the camp in Rochester. The drive is more than two and a half hours today—you can imagine how long it took back in 1940, before the existence of I-81, in a 1936 Ford.

Kissell wore number 385 on his back and fielded five balls at shortstop.[1] He showed the Cardinals enough that they signed him to a contract. A Rickey scout asked Kissell how much money he'd spent to get to the tryout. Kissell added the hotel room, meals, gas, and told the scout: $19.80. The scout handed him a twenty and said, "You got a twenty-cent bonus."

To place the start of Kissell's career within the framework of Cardinals history, here's what 1940 meant. It meant Kissell was a Cardinal before Stan Musial had collected the first of his 3,630 major league hits. It meant Kissell was a Cardinal for most of Terry Moore's tenure in center field and overlapped the careers of Pepper Martin and Joe Medwick. Johnny Mize led the team before World War II and would play for more than another decade in the major leagues. Dizzy Dean was still active with the Cubs and had been traded only two years earlier.

All of the players in the preceding paragraph had been signed and developed by the Cardinals. So clearly, by the time Kissell arrived on the scene, the system had already figured out a way to provide the Cardinals with a steady stream of elite talent.

As he began immersing himself in this environment, Kissell was doing something else: he was writing it down. In the summer of 1941, rookie third baseman George Kissell traveled to Hamilton, Ontario, to play for the Cardinals' Pony League affiliate there. He hit .350 as Joe DiMaggio hit in 56 straight and Ted Williams cleared the .400 mark. Then Kissell returned to Ithaca College, where he was an undergraduate, and continued working toward his degree.

He earned it, a baseball-playing member of the class of 1942. His senior thesis, sadly lost to history, was nothing less than a road map for his journey to come: a manual on how to play, and properly instruct, young baseball players.

Might Kissell have been one of those players? We'll never know. World War II intervened, and Kissell spent most of the next four years out in Guadalcanal. He returned stateside in 1946, and then the Cardinals did something with the born teacher: they made him a player-manager, at the age of twenty-six.

So Kissell kept on playing, hitting .281, then .289, with the Lawrence Millionaires, the Lowell Orphans, and then back down the ladder as Kissell the player took a backseat to Kissell the manager, Kissell the molder of young men, in Hamilton, Ontario. He earned his master's degree from Ithaca College. In 1950, the Winston-Salem Cardinals in Class B won 106 games with Kissell managing. This was hardly a team stacked with future major league stars—though Vinegar Bend Mizell did pitch to a 2.48 ERA for them—but Kissell had the kind of year that eventually got him honored by the Winston-Salem Hall of Fame.

And how he did it, through personally connecting with his players, became a hallmark for Kissell every bit as important as that book of his, which was a living document. To know Kissell then, or any day of his life until the end, was to see him perched in a dugout, watching, writing. His papers are overflowing with observations, from long-lost games in the 1950s, or the 1970s, or the 1990s, or the 2000s.

> *I've always enjoyed working with the kids. I still do.*
> —George Kissell, 2004, at age eighty-four[2]

> *Hi George, This note from Dick Schlueter, member/catcher, Hamilton Ontario, Cardinals—Class of 1948—I think the last time we talked was spring training in Albany, GA in 1949. . . . But my prime reason for this note—for old times sake (to be sure) but to thank you for your help/guidance as a baseball coach/manager and of greater importance guidance "in the game of life."*
> —Letter to George Kissell from Dick Schlueter, 2000

The Cardinals, short on infielders at the end of the 1950 season, offered Kissell a chance to come up and play in St. Louis. Kissell was married to Ginny (Virginia) by then and had two small children. He turned the Cardinals down, preferring to stay at Winston-Salem and manage the youngest pros.

"I should have gone up and had the cup of coffee when I had the chance," Kissell told a reporter, staring out onto a back field in St. Petersburg, according to a 1994 partial clipping I found among his papers. "But I did what I thought was right at the time."

The Cardinals hardly begrudged Kissell for his selfless decision. Instead, they gave him a project—a raw converted pitcher out of Alba, Missouri, who the Cardinals hoped could make the transition to third base. His name was Ken Boyer, and if you'd gotten up early and made your way to Al Lang Field in St. Petersburg that spring, you'd have seen a small man with a booming voice showing Boyer every possible ground ball a third baseman needs to learn how to field.

It worked out for both Boyer and the Cardinals. Six All-Star Games, five

Gold Gloves, and the 1964 NL MVP of the World Champion Cardinals isn't a bad return on a spring project.

Not that Boyer enjoyed all that hard work at first, chafing at Kissell's instruction at times, and complaining to his minor league teammate, a second baseman (and Kissell's roommate) named Earl Weaver. Kissell benched Boyer.

"And I told Weaver, 'You tell him when he's ready to take advice, then he's ready to play,'" Kissell said in 1994.

Thirteen years later, the Cardinals sent the reigning NL MVP to the Cardinals' Winter Instructional League, to tell a new generation of young players what George Kissell had made possible.

Boyer called the coaches together and pointed to Kissell. "I just want to say a word. You know this little guy here, I couldn't stand him when I played for him. But he taught me, more than anyone else, the meaning of one word—*respect*. I just want to thank him."

> *Dear George: In the 1960s, I played in the Cardinal organization (1964–1968).... You were a roving coach ("ambassador!!!") and I always thought we had a pretty good relationship.... As a college graduate, we talked about one of your children who, at the time as I recall, was either in medical school or trying for acceptance.... George, I have always remembered your professionalism and the extent of your knowledge.... It has taken me more than 30 years to write this letter, but I want you to know that you were an influence on me at a time when I was a bit cocky for someone with low average ability. I wish I would have been as smart at 21–25 years old as I am now.*
> —Letter to George Kissell from J. Dale Meier, June 20, 2000

By 1967, Kissell had already been with the Cardinals for twenty-seven years. Red Schoendienst, the Hall of Fame second baseman who'd become manager of the Cardinals, wanted Kissell on his major league staff. Both were Rickey acquisitions; both were schooled by how Rickey had set up his minor league system.

The Language of George Kissell

"You as a player are sitting there, and you as a player want to get out there and start playing," Schoendienst told me as we sat and talked in an office off the Cardinals clubhouse in August 2014. Schoendienst, ninety-one at the time, is still at the ballpark constantly, coaching and passing on the collected wisdom of Rickey, Kissell, and so many others. He's no mascot or honorary presence. He was still in the building, well after 1:00 A.M. following a World Series game back in October 2013. He was there early the next morning, too.

"The thing was, you'd sit there for maybe an hour, and sit and talk," Schoendienst explained, referring to the classrooms Rickey, a teacher by training and in temperament as well, incorporated into spring training as part of season preparation, and which remained after Rickey left for the Brooklyn Dodgers following the 1942 season, run by Kissell. "It sketched different things out—this guy, he's gonna go first to third if the ball's hit here. If you're an outfielder, we're teaching the left fielder, center fielder, right fielder, for when the ball's hit to the left or right of you. Every day, in spring training, before you went out in those days, and still, when I was in the big leagues. You sat there and talked about what you were going to do that day. And the manager, and the coaches, we're gonna practice rundowns, cutoffs, and then we'd go out and do it."

That meant Cardinals players were not merely put through the paces, but by the time they'd mastered these skills, they'd also know why. This approach, implemented by Kissell, Schoendienst, and others, came directly from Rickey.

By the time Branch Rickey returned to St. Louis for his second stint with the Cardinals, he had this to say about Kissell in a November 8, 1962, report, after observing him: "This fellow, George Kissell, is doubtless a good manager and all that. But he is also a darn good employee. He looks after details. He is a 'cleaner-upper.' First man out, last man in. Impresses me as having a sense of responsibility for anything and everything; even to the insignificant things such as locating early and picking up later stray balls. I would hire him in any camp."[3]

And Kissell, the Rickey hire, certainly didn't lack an understanding of the great baseball man who brought him to the Cardinals. Kissell wrote down his recollections of Rickey in 1994, on Cardinals stationery. I found this among his papers. It reads like a how-to guide on Kissell's own approach to the game.

> Mr. Rickey had a very demanding presence....
> 1. He was very punctual and demanded it of others.
> 2. He was a very persuasive speaker and had a remarkable vocabulary.
> 3. He was extremely knowledgeable about <u>every</u> [with two underlines] phase of the game. He knew all positions equally well. He would challenge your method or play but would accept and use it when you could prove it superior to others.
> 4. He was very observant + a stickler for details—from the way the athlete dressed on the field to how the hot dogs were made.
> 5. He had a few mottos a ballplayer could live with: You reap what you sow. No athlete ever became great without practice, practice, practice. Luck doesn't just happen. Luck is the result of hard work.
>
> He was probably the most astute baseball man of all time and I feel enriched for having known and worked with him.

Rickey signed Schoendienst. Rickey signed Kissell. And the two men taught generations of Cardinals, players and coaches who are helping the Cardinals win to this day.

> *Dear George: Thank You! It is a very belated thank you I can assure you. Thirty-seven (37) years ago almost to the day, I walked on to the Brunswick, Georgia baseball diamond. I had just graduated from college and felt sure I knew everything there was to know about baseball. I met a guy named Kissell, who told*

me that he had probably forgotten more about baseball than our college coaches knew. Boy, was I ever shocked to hear something like that. And in a very short time, I knew your statement was true in every way.... You are the most unselfish man in baseball that I ever met, and I know you have touched thousands of players in your career.... I also know that you had something to do with my being a part of the 1970 Cardinal team, and I also thank you for that. I know I was not a star, nor was my name a household word... however I was never so proud as I was during opening day in 1970 when I was warming up Bob Gibson. Those are memories I will carry with me forever.

—Letter from Bart Zeller, June 14, 2000

The qualities of a good third baseman are a good pair of hands, a strong arm, and quick reactions to all situations. He must also be able to charge either way and throw the ball to first base, off balance, with something on his throw.

—From George Kissell's managers' syllabus, 1968

In 1951, Franklin D. Roosevelt's former vice president Harry Truman held the Oval Office. In 1967, Lyndon Johnson did, and he'd shortly be challenged for it by Bobby Kennedy, who was seven years old when FDR was first elected.

In 1951, *Billboard*'s Top 10 included "On Top of Old Smoky" by the Weavers and "Come on-a My House" by Rosemary Clooney, with "Too Young" from Nat King Cole on the top spot.

In 1967, the *Billboard*'s Top 10 included "Light My Fire" by the Doors, "Windy" by the Association, and "To Sir with Love" by Lulu, who was three in 1951.

In 1951, you'd have found George Kissell at Al Lang Field in St. Petersburg, Florida, teaching a young Cardinal how to play third base.

In 1967, you'd have found George Kissell at Al Lang Field in St. Petersburg, Florida, teaching a young Cardinal how to play third base.

This time, it was Mike Shannon, picked to be Boyer's replacement at third base for the Cardinals. For those keeping score at home, that's the 1964

NL MVP getting replaced by a third baseman who homered for the 1967 World Series winners and finished seventh in the 1968 NL MVP voting for the 1968 NL pennant winners.

"We would try to teach him everything that would happen in a ball game," Schoendienst said of Shannon when we talked in August 2014. "I could handle the bat pretty good, could still handle it pretty good, and we'd put him in situations, you know—a man on first, man on second, nobody out. Bunting, playing third base. So George would toss 'em in, nice and easy, and I'd hit them to him. And then, George had more good ideas—hell, he wrote things out and had them in the book!"

Schoendienst made it clear he subscribed to Kissell's ideas. Like any good actor, and all the coaches in the Kissell tradition, the two men had long since internalized the book. So Shannon was hearing two voices, but one set of ideas about how to play the position.

"He taught me how to play third base," Shannon said of Kissell when we talked in the Busch Stadium television booth in August 2014. Shannon's now been a Cardinal for fifty-five years, though, really, longer than that—as a high schooler, in St. Louis, Shannon played football with Stan Musial's son and found himself often in the presence of the finest hitter in Cardinals history years before the two men were teammates. "He taught Joe Torre how to play third base. And that's just two of us. Who knows how many there've been! And it goes on and on and on. And then you talk to the managers, and it's the same thing. It's unbelievable!"

It didn't take Shannon long to understand how important it would be for his career to listen to Kissell:

"He commanded respect. You didn't know who the heck this guy was, but you'd listen to him for five minutes, you'd go—'Oh! This guy! I'm gonna pay attention to him.'

"He did it very simply. The great teachers, they don't need flowery words. They can come down to almost any level, they can go up to any level.

"He gave me the fundamentals. If you don't have legs on a table, you don't have a table. George would explain that to you. Now after that, you had to work for it yourself. He'd show you how to do it. And then Red took over and hit me eight million ground balls." Shannon chuckled at the memory of his sore legs. "And practically killed me. But George was the guy. He not only taught me how to play, he taught you how to live."

For a few years, Kissell taught lessons on those parallel tracks to the Cardinals in St. Louis, not the Cardinals in Johnson City or St. Petersburg or Modesto or Lewisburg. After twenty-seven years, Kissell had been promoted, brought on staff by his old friend and the manager of the Cardinals, Red Schoendienst.

"He's been in the boonies all his life," Schoendienst recalled telling then Cardinals general manager Bing Devine. "And we've got to get him up here. So I called George—'Oh, I don't know if I could do that,' he said. I said, 'George, with all the inexperienced kids that you taught there, that know now, these guys got experience up here. It's not as much teaching as doing the right thing. You talk it over with Ginny.' . . . I wanted to get him out of there. Hell, how many years did he spend down there? I think he deserved it."

It was fascinating to hear Schoendienst talk about the minor leagues as something to grow from, to move on from, while for Kissell, the minor leagues served as his home, ultimately, for almost seventy years. The combined wisdom of two Cardinals greats—with a combined 140 years of service to the club—thus covered different ground at the same time. Schoendienst had made quick work of most of Branch Rickey's minor league ladder in a single year.

The two collaborated on strategy in 1967 and 1968. The Cardinals had two NL pennants and a World Series to show for it.

"He wanted to be a big part of everything," Schoendienst said. "Which was good. He'd be in my office. We'd go over the lineup. He looked over a lot of things, this and that. And in the game, he'd watch—he'd think a guy should be playing over to his right more—George was very alert, very astute in the game."

Kissell's career had lasted nearly thirty years by then, and still had more than forty to go. You didn't have to look hard to find Kissell's impact on the game already, and not just in St. Louis.

A young minor league manager in the Cardinals system got a job as third-base coach for the San Diego Padres. On October 8, 1969, he'd get the major league managing gig with the Cincinnati Reds. His name was Sparky Anderson. He learned how to manage from Kissell, once saying of him, "A man named George Kissell: The greatest single instructor I ever seen on fundamentals in my life. He could teach a snake to box."[4]

Anderson's Reds, in his first season at the helm in 1970, won 102 games and the National League pennant. They won 99 games in 1973 to win the NL West, 98 games in 1974, then a pair of World Series titles in 1975 and 1976.

Over in the American League, Kissell's old roommate who then played under him in the Cardinals system, Earl Weaver, took over as Baltimore Orioles manager. His Orioles fared okay, too: they won 109 games and the AL pennant in 1969, 108 games and the World Series in 1970, 101 games and the AL pennant in 1971. His Orioles won 97 games and the AL East in both 1973 and 1974, and 90, 88, 97, and 90 games in four other close AL East races. Then, 102 in a 1979 AL pennant campaign, and 100 in a 1980 season that saw the Orioles finish second to the Yankees in the AL East and miss the play-offs, despite finishing with the second-best record in all of baseball that year. Another 94 wins in 1982, then 98 for the 1983 Orioles, who won another World Series.

Then, in 1984, it was Anderson's turn again: 104 wins and a World Series with the Detroit Tigers.

From 1969 to 1984, while George Kissell was training Joe Torre—a manager who had some success himself—to take over at third base for Mike Shannon, just two of the Kissell disciples won nine pennants and four World Series titles. More significant still, between Weaver and Anderson, a Kissell disciple won at least 90 games every year between 1969 and 1984.

The Language of George Kissell

Earl Weaver said Kissell, along with Paul Richards, had been his greatest influence.[5] Anderson said this at his Hall of Fame induction in 2000:

"A man named George Kissell. The greatest single instructor I ever seen on fundamentals in my life. Fiftysome years with the Cardinals. And Georgie... he was something special to me."

George was instrumental in my development as a professional baseball player. George was a great teacher of the game who taught me how to play every aspect of the game correctly and, above all, how to win the Cardinal way. George demanded—and never accepted—anything less than 100% effort from all his players. Most importantly, George instilled in each of us a strong sense of pride in being a Cardinal. Thanks to George, we were steeped in Cardinal tradition and understood what it meant to wear the Cardinal uniform.

I still carry this proud tradition with me. I was never as comfortable in a New York Mets uniform.... Thanks for everything, George. You helped mold me into the player I became. I believe in time and space, and I was truly blessed to have had the benefit of your tutelage in the early stages of my career.

—Letter from Keith Hernandez, September 29, 2002

The Cardinals drafted Keith Hernandez in 1971. He went on to win 11 Gold Gloves at first base, the most of anyone at the position in the history of baseball. But Kissell didn't just work with the future greats. Kissell had returned to the minor leagues once Red Schoendienst was replaced as manager by Vern Rapp. It was where he was most comfortable, most effective, and it allowed him to teach again.

"He could've left twice with Sparky Anderson," Kissell's grandson Tommy Kidwell recalled as we talked in St. Petersburg in September 2014. "He could've gone to the Big Red Machine, he could've gone to Detroit, and he said thanks but no thanks.

"He could've gone from the minor leagues to the big leagues a second time, and he didn't want to. He wanted to stay with his family. His loyalty to the Cardinals—he was not a threat to anybody else's job because he didn't want anybody else's job. He wanted to do what he was there to do, which was coach and help young guys. Even in his last days, when I was managing in rookie ball, his love was for rookie ball and the lower levels, more so than Double-A, Triple-A, where guys are less coachable, think they know it all, more set in their ways, and less likely to learn. So he was always better at the lower levels, where most guys, frankly, don't want to be for a long time. They want to move up."

And in 1978, another of Kissell's projects was an undrafted free agent who'd struggled to get playing time in college, a young infielder named Steve Turco, discovered at one of those tryout camps Branch Rickey created, and which had allowed the Cardinals, thirty-eight years before, to discover George Kissell.

Turco had been drafted by the Indians out of high school, but elected to go to Florida State. However, he clashed with the coach there, who wanted to move the infielder to the mound. Finally, when he arrived in the Cardinals' Instructional League, George Kissell was waiting for him.

"When I think about the first time I ever saw George, I was down in St. Pete, hitting in the batting cage," Turco told me in May 2014, as we sat and watched the extended spring-training Cardinals face the Mets on a back field in Jupiter, Florida. A sign honoring George Kissell was visible from the silver bleachers where we sat. "I happened to be taking batting practice, and George comes by. I don't know who he is, and he says, 'Hey, we need to go pick 'em up'—he's telling us about picking up [stray baseballs in the cage]. He says, 'You don't pick 'em up, you don't get to hit.' I said to somebody, 'Who is that?' Someone said, 'That's George Kissell.'" Turco shrugged, as he had that day. "'No,' he said, 'That's the Man.'

"After that, knowing who he was—I think what George saw in me was somebody who worked hard. When you're somebody who put in the extra time, the extra effort, I think George appreciated that. And in my case—he was there for me in every way."

For Turco, that meant on-field things, but it meant other things, too—how to carry yourself, little details as seemingly insignificant as wearing socks in the clubhouse. Talking the game for hours. But it all began with endless repetition on the field.

"I remember that first spring training," Turco said. "We'd have to take a bus, and they'd drop us off across the street from the hotel, a busy road. I had trouble even walking across, my leg was so sore, after we were done for the day. Bucket after bucket of ground balls. Things we don't necessarily do as much anymore because we're sensitive to things—the arm care of players. But back then, though, it was bucket after bucket. And George liked the work. Not only the time he put in with us, but the appreciation we had for him doing it for us. It was one of those things where I was indoctrinated quickly into George's style.

"The things I am in the game today, I owe to George."

Turco held his own in 1979, putting up a respectable .254/.326/.303 line, playing shortstop for the Gastonia Cardinals of the Western Carolinas League. He also took the opportunity to go to the league's All-Star Game, mostly to sit and watch with Kissell.

"I'll never forget, the first year I was playing, we played 138 games in 140 days. We only had two days off, and one of our two days was the league All Star Game. The game was being played in Gastonia, which was our home field, and George was there. So I went to the game—I was the only player there who wasn't playing in the game.

"So I sat there with George, and he said, 'Look out there.'"

Everyone I ever spoke to who knew Kissell immediately slipped into an impression of Kissell when quoting him. It's generally agreed that John Mabry, the St. Louis hitting coach, is the best of the Kissell imitators, but they are omnipresent around Kissell stories. Anyway... "'Look out there. See that shortstop?' I said, 'I see him.' 'What can he do that you can't? He can't run with you. He can't throw with you. He may have better hands, but you can hit like he can. So what can he do that you can't do?' Well, it turned out, it was Ryne Sandberg. He only went on to be a Hall of Famer. But especially if he thought you had some ability, he pushed you."

That continued into the 1980s, Kissell's fifth decade with the Cardinals. Ask Terry Pendleton about the year he came to camp overweight. Kissell said nothing, but had him come in early, stay late, hit him about ten thousand ground balls. You didn't say no to Kissell. The pounds melted away in the Al Lang Field sunlight. Pendleton went on to win three Gold Gloves at third base, the 1991 NL MVP, played in five different World Series.

Kissell-trained Cardinals helped St. Louis win National League pennants in 1982, in 1985, in 1987. And those who went to other organizations didn't forget Kissell's help, either.

> *I could not be in the big leagues if it weren't for Mr. Kissell.*
> —Andy Van Slyke[6]

Dear George,

Here's a letter to let you know I'm alive and kicking in San Diego. Things are looking up for me now, and I'm about to turn the corner.

I wanted to write and tell you how much your tutelage and instruction meant to me. While everybody else is busting their tails to learn them, the fundamentals are coming second nature to me. It is mainly because of your time and effort that I am ahead of the game there. I used to dread your chalkboard sessions in instructional league, but now I see they were of great necessity....

Say hi to your wife, and good fishing!

Gratefully,

Terry K

—Letter from Terry Kennedy to George Kissell, 1980. Kennedy went on to make the All-Star team for the Padres in 1981, then another three times. He was the starting catcher for two National League pennant winners: the 1984 Padres and the 1989 Giants.

The Language of George Kissell

Jim Leyland took the Pirates to three straight NL East titles in 1990 to 1992. He also had a spring ritual: en route to camp, he'd stop in St. Petersburg and have himself a fishing trip/study session with George Kissell.

As Kissell taught John Mabry to play third base, another project, another decade, another Boyer stand-in doing the same things in the same way more than forty years later, one of Kissell's other third basemen, Joe Torre, managed the Cardinals, then the Yankees. He had a bit of success in New York: World Series titles in 1996, 1998, 1999, 2000, and a string of postseason appearances unbroken from 1996 to 2007.

The only other manager to win a World Series during that 1996–2000 Torre run? Kissell's fishing partner, Leyland, with the 1997 Marlins.

Meanwhile, Turco's career did not take off the way Sandberg's did. He reached Double-A, but found himself playing in St. Petersburg, in the Florida State League, for several years. Finally, the Cardinals released him in 1984, and he made up his mind to go play overseas, accepting a chance to play in Italy.

George Kissell had other plans for him.

"I knew it would be a nice way to go and see Europe," Turco told me. "Particularly Italy. I'd stay there for a year. They played twice a week, they had two practices, you'd sightsee three days a week.

"Anyway, I had it all set, and [then Cardinals minor league manager] Jim Riggleman calls me. And he said, 'Listen, they called, and I told them you can do whatever their needs are. But before you make that decision to go, why don't you give [then Cardinals director of player development] Lee Thomas a call?'"

The Kissell plan for Turco had been set in motion.

"I'd played with Lee Thomas's son, Darren Thomas, and he said, 'Listen, why don't you give Lee a call?' This is all the same day, I get three phone calls.

"And finally, it was George. And George says, 'Give Lee a call,'" with Turco slipping into a Kissell impression.

"And I knew that George was instrumental in my getting that job. Because this is what he did. You talk about continuity—what George always believed was that you don't always groom players. You groom coaches and managers."

Turco has been with the Cardinals ever since. He managed Glens Falls, then the Cardinals' short-season Appalachian League team in Johnson City, Tennessee.

Kissell kept right on coaching. It was amusing, in retrospect, to read all the letters and articles that talked about his imminent retirement. The reporter from the *St. Petersburg Times,* back in 1996, sounded pretty sure that would be Kissell's final year. Virginia told that reporter Kissell, then seventy-seven, had been threatening to retire every year since he was sixty-three. The Hernandez letter from earlier in the chapter is in conjunction with a free trip the Cardinals gave to Kissell in 2002, to be used once he retired. (Tommy Kidwell confirmed that Kissell never went on the trip.) Kissell kept on working right until the end.

This is not to say that he and Virginia were separated all those years. Every season, Kissell would get into his car and travel the country, making stops wherever Cardinals minor leaguers played. And Ginny was right alongside him.

"To my lovely wife," Kissell inscribed a picture of himself. "The success I've achieved in life and in this game has been entirely through your patience, inspiration and love." They estimated they'd make about two hundred stops every summer.

Kissell never missed a day of mass, either. The lifelong Catholic made a promise back in 1964 to God that should his son, Richard, get admitted to medical school, he'd go to mass every morning for the rest of his life.

For Sunday day games, he used to have the socks and other baseball accoutrements on under his church clothes. It was for efficiency, his grandson says, but it represented more than that.

The Language of George Kissell

No one around baseball who knew him doubted the importance of his family to him. Bobby Valentine heard how amused Ginny was by his stunt, after an ejection, of returning to the dugout in a Groucho Marx disguise. He sent her a signed photo of himself in disguise, inscribed, "Have a laugh on me."

Kissell got the call back to the major leagues in 1999, when Tony La Russa asked him to return and be his additional coach.

The 2000 Cardinals won 95 games and advanced to the NLCS. The 2001 Cardinals won another 93 games. La Russa credited Kissell for much of his own managerial thinking piloting the 2006 Cardinals and then the 2011 Cardinals to World Series wins.

The way that he taught engaged and involved players. George had a love for the game, a love for the people who play the game, a love for teaching the game, a love for understanding the game, and relaying that and teaching that to people—every day. There were instances every day. Personally, the way he rooted for me to succeed, more than I rooted for myself sometimes. Understanding that he gave, no matter what, his time, and that, to me, is more important than anything, ever, that somebody would care for you that much that they would take their time, and teach you what they knew.
    —Cardinals hitting coach John Mabry, in August 2013 interview

Hitter grasps bat in both hands balanced by choking bat.
1. *Takes ball in right hand. Tosses it up and hits and runs, swinging down on ball. Repeats 15 swings. (Does it slowly.)*
2. *2 hands on bat—roommate/coach soft tosses 20 pitches and hitter hits and runs swinging down on ball. Repeat 20 times.*
3. *Hitter on floor or ground with left arm at 1 o'clock (5 pound weight).*

—George Kissell drill for switch-hitters, as recorded on Virginia Kissell personalized stationery, likely by Virginia

Dear George,

As I look forward to spring training and the upcoming year in Louisville, I didn't want another season to start without thanking you for everything you have done for me.

I know my assignment to Louisville would have never happened without you. I can't begin to tell you how much I fully appreciate being in your presence and I fully appreciate the personal interest you have taken in me.

Your knowledge of the game of baseball, that you passed along to me, is absolutely priceless. In fact, your knowledge of the game, along with your enthusiasm, dedication and loyalty certainly go unmatched by anybody in baseball.

George, I came to the Cardinal organization because of you and that decision has become the wisest one I have ever made.

In my eyes you are the greatest Cardinal who ever put the birds on. You have helped me make my five years as a Cardinal the best years I've had in baseball.

I love you, George. Looking forward to seeing you.

Your adopted son,

Mark DeJohn

—Letter from current Cardinals minor league field coordinator Mark DeJohn to George Kissell, January 25, 1991

Mabry is the hitting coach in St. Louis now. Since 2009, Turco has been managing the Gulf Coast League Cardinals. His tenure with the organization is now thirty-five years, or just over half the sixty-eight seasons Kissell gave the Cardinals. Turco's usually the first manager any Cardinal plays for. Kissell disciples Mike Shildt and Ron "Pop" Warner finished off Cardinals prospects at Double-A and Triple-A in 2014. DeJohn is everywhere, doing what Kissell did for so many decades. He entered his thirtieth season with the Cardinals in 2015.

"As I get older—and I don't want to compare myself to George—but as I get older, my perspective on things, to these kids, it changes," Turco told me.

The Language of George Kissell

"I have two sons, who are eighteen and seventeen, and I'm fifty-eight years old. I could be their grandfather. And they start to look at me, maybe, the way I looked at George, because of the age. And maybe, with the age, comes wisdom? But the wisdom that I have, in life and about the game, really came from George. The wisdom I can impart to them has come from experience with George, experience in the game, experience in life."

Kissell, in his three seasons with the Cardinals from 1999 to 2001, took on a couple of projects that Tony La Russa didn't want. The first one was a twenty-eighth-round pick from Morris County College in New Jersey, the kind of hardworking overachiever that Kissell lived to help: Joe McEwing.

"My rookie year, he was on the bench with me," McEwing told me at a St. Petersburg hotel in September 2014. The White Sox were in town to play the Rays, and McEwing, who'd heard about my book, volunteered to simply talk about George Kissell for hours late into a Friday night/Saturday morning.

"I'd had him in the minor leagues for years. So George was with me every single day. And he prepared me every single day. So basically, I learned to play second base from him in the big leagues. He wore me out, every single day. And that's who I would go to with questions. Was I in the right place? Should I have been here, should I have been there?"

As Kidwell explained, "Tony didn't like young guys." So it fell to Kissell, nearing eighty, to connect with the twenty-six-year-old McEwing.

The two had formed the bond years before.

"When you first sign, you're new to everything," McEwing told me. "When I signed, I went to instructional league. And so George walked in—you know, we play ten o'clock games 'cause it was so hot. So we were on the road, we were playing the Angels. And we had a terrible game, defensively. We get back, off the van, nobody went to the clubhouse. We went back on the field, took infield until it was perfect. Took a whole infield, and until it was perfect, nobody was getting off the field. And that's when you understand the importance of every single play that goes on in each game."

But it wasn't as if Kissell stood there, book in hand, and read from his manual, crafted all those decades before on snowy Ithaca, New York, nights. Kidwell echoed McEwing's stories as the hours went by, pointing out that while McEwing heard them since he was twenty, Kidwell had been hearing them since he was six years old.

"George simplified," McEwing said. "You didn't know what you were going through. When you did your routine, he did not let you know what you were going through. So you were just getting to every ground ball, but at the end he would let you know, you just fielded every ground ball you could possibly have at second base."

A year later, McEwing had been traded to the Mets. Kissell took charge of improving the defense of Fernando Viña, the new Cardinals second baseman. He went on to win the 2001 Gold Glove. And he had a replica made for George Kissell.

McEwing looks like another direct Kissell product who will get a job managing at the big league level, though even now the Cardinals are hiring and training young managers such as Ollie Marmol, their State College Spikes skipper in 2014, promoted to Palm Beach in 2015, with the Kissell ideas in mind, and usually by those who were trained by Kissell himself. McEwing is the third-base coach for the Chicago White Sox. The Cardinals interviewed McEwing after 2011 to replace La Russa, before choosing Mike Matheny. Both the Diamondbacks and the Twins interviewed McEwing for their managerial openings after the 2014 season, and it seems more like when than if for McEwing to get that chance to manage.

He speaks fluent Kissell, and you better believe that's a language, one that has outlived Kissell himself, who died in 2008. It's hard not to feel that baseball was robbed of some more years with Kissell, who was in fine health when he died, the victim of injuries sustained in a car accident.

McEwing told me he not only thinks of Kissell every day, he thinks of what Kissell would do when he makes any decision on the baseball field, and many of them off it.

The Language of George Kissell

Turco's final words to me, as we left the playing field in Jupiter following a three-hour conversation: "Make sure you say nice things about George Kissell in that book of yours!"

"Luis Alicea—my last year playing was in the Red Sox organization," McEwing recalled. "So I went to big league camp with the Red Sox [in 2007], [Dustin] Pedroia's rookie year. So I'm listening to Luis—I'm kind of a veteran at that time—I listen to Luis describing double-play depth with Pedroia. And I go, 'I don't want to interrupt, but do you want me to finish this?' He goes, 'What do you mean?' I go, 'Do you want me to finish this speech?' He's, like, 'You grew up under George. You know exactly what I'm gonna say.' I said, 'You're right.'"

White Sox hitting coach Todd Steverson then joined us. He'd heard Kissell stories were being told and wanted to add his. He'd spent only a few years in the Cardinal organization, but he found that his exposure to Kissell allowed him to become the go-to guy on fundamentals for every staff he'd joined since, from Oakland to Detroit.

We all kept talking until after 2:00 A.M., and then I left, and Kidwell told me they kept on talking baseball, story after story, until the sun came up, remembering the past and applying it all to the present. They were the same conversations coaches and players have had all over this country, at every outpost found by Rickey and developed by Kissell and all who have come after him.

It's the book, sure, but it's the conversation that the book starts, the repetition that allows players and coaches to work from the text rather than being slaves to it. Or as Joe Torre says Kissell used to put it:

"Who wrote the book, Joe?"

"Who?"

"Nobody, Joe. Nobody wrote the book."

Kissell did, though. And the ideas, the diagrams for where to go and what to do for nearly every conceivable baseball situation, the drills that coaches from other organizations have admired without knowing how they'd even file them in reports if they appropriated them, are not just in English.

It is the language of Branch Rickey. It is the language of George Kissell. And it's how the Cardinals talk to each other and have for nearly a hundred years.

3

BILL DEWITT JR.

Player development is essential to the success of a Major League ball club. It is probably the most vital ingredient in putting a team on the field.

—BILL DeWITT JR., 1965

In 1965, a twenty-three-year-old graduate student at Harvard Business School, Bill DeWitt Jr., submitted a paper to his Business Policy professor, Joseph L. Bower. In it, DeWitt detailed how a professional baseball team, the Cincinnati Reds, could improve overall business practices. Both the recommendations and the source are striking for their accuracy and provenance.

"Bill was quiet in class, so I was surprised when his paper for the 'personal strategy' assignment was really strong," Bower told me in a November 2014 e-mail when I asked him about the paper. "For purposes of the book, you can say I gave him a Distinction grade, although it may have only been a High Pass. I only remember that it was strong, and that I invited him to my office to talk about it."

DeWitt Jr.'s paper probably earned more of a hearing from the upper tiers of Cincinnati Reds management than other academic exercises of the time, since a Bill DeWitt Sr., the sole owner, also served as the team's president and general manager. By then, the Branch Rickey diaspora was everywhere, in what would be the last year of Rickey's life.

Rickey had returned to the Cardinals in an advisory role. DeWitt Sr. ran the Reds. Warren Giles, who'd been president of two top-level Cardinals farm teams under Rickey, rose to the presidency of the National League. Lee MacPhail, son of Larry (who'd gotten his first executive job in baseball under Rickey), was building the Orioles for three decades of success.

But no one, even those who'd worked in the Cardinals organization, could claim as direct an intellectual line of success from Rickey than that young graduate student.

DeWitt Sr. had worked for Rickey for two decades, indebted to Rickey for his first job in baseball beyond that of peanut vendor, for much of his formal education, and for his intellectual framework for the game of baseball. Bill DeWitt Jr. grew up, then, with "baseball in his blood," as the current Cardinals general manager, John Mozeliak, put it about DeWitt in an October 2014 interview.

DeWitt Jr. was born in St. Louis on August 31, 1941. When he was three years old, the Cardinals DeWitt Sr. helped build with Rickey faced off in the World Series against the Browns—the Browns' only pennant—DeWitt Sr. built after leaving the Cardinals.

Just prior to DeWitt's tenth birthday, the Browns of DeWitt Sr. and Bill Veeck needed a tiny uniform, stat. Veeck had hired Eddie Gaedel, a little person standing just three feet seven inches, and the Browns hadn't, understandably, planned for such a player.

"I had an official Browns uniform that was issued, sized to fit me," DeWitt Jr. told me back in August 2013, as we chatted in his office at Busch Stadium. "It's not like today, when you have different uniforms for different days. You'd get 'em at the beginning of the year, and at the end of the year, you'd give them to minor league clubs. My father [had] sold [the Browns] to Bill Veeck, but was still active in the operations.

"It was 1951. So I was nine. And my uniform was actually a little big on him, as a nine-year-old," DeWitt recalled, laughing. "So I still have it, with the 1/8 on the back." After spending time on display in Cooperstown,

DeWitt/Gaedel's uniform is now in the Cardinals Hall of Fame, which opened in 2014.

This was the childhood of Bill DeWitt Jr.

"I remember the stories about him," DeWitt Jr. said of Rickey over lunch in New York in September 2014. "The stories about him, and the Cardinal office." DeWitt pointed out that at the time Rickey became president of the Cardinals, a person working directly under him was DeWitt Sr.

By the 1950s, the Browns had been sold again and moved to Baltimore. DeWitt Sr. took a post with the Yankees under George Weiss. In Weiss, the Yankees had a man who'd been hired in 1932 to try to replicate what Rickey and DeWitt created with the farm system. Weiss had been farm director for the team, then took over as general manager in 1947 when Larry MacPhail was let go.

But DeWitt was told by Yankees owners Dan Topping and Del Webb that Weiss would be retiring soon, at which point DeWitt would become general manager. So DeWitt signed on as an assistant to Weiss, which gave the younger DeWitt a chance to learn the game at a granular level.

"We still lived in St. Louis, since my sisters and I still were in school," DeWitt Jr. told me of that time. "We'd stay in a hotel here in New York. And my mother would come up during the week, we'd be here [in New York] all summer. So that lasted a couple of years. I used to travel with my father when he was with the Yankees. As the assistant GM, he used to go scouting all over the place. I would go with him. He used to give me the stopwatch, to clock runners from home to first. I got to meet a lot of scouts, and high school and college coaches."

This is where the other thread of the Cardinals' succeeding today can be found, in events six decades before. DeWitts on the road, sharing stories of what to look for. The younger DeWitt, holding the stopwatch. George Kissell is teaching Ken Boyer how to play third base in St. Petersburg, and Bill DeWitt Sr. is teaching Bill Jr. how to properly judge which players Kissell ought to train.

"As a kid growing up, my first recollection is with the Browns. And I just grew up in that world. My father was running the Browns, and he and his brother owned the team. Again, that was a small operation. But I got the sense, as I got to be a little bit older, how he operated, and Rickey's was the model that he used. It was an area I always thought in my mind I would follow. I always wanted to get back."

While DeWitt Sr.'s somewhat nomadic existence as a baseball executive followed—Weiss did not retire, so DeWitt moved on to Detroit as president/GM, then to Cincinnati—DeWitt Jr. graduated with a degree in economics from Yale, then got his MBA from Harvard in 1965.

He doesn't remember what grade he earned on the paper, but the document is a largely accurate portrait of where the game of baseball would go in the next fifty years. DeWitt cites the increase in television revenue as a driving factor in changing the economics of the game—his paper includes a citation of a *New York Times* story from February 14, 1965, with the adorable subhead "A $23.3 million bonanza," referring to the total radio and television revenue collected by *all* the MLB teams in 1965.

DeWitt cites the "recent trend in Baseball legislation toward the equalization, among clubs, of the ability to secure playing talent." (You can argue the last hundred years of MLB history is primarily about the struggle to combat the money of the New York Yankees.) He predicts further expansion, a greater emphasis on international sources for players, even interleague play, which DeWitt describes as "a certainty in the near-future."

Significantly, DeWitt speaks to the oncoming *Moneyball* evolution still decades away (though, really, a return to the kind of reliance on statistics practiced by Branch Rickey) in player development. "Broad coverage will become relatively less important (since everyone will have it) and judgement on ballplayers and on standardized reports will become increasingly important," DeWitt wrote. A balanced approach between scouting and statistical analysis? Yes, the template for the success of the Cardinals today could be found in a Harvard Business School paper fifty years ago.

But the greatest area of emphasis for DeWitt came from an innovation that he believed held the key to a team's future success: the amateur draft.

"Another requisite... is the development of a system by which the abilities of players and the needs of the organization can be integrated into a preference rankings of ballplayers for the purpose of selection at the free-agent draft. Concomitant with this requirement is the need to 'feel out' players considered, i.e. do they want to play baseball, how much money will they need to sign, etc."

In his recommendations, he put cost certainty, along with making sure there was value to be gleaned from every pick, in the starkest possible terms:

"All free agents who are Major League prospects should be contacted, before the draft, with a determination made of the amount needed to sign them. Those wanting more than they are worth, in terms of their potential and the budget of the farm director, should be put at the bottom of the list. Those wanting what they are worth, or less, should comprise, basically, the draft list." DeWitt's new system called for plotting all minor league prospects on a graph measuring level and age, with an accounting for team needs in various positions, with the completed draft list rating player potential—Exceptional, Good, Average, and Below Average—as a guide for where a player should begin his professional career.

This may seem fairly straightforward, but plenty of teams, even now, fall in love with individual players and ultimately pay too much for them or don't do the proper legwork to know how much a player they draft will cost. So putting these best practices to paper not fifty years after the draft began, but the very year it was created, is both significantly forward-thinking and an astonishing foreshadowing of the kind of changes DeWitt's Cardinals would make after hiring Jeff Luhnow in 2003.

Another way DeWitt's 1965 paper parallels the St. Louis changes four decades later comes in his primary financial recommendation. He noted that Jim McLaughlin, the Cincinnati farm director, was directed to trim $270,430 from his operating budget for 1964 from 1963's. Since that budget—for both player procurement and player development—had been just over $800,000, that was a 33 percent cut. DeWitt took exception to this decision:

"In one area, however, there appears to be a conflict between two of the [team's] stated goals. This is the area of player development. The conflict arises between profits now and winning later. While the Reds have attempted to continue to sign and develop good ballplayers, bonuses have been cut, Minor League teams have been cut (from five to four, lowest in Baseball), Rookie League participation has been eliminated, and scouting has been curtailed. These cost saving measures must have an effect on both the quality of players signed and the development of those in the organization."

DeWitt Jr. graduated from Harvard Business School in 1965. His father, in his final year overseeing the Reds, managed the draft with significant success. Top pick Bernie Carbo finished a twelve-year career with an OPS+ of 126, though his most famous home run, a 3-run shot in Game 6 of the 1975 World Series, actually came against the Reds. The second pick played somewhat well in Cincinnati, too: catcher Johnny Bench. And sixth-round-pick Hal McRae hit 191 home runs over a nineteen-year career with the Reds and primarily the Royals.

DeWitt had every intention of making a career of baseball. The Reds, with the elder DeWitt in ownership and the younger one in the front office, were well positioned to inherit the Rickey approach. The Reds even hired DeWitt Jr. officially in January 1967, in a role similar in description to the position Jeff Luhnow received from DeWitt and the Cardinals in 2003.

In a memo to new Reds owner Francis Dale outlining his responsibilities at that time, DeWitt's first task is "to work very closely with the farm department with which I have a very good relationship. I will assist in the preparation for (and will attend) the Free Agent Draft sessions, the analysis of free agents through scouting and interviewing, the further development of our scouting and managerial staff, and the handling of our minor league affiliated clubs and players."[1]

The memo provided a wide-ranging set of areas, from team finances to overseeing radio/TV coverage, even handling player accident insurance. The memo describes DeWitt's title as "treasurer," a title his father once held under Rickey, though like DeWitt Sr.'s job "this certainly does not fully define the broad scope of my job." DeWitt Jr. was to report "directly to the General manager."

But just as with a few slightly different outcomes in the 1910s this book could easily have been about the Browns, the same is true of the Reds in the 1960s. It was not to be, though the seeds planted by DeWitt Sr. played a major part in a Reds team that won four National League pennants and two World Series trophies from 1970 to 1976.

As DeWitt Jr. put it to me, the new general manager "had his own ideas." Bill DeWitt Jr. in 1967 didn't get the chance to be Bill DeWitt Sr. in 1926, or Jeff Luhnow in 2003.

Instead, nearly three decades followed, with a decent consolation prize: Bill DeWitt Jr. went out and became extremely successful in the investment business with the firm Reynolds, DeWitt and Co., which he formed with Mercer Reynolds. The firm specialized in private equity investments in multiple industries, including oil and gas exploration, waste management, Coca-Cola Bottling, Arby's Restaurants, and property and casualty insurance. The firm is most well-known for investing with George W. Bush in oil and gas exploration in the 1980s.

But for baseball, it meant that when Bill DeWitt Jr. finally got himself a baseball team to run, he wouldn't be forced to pinch pennies the way his father and uncle had needed to with the perpetually underfunded Browns back in the 1940s, or with the Reds in the 1960s, cutting their farm-system expenditures in an effort to retire debt.

Yet even a man as well connected as Bill DeWitt Jr. had some trouble getting that majority stake in a major league team.

"I was interested, and pursued, back in the early eighties," DeWitt recalled. "Back when Marge Schott bought the team." Take a moment and let that sink in, Reds fans: Bill DeWitt Jr. could have been the owner of your team instead of Marge Schott. "But she was already a partner. So she had first call."

Those efforts continued, each time bringing DeWitt Jr. closer to, yet short of, owning a major league team.

"I lived in Cincinnati," DeWitt Jr. said. "I reached out to the Reds—ended up buying a small stake, sort-of-undisclosed partnership in the Reds—around the early eighties. But I'd gotten close to George Bush because we'd been partners in the oil business. So when [the Rangers] became available, and I found out about it, I called him. We'd sold our oil and gas business, he was working on his father's campaign." That would be George H. W. Bush's 1988 campaign to be president of the United States.

"And when we were in the oil and gas business, he and I used to travel around, getting investors. So he and I would go to ball games—he was a huge baseball fan. And we always said, someday maybe we'll own a team. So when I found out about the Rangers, I called him. And we worked together on the Rangers acquisition."

But DeWitt's role with the Rangers was more financial than executive, and so by 1993 he took an opportunity to finally become a majority owner of a major league team. And thus, the book you are reading today is all about that team he purchased... the Baltimore Orioles?

"I had a contract with Eli Jacobs to buy the Orioles," DeWitt said. "Then he went personally bankrupt. The creditors didn't honor the contract. It went into bankruptcy court. It's really an interesting story."

But not a story that ends with DeWitt at the helm of the team. Instead, the Orioles got Peter Angelos, who paid $173 million.[2] DeWitt had a minority stake in that team, too, part of the spoils for solving the bidding for the Orioles by four different entities, including eventual Miami Marlins owner Jeff Loria. But shortly thereafter, DeWitt recognized that, as a minority owner, he wouldn't have the baseball role in Baltimore he still sought. I asked him whether he'd come to worry he'd never get the opportunity to fulfill the work he'd originally sought nearly three decades earlier.

"At that point, I was still in the Rangers deal," DeWitt said. "I would weigh in on things from time to time. Not active, but enjoyed it. I was in the private equity business. But I always wanted to get back, in a control-ownership role. I was in the game one way or another from the early eighties, straight through. And I stayed in touch with all the people I knew throughout the game. Had the Oriole deal gone through, I would have moved to Baltimore and actively run the team. But it motivated me to get back on a full-time operating basis."

Not that DeWitt thought it would be the Cardinals. For as appropriate a fit as it all seems in retrospect—the strands of Rickey's original plan, Kissell and DeWitt Jr., brought back together within the organization where the ideas of statistical revolution and player development originally thrived together for a quarter of a century—DeWitt never thought the club would be available.

The man who hired Rickey, Sam Breadon, sold the club in 1947. Six years later, Anheuser-Busch (A-B) purchased the team from Fred Saigh, who'd been pressured to sell due to a minor inconvenience of federal tax-evasion charges.

And for more than four decades after that, few owners were more synonymous with the team they owned than Busch (as in, the Stadiums) and the St. Louis Cardinals.

"The interesting thing about Baltimore was, it was the old Browns," DeWitt said, raising the connection to the franchise his father and uncle had run five decades before. "So it was intriguing. They had a new ballpark." DeWitt laughed at the notion that he'd have moved the Orioles back to St. Louis, but the lineage wasn't far from his mind.

"I'm lucky that the Baltimore deal didn't work out. Because the Cardinals turned out to be a much better fit. [DeWitt's wife] Kathy and I grew up there, my father's history, everything I knew about the city. But I really didn't think the Cardinals would ever be for sale. It had just been part of that corporate structure forever."

Once again, DeWitt's personal network helped him facilitate a transaction. He got a call from Fred Hanser, an old friend and classmate, who had heard secondhand that the team might be for sale. He called Sandy Warner, a good friend, who was on the board of A-B, to find out if it was true. Warner suggested DeWitt contact longtime A-B executive Jerry Ritter, whom DeWitt also knew well because Ritter and DeWitt each owned a house in the same development down in Florida, just outside Vero Beach.

"We negotiated a lot of the deal, down there," DeWitt said.

By the end of the 1995 season, DeWitt could see his quest was nearly over, though the announcement came in January 1996.

"It was quite a thrill," DeWitt said. "I remember, we hadn't quite reached an agreement on the last day of the season, back in '95. I went to the game, and I remember walking around the outfield. You know, just sort of getting a feel for the opportunity, what it would be like. And I'd gone to games over the years, when I came to town."

This, however, was very different from attending the game as a fan. The DeWitts had themselves a major league team again.

"Well, Bill the Third had gotten out of Harvard Business School in '95, which was really when we were negotiating the deal," DeWitt Jr. said. "And he was working in private equity. And we had talked—that if this deal went through, it would be a great opportunity for him to get involved in the business. He was a great age, and he'd obviously been a huge fan growing up, so it was an ideal situation for him. And for me, to have him continue on."

To be clear, though, Bill DeWitt Jr. doesn't believe the Cardinals are his family's birthright. As perfect as the combination seems in hindsight, a family returning to finish the work it started decades before, nothing about it was preordained in DeWitt Jr.'s mind.

"The reaction in St. Louis to the history, particularly the baseball history, was a positive and made Anheuser-Busch comfortable," DeWitt said. "Also, we had five to six St. Louis investors in the group who were all highly regarded in the community. That was very helpful, and they have been great partners and very supportive of how the franchise has been run. I wouldn't go as far as to say 'rightful place.' It was just exciting to get back in the game, and in an active way. To run a team—to continue the family legacy."

But doing that in precisely the way Bill DeWitt Jr. once wrote about back in 1965, or the way Bill DeWitt Sr. once ran the franchise's farm back in 1925—well, that didn't happen right away.

DeWitt had his team. And he didn't shy away from investing in the farm system. But early on, it happened more at the top of drafts, in one-off situations, as opposed to the comprehensive way we'd see the Cardinals incorporate this imperative from DeWitt later in his tenure.

"First off, we used to have organizational meetings, where all the scouts would attend," DeWitt Jr. said. "And it was a little bit different from what we do now. Mike Jorgensen was the farm director at that time. So when I first took over, I went to the meetings, and I spoke to the scouts. I said, 'One thing you should know is, I'm totally committed to drafting and signing the best players. We will never back off from a player who is a talent because maybe there's some signability issues—I mean, within reason. But this is the lifeblood of the business. I know what you go through—the long hours, the travel. But it's an important job. It's hard. You see all those players, and then there's a draft—you love a player, and somebody else takes him. So it can be a thankless job.'

"I wanted to let them know I understood that. I always delivered that message, and I'd like to think they knew it was true."

DeWitt had a chance to prove it the year after he bought the team. He recalled sitting in the 1997 draft room. Both DeWitt and Mozeliak described a draft board set up traditionally, with 100, maybe 125, names up there in order.

"So we made our first pick, and then, as the pick's made, you take the name off the board and throw it in the waste can," DeWitt said as we chatted in his office a few hours before the 2014 draft began in June. "He's gone. And as we were approaching the second round—and we picked kind of low because we won the division the year before, and we'd picked Adam Kennedy.

"In the first column, all the names were gone except for Rick Ankiel. As the second round began, the group's talking about 'Well, are we going to take this guy or that guy, if he's available,' and I said, 'What about Rick Ankiel? Tell me about Rick Ankiel.' I didn't know Rick Ankiel. And they described him as this impact, great, left-handed high school pitcher, and I said, 'Why aren't we taking him?' They said, 'Well, you can't. He's not signable.' And I said, 'What do you mean he's not signable?' They said, 'Well, he's got Scott Boras for an agent, and if he doesn't get a multimillion-dollar contract, he's going to go to college.' I said, 'Oh, really? Is he a good student? Does he really want to go to college?' And they said, 'No. He wants to play.'"

The price tag Boras floated was based on the year before, when Travis Lee, an elite prospect, had been declared a free agent and received $10 million from the Diamondbacks. Boras told teams it would cost something similar to keep Ankiel out of school.

"And then I kept probing," DeWitt said. "And they said, 'Oh, well. It's going to take at least three million,' and I said, 'Well, we'll see. But I think we should take him,' and so they took him."

The signing of Ankiel, who would become of the elite young pitchers in the game as a twenty-year-old for the 2000 Cardinals, before arm and psychological difficulties forced him from the mound and into a productive career as an outfielder, came down to the final day.

"It was a typical Boras scenario where he's going to enroll in the University of Miami if he didn't get three million," DeWitt said. "And we said, 'Two and a half million or have a good time in college,' and he took the two and a half."

Mozeliak described this approach as a huge change from previous practices, which were, in his words, "almost penny-pinching, if I may say so."

No longer. The Cardinals grabbed another Boras client in the 1998 draft, J. D. Drew, who'd sat out an entire year rather than sign with the Phillies in the 1997 draft. They went above and beyond in 1998 to bring in the multisport star Chad Hutchinson.

"But my point of all of this is we were aggressive then," Mozeliak said.

The problem with the strategy change wasn't the going-above-slot for players. But the failure to make the draft focus comprehensive didn't change the overall quality of draft hauls beyond them.

Ankiel and Drew paid off. Ben Diggins, drafted but unsigned in 1998, and Hutchinson didn't. But the Cardinal drafts throughout the rest of the 1990s, into the early 2000s, left the franchise without the kind of steady pipeline of talent that helped the teams from that era compete. This was a minor problem within that era, but not one Cardinals GM Walt Jocketty couldn't overcome, primarily through free agency and the salary dumps of other teams.

As the twenty-first century commenced, that began to change, notably with the 2002 collective bargaining agreement (CBA).

"Back then, the environment was such that a lot of clubs, for whatever reason—whether it was going younger, or financial constraints, or other reasons, were a little more willing to give up players we thought could help our club," DeWitt said back in August 2013. "So we were able to make trades for Jim Edmonds, and Mark McGwire, Scott Rolen and Darryl Kile—really key players who had great seasons with us and really elevated the franchise over that period of time.

"But we could see the landscape changing. And frankly, we pressed the draft and were aggressive in the draft... but there wasn't a lot of depth to that. When you sign free agents, you're giving up draft picks. And when you make deals, generally you're trading younger players."

Meanwhile, the 2002 CBA, which DeWitt describes as the same "intellectual underpinnings" as the subsequent 2006 and 2011 agreements, added revenue sharing at a level that allowed many more teams, even the bottom-feeding financial franchises, to keep more of their young players. Gone were deals to dump salary expenses out of necessity. And teams could extend their valuable young players to keep them from free agency.

"The implications are, I can't go get Jim Edmonds because they can't sign him," DeWitt said. "Player resources become much more valuable."

So the Cardinals found themselves, in 2003, with a payroll of $83.4 million, good for eighth-highest in baseball.[3]

But DeWitt recognized that $83.4 million wasn't going to buy what it once did. And it wasn't just that the Cardinals would have to spend more, though that would prove to be true. It's that those players they once bought with their $83.4 million wouldn't even be available.

The Cardinals were winning. Everything looked great on the field. But their ability to compete with the New Yorks and the Bostons would disappear if they continued with their current plan, especially with the low picks that come with winning. And they'd fall behind even those who spent less but did a better job of producing young talent. To guard against this, DeWitt began encouraging offering arbitration to would-be free agents, in large part to collect draft picks if they signed elsewhere. Current Cardinal standout starter Lance Lynn, drafted with a compensation pick for losing Troy Percival after 2007, is a fine example of this strategy in action.

Still, the Cardinals had a problem, though few other than Bill DeWitt Jr. realized it. Even within his own organization. Even in the eyes of his own team's general manager.

It was time for DeWitt to call for some help from the outside. He went with a guy who'd redesigned the way Lands' End did business, played fantasy baseball, and had never before spent any time in professional baseball.

4

LUHNOW ENTERS

He that will not apply new remedies must expect new evils; for time is the greatest innovator.

—Francis Bacon

So I'm thinking, "What is Tony [La Russa] thinking? Here's the PetStore.com marketing guy in with DeWitt."

—Jeff Luhnow

Jeff Luhnow had far more in common with you in the summer of 2003 than he did with the decision makers in Major League Baseball.

You know that famous Billy Beane quote from *Moneyball*—"We're not selling jeans here"? Luhnow had actually sold jeans. More specifically, he'd been hired by Lands' End to improve how they sold jeans online.

Luhnow was a business-consulting specialist. He'd done this work first for McKinsey, then struck out on his own for several years. He was three rounds of investment into the work at his newest start-up, Archetype Solutions, described by Luhnow as "mass customization of apparel for brands like Lands' End" in August 2003 when an old colleague of his, Jay Kern, sent him an e-mail.

"I forgot who his father-in-law was so I did a little bit of research and figured out it was Bill DeWitt Jr. because I knew him before he married into the family," Luhnow told me as we sat in the visiting manager's office at Citi Field in September 2014. "And I was perplexed as to why the owner of a baseball team would want to talk to me.... But it was, like, 'Hey, Jeff. It's Jay. How's everything going with the business?' Blah, blah, blah, you know. 'By the way, my father-in-law, Bill DeWitt Jr., wants to talk to you.' And I was, like, 'Who is this?' Like, took me one Google search to figure out who it was. And then I remember and I started going, 'Yeah, Katie DeWitt and he married her, and her father ended up buying the team a few years later.' And I'm, like, 'Okay. This is a baseball guy.'"

Luhnow, like so many of the most influential figures in baseball's evolution over the past decade, had just read *Moneyball*.

"My ex-wife bought it for me. My birthday's June eighth. The book had just come out. I was in the Bay Area so there was a lot of talk about it on the radio. I got the book. Read it front to back. I was interested but that was about it."

This is not to say that reading *Moneyball* was the sum total of Luhnow's interest or background in the sport. His interest dated back to his parents—especially his mother, Luhnow says—and a childhood following the Dodgers from Mexico, with trips to the Astrodome thrown in when he attended summer camp. Accordingly, he'd reached out to fellow Penn alum Peter O'Malley after graduating: "Is there room for any person who has an engineering and business degree? Are there any jobs in baseball that are interesting?"

Luhnow never heard back. It didn't stop him from doing the parallel work that so many of his generation did, these shadow front offices making their way ultimately into journalism, finance, law, and other high-profile nonbaseball industries—but always, as Bill DeWitt put it, "looking to get back." Baseball in the blood.

These were not people, though, who generally ever got the chance to make decisions for Major League Baseball teams. So instead, Luhnow sat in the bleachers at Wrigley Field.

Luhnow Enters

"When I was in business school at Kellogg, I took a class in management strategy, and I chose to study the Cubs," Luhnow said. "So I did a whole paper on the Cubs, and when I did that, I did a lot of research into the industry, what the key success factors were to compete for a team like the Cubs. I was also spending many afternoons in the bleachers drinking Old Style beer and yelling at Sammy Sosa. So I learned a lot about the business side of baseball, as well as the fan experience. And I've been playing fantasy baseball for close to fifteen years and knew every player up and down every system. But I really had no intention or thought of venturing into baseball."

Luhnow in his career, instead, bounced from start-up to start-up, got them up and running, then moved on to the next challenge. So, three investment rounds into Archetype Solutions' development was the ideal moment for him to take on something new, intellectually and emotionally.

"I was pretty close with a lot of venture capitalists because we went through a lot of funding for both my companies, and I really thought my next step was going to be, they were going to insert me into one of their companies because VCs always need CEO types to run companies," Luhnow said. "So I figured that would be my next step . My career was fine without baseball. Jay calls and I end up having my first call with [Bill]. Jay introduced us and was on the call and we really [connected]—it was supposed to be a forty-five-minute call. It wound up being about two hours. And it was really just a very pleasant conversation. I shared a lot of my thoughts and he asked a lot of questions, and at the end of that conversation he asked me to come to Cincinnati to see him."

"I was talking to my son-in-law about the type of person we needed," DeWitt recalled in a May 2014 interview with me. "Because I thought we needed a fresh look. We were a pretty traditional team, doing things pretty traditional ways. And I wanted somebody fresh, to give an outsider's perspective. And to do more research and analysis. And [Jay] said, 'I've got the perfect guy. He's a baseball fanatic. He's a great analyst for McKinsey. And I know he would love a project like what you are proposing.'"

So Jeff flew to Cincinnati to give what turned out to be a life-defining presentation. In the middle of fantasy-baseball season, Luhnow told the owner of the most successful franchise in the National League how he'd change the way his ball club operated.

"We talked through all different elements of baseball and the club and where it was going," Luhnow said. "And he gave me some background on who the characters were from the organization to the ownership though the general manager. Everybody else. And by that time I had done a lot more research because I had three or four days to prepare.

"So I came in with—I kind of treated it like I would a McKinsey study where you just kind of figure out—if I were the owner of a baseball team, what would I be concerned about? Where are the Cardinals today? Where is the industry going? How are the Cardinals thinking? And a lot of the things that I had prepared to talk about, Bill was very much on the same page about these things.

"And so we had a really good conversation. And then I don't remember all the sequence of conversations, but I do know at one point he said, 'I want you to come to St. Louis and meet Walt [Jocketty] and meet some other people.' Some of his partners. And so I remember we were playing, interestingly enough, the Astros. The Cardinals were at home. It was the end of the '03 season and I met Walt."

Luhnow even met Cardinals manager Tony La Russa, though it wasn't their first meeting.

"Tony had just gotten the win that made him third-winningest manager, so they were going to present him with a watch on the last week they were with him," Luhnow recalled. "I went into the club to watch them present Tony with a watch, and interestingly enough, Tony and I, our paths had crossed in '99. I was head of marketing for PetStore.com and we were trying to do a relationship with the ARF, which is the foundation he runs, and I had supported their fund-raiser. He came to our warehouse, and I met him. I remember talking to him, and he had gotten on the phone with Walt Jocketty, and they were thinking about a trade where they got [Pat] Hentgen and [Mike] Matheny. And he said, 'What do you think?' And I knew enough about all these players where I was able to give me my point of view. He was, like, 'Oh, you actually know something about baseball.' And Tony gave me tickets to go to the game when the Cardinals were in town against the Giants.

"So we had that connection and I remember giving Tony a bag. Like a briefcase. And fast-forward [four] years and I'm in his office and Bill DeWitt's giving him this watch, and Tony says to me, 'I still have the bag.' And I thought, 'Oh my God. He remembers me. Like, how is that even possible?' I didn't say [anything about the last meeting], and he was, like, 'I still have the bag.'

"So I'm thinking, 'What is Tony thinking? Here's the PetStore.com marketing guy in with DeWitt. What is going on here?' And it was strange."

Bill and Jeff first talked in August 2003. At the time, the Cardinals were locked in a three-way race in the National League Central with the Astros and the Cubs. They'd finish 85-77, three games out, the only season between 2000 and 2005 when they'd fail to win 90+ games. They slipped to 83 in 2006, but it's hard to call that a lost season: the Cardinals made the play-offs and won the 2006 World Series.

"I think what led up to it, Bill just had some ideas," Walt Jocketty, the team's general manager from 1995 to 2007, recalled in a January 2015 interview. "And he wanted to try some different ideas. And at first I resisted, because I thought we were pretty successful in the way we were doing it.

"And I think as time passed, one thing I did regret, in hindsight, was probably not agreeing to adapt more quickly than I did. We really hadn't done a lot with analytics, and that type of information. And I think it was also working with a manager and a coaching staff that weren't really that adept at that either. And they resisted it initially as well."

So consider for a moment how Bill DeWitt Jr. might have been thought of in St. Louis as he changed what was working with the Cardinals. The coming years provided scores of critics, both within and outside the organization.

If the new direction for the team had faltered, the change would have seemed like the reason.

"I never thought about my legacy if success had not followed what I believed to be the optimal process," DeWitt told me in November 2014. "Of course you are right that there was no assurance that good outcomes necessarily follow good process. The challenge at the time was to change the organizational culture, and it wasn't easy, particularly with the on-field success we were having. It was easy for those who disagreed with the approach to be critical, and this worked its way into the media. There was never any question in my mind, however, that this was the correct path for the Cardinals, and I was prepared to live with the results despite the disruption and scrutiny."

Or as former Cardinals executive, now Athletics Assistant General Manager Dan Kantrovitz put it to me, "The bottom line is, Bill had the courage to fix something that wasn't necessarily broken."

A month after his initial meeting with Jeff, Bill DeWitt prepared a memo, which he shared with a few senior members of the organization, about his new hire, Luhnow. His proposed role bears more than a passing resemblance to that Bill DeWitt Jr. signed up for with the Reds back in 1967.

I asked Bill why he didn't take on the role himself. After all, implementing these principles had been a lifelong pursuit of his. Plenty of owners with far less expertise meddle with their teams or flat out ruin them. But perhaps it is precisely the intelligence that separates DeWitt from a James Dolan of the Knicks or Jerry Jones of the Cowboys that convinced him to delegate that role.

"No," DeWitt said, laughing, when I posed the question to him in September 2014.

"First of all, I was running the overall franchise. We had a lot going on, especially efforts to build a new stadium. That was a specific, full-time job at the time. I just figured I'd get the right person in there. And I'm not sure I could have done it. Someone at that age, with those computer skills, is what we needed. I always, in everything I've done, I've tried to get smart people around me. The smarter the better. And let them figure it out."

DeWitt returned to this himself, later in the same conversation. "Jeff hired Sig [Mejdal]. It's kind of, like, why didn't I do Jeff's job? Why didn't Jeff do Sig's job? Because you want to bring in smarter and smarter people."

MEMORANDUM

FROM: Bill DeWitt
RE: Proposed Organizational Change
DATE: September 16, 2003

I have been concerned for some time that our player procurement process and professional player evaluation system have not been at a level to give us a competitive advantage within Major League Baseball and in certain areas have in fact been below average. It is critical to the success of our franchise that we endeavor to correct this, and my goal would be to put us at the forefront in these areas to take advantage of what is certainly an inefficient market.

I would propose to establish a position under Walt titled Vice President of Baseball Development. Enclosed is a description I have developed of what this job would entail, and I am very excited to have come across an individual who, I believe, is ideally suited to take on this important role.

His name is Jeff Luhnow, and he is 37 years old. Although his family is originally from the East Coast, Jeff grew up in Mexico City and, of course, is very fluent in Spanish. He is a graduate of the University of Pennsylvania with a joint degree in Economics and Engineering and has an MBA from Northwestern. Following graduate school, Jeff worked for McKinsey and Co. in Chicago for five years where he was ranked at the top of his class, achieved pre-partner status at the earliest possible age, and was on track to become a partner when he left to pursue an Internet opportunity in California. From there he became a founder and C.O.O. of an Internet startup which has grown, appears to be on a successful track, and has continued to be funded by sophisticated venture funds in a very difficult climate. Jeff designed and implemented the information technology system and currently manages 35 employees.

The reason Jeff would leave his current position, which has substantial upside with his management warrants, is he is a baseball "nut." He has always been a huge fan who follows and studies the game in his spare time including the extensive scientific work which has been developed over the last 20 years. He almost bought a minor league team a couple of years ago and has always wanted to be involved in baseball. I became aware of Jeff through Jay Kern, who worked with him and vouches for his talent and importantly, his personal qualities. He would fit in very well with our organization. I think he presents a unique opportunity for us to bring to the Cardinals a high level McKinsey talent at a below market price to fill a very challenging and important position.

VICE PRESIDENT OF BASEBALL DEVELOPMENT

Responsibilities

1. Establish methods of evaluation for amateur players.
   A. Based on existing data and history, what are best predictors of success, e.g., tools, intangibles (makeup), performance, etc. Look backwards from MLB and forward from amateur signings.
   B. Determine risk/reward parameters for various categories of draft, including high school, college, pitchers, position players and combinations thereof.
   C. Research and assess cost/benefit analysis for outside U.S.; Dominican Republic, Venezuela, Asia and elsewhere.
2. Based on information generated from the above, determine the best organizational structure and allocation of resources to

achieve our basic goal: to acquire players on a real value basis with maximum market efficiency.
3. Develop and establish information technology system relative to professional player personnel.
   A. Build data base for professional players with maximum relevant information for each player.
   B. Establish a model to evaluate a player's contribution to winning which will help quantify a player's financial value and therefore determine what he should be paid.
   C. Model would include a forecast or a prediction of future success. Types of relevant information will include age of increasing, peak, and declining performance, ball park impact, performance to date, likelihood of injury, length of time in minors, etc.
4. The overall objective of this knowledge based and systematic approach is to enable the Cardinals to make the best possible player decisions, including financial commitments, and to take advantage of the inefficient market.

Luhnow soon had to employ one of the most significant attributes Kern touted to his father-in-law: an ability to withstand criticism.

"I was in charge of recruiting for both Northwestern and from Chicago," Luhnow said. "From the McKinsey Chicago office. And [Kern] was one of the top recruits. He did a summer internship. I recruited him to come back full-time. He had offers to go work in Wall Street. We got him back full-time. I was working for a manager who was known as one of the toughest managers in the office. She was really, really tough on people. And I didn't have any problem with her at all. Jay rolled onto a study that I was rolling off of and took my role on the study with an insurance company, and this woman became his manager, and he sort of freaked out. He had a tough time handling her because she was a micromanager. Jay's a really smart guy, I mean he's really capable, but they didn't get along at all. And I remember Jay saying,

'I can't believe you survived under this manager. You must have a really thick skin. You must have a really great way of getting along with people that I don't have.' Because I'm not sure that's the study that drove him from the firm, but he ended up leaving the firm shortly after that.

"I think he felt that if I could survive under her that I could probably survive the rough-and-tumble baseball world. He anticipated some negative reaction to someone like me coming in. He communicated to Bill that this guy, one of his strengths is that he's got a thick skin and he's not going to be easily pushed aside by some of the traditional baseball guys."

Understand this: over the past decade, baseball has come a long way on the idea that those who didn't play the game can eventually run it. When Luhnow was hired, the use of statistical analysis by the A's was an anomaly. Now, clubs that *don't* rely on such analysis are very much the anomaly. Clubs without an analytics department don't exist. Theo Epstein, don't forget, was a widely mocked hire back in 2002. That he was a breakthrough in any number of ways for the sport didn't gain widespread acceptance until he broke a little eighty-six-year-old streak in Boston.

But even today, someone with Jeff Luhnow's background, brought in with a relatively senior title (vice president of baseball development) and an expansive portfolio, would be looked upon suspiciously by many people within a major league organization.

And this wasn't just a major league organization. This was the St. Louis Cardinals. And while there were a few around who'd internalized what George Kissell stood for—the constant innovation that he'd learned from Branch Rickey, the consistent adding to and changing of his manual first scripted decades ago during a snowy Ithaca winter—for many others, the Cardinals were this static, successful thing.

"When you think about the timing—okay?—'03 was not a great year for us," Mozeliak told me in a January 2015 interview. "Wasn't awful, but wasn't great... and Walt at the time was probably considered one of the top five general managers in the game. And then subsequently, Bill brings in Jeff, and I think Walt had a hard time with that because it wasn't his decision to bring him in. It wasn't necessarily his type of person to be around from a personality standpoint. And now fast-forward from October of '03 to now, say, July of '04, guess what? The St. Louis Cardinals are a pretty damn good baseball team all of sudden. Right? And so I think, in Walt's case, he was, like, 'We knew what we're doing.' We subsequently win 105 games. We go on to the World Series. And I think he felt, like, 'Jeez, maybe we weren't that bad off.'"

And some guy from McKinsey was going to come along and ruin it.

"But if you think of it from Jeff's perspective, that he was brought in by the owner, you know? The owner," Mejdal, who joined Luhnow with the Cardinals in 2005, told me in an October 2014 interview. "At a time the team was winning. There weren't many people with his background in baseball at that time. I can say that the resentment of the portrayal of scouts in *Moneyball* was quite fresh in people's minds. And Jeff was brought into a system that wasn't particularly interested in having him in that system.... I think that's a description of what ground rules were like when he came in."

Or as Mozeliak put it, "I don't think Walt trusted him, and I don't think Walt liked him. And from that standpoint, that was where it began."

Precisely how huge an advantage the Cardinals had just given themselves came into focus early on, in a meeting with the analytics team.

"When we first did the retrospective study, I could see the improvement to realize with the proposed methodology and felt compelled to convince anyone I could that we needed to take advantage of this." Mejdal recalled. "I remember we presented that to the owner, La Russa, and [then–pitching coach Dave] Duncan, and [team president] Billy DeWitt [III] was there, too. I remember the look on Billy's face very well. I didn't know if there would be skepticism or even a dismissal of the idea, but instead I saw a look of excitement. He and his father both appreciated that the inefficiency was there, and I remember feeling a great relief. It was just a question of how much of it could we grab and how long would the inefficiency remain."

Also, how quickly the team could implement a system to capture that inefficiency without the support of some key stakeholders, such as the general manager. Jocketty, who'd led the Cardinals to significant success that continued as Jeff was brought in, had a hard time fathoming that he'd be more than an advisory hire.

"Initially, I was told, in fact by Jeff himself, that he was there to observe and [find] ways that we might do things better, and how we might make better decisions, however the process was," Jocketty said. "And it was something that was more an informational piece as much as anything. But then, through the years, when he was brought in full-time, he got more involved with scouting, then player development, it became obvious that it was a change in direction, in philosophy, that they were eventually going to go to."

Luhnow lacked the credentials that would have made him palatable to many in the organization already. Several people I talked to, including Jocketty, believed that Luhnow's receiving a senior title right away created additional friction as well, though Mejdal believes, with good reason, that Luhnow's ideas would not likely have been heard at all without that title and his direct line to DeWitt.

Every single person I interviewed told me that Luhnow's ideas would have been a huge problem regardless of who advocated for them. Luhnow worked hard to implement these ideas slowly enough to avoid more significant conflict, often to the frustration of his analytics team. But if he'd slowed them any further, he would have been operating at a suboptimal level for the man who hired him.

"I felt like the mandate from Bill was 'Let's make sure that we put together a system to provide information to the decision makers, especially on the baseball side, so let's make sure that we're not flying blind when it comes to all of the GM stuff,' all of the sabermetrics, if you want to call it that," Luhnow said. "Information that front offices are clearly starting to use to make better decisions. Let's make sure that we're up to speed. And Bill's instinct was that we we're not up to speed. And he was correct. And so there was not a lot of information that looked at—at performance in a different way than just looking at the scout sheets."

While the organization was not monolithic in resenting Luhnow, it must have felt that way to him, particularly early on.

"I thought it was good that we were starting to take a more analytic view of the game," longtime Cardinals front office executive John Vuch told me in a December 2014 e-mail. "But for a long time, I was the closest thing we had to an analytics department—at one point my title was something like Manager of Baseball Information. So I was all for us ramping up the statistical side of things, as I thought we underutilized the stats in our decision-making process."

Luhnow concurs, crediting Vuch for doing what he could within the system. But Luhnow added, "There was nobody—it wasn't like I was encroaching on anybody's territory because there was nobody really to do any of these things."

Yet, at least the implied threat was obvious to Jocketty, according to John Mozeliak, who was hired by Jocketty in 1995. Jocketty had succeeded in his role. But his method for doing so was not dramatically different from that of the Cardinals GMs who'd preceded him.

"My first thoughts were—one was, I was scared. Because I could tell Walt wasn't happy," Mozeliak said in an October 2014 interview. "So I didn't know what all of this meant, or how this would affect us. But there was a part of me that also saw it as a wonderful opportunity. I was curious. I understood how the old model worked. I got it. I could do that. But I also saw that the world was changing."

Or as Jocketty put it, "I think my feelings then and now are much different. I still have a lot of respect and admiration for that organization, for the people there, and the utmost respect for Bill DeWitt, and what he's done for that franchise through the years. But at the time, I didn't understand. Because I thought we had been very successful with what we had been doing. But Bill had the vision to see that things were changing rapidly."

> *To a certain extent, I'm not going to call them all social outcasts, but they're not exactly people you'd find at a bar, you know, late at night.*
>
> —JEFF LUHNOW

If the entrenched forces that made up much of the Cardinals front office rejected Luhnow himself, you can imagine the response to the advisory board Luhnow immediately put together to begin analysis of any inefficiencies in the team's operations.

"I read a lot," Luhnow remembers of this time. "I researched a lot and I found people that resonated with me that I thought were smart and could help, and I started asking them for advice. If you were the baseball team, what capabilities would you want to build with? Things you'd focus on, et cetera, et cetera. Also really enjoyed reading because I was into fantasy, [innovative fantasy-baseball writer] Ron Shandler's stuff about how to predict the future from stuff from the past. And so I got Ron Shandler involved and I actually created this advisory board. When you're in the start-up world, you create an advisory board of people that are in your sector just to get credibility, and you use them for advice as well. You don't pay them anything. We had a great advisory board at Archetype of, like, [high profile businessman] Arthur Rock... so people with clout and knowledge.

"And so I figured, let me get in this little area of baseball information, advanced baseball information. Let me pull together a little group of experts and let them feel involved in what we're doing, but more importantly get access to their brains and figure out what we can do."

Luhnow didn't start bringing this group to meetings or anything—as he put it, "Walt wouldn't have known Mitchel Lichtman from Tom Tango from Ron Shandler from any of these guys.... So it didn't matter who I presented. It was going to be weird and different and odd no matter what. Now, these are some odd characters. You know, none of them played. The analytical crew is a unique breed of people.... To a certain extent, I'm not going to call them all social outcasts but they're not exactly people you'd find at a bar, you know, late at night."

But while Luhnow gathered information about how he'd recommend changing the team's process long term, "At the same time, I was getting myself as up to speed as possible on how I could help the baseball decisions that fall," Luhnow said. "And there were a lot. There was trading J. D. Drew and what we were going to get back from that. There was signing free agents like [Jeff] Suppan and [Reggie] Sanders and—how can we make sure that if we're going to go out and sign a free-agent pitcher that we get the right guy? Obviously we had scouting reports from pro scouts on all that, but I felt like my responsibilities were to make sure that we didn't make a mistake, by really understanding their performance history. And so Suppan was probably one of the first signings that I felt like I influenced.

"But I do remember, in particular, it was Suppan, I was really intrigued by the consistency of his win-share production year over year. And the fact that he was kind of money in the bank to earn between ten and thirteen win shares every year regardless of environment or—and to me, on what I thought was a play-off-contending, championship-contending team, that would translate into ten to fifteen wins. Which when you add it to Matt Morris—it just seemed like a number three starter that would stabilize the rotation, and that's what I argued. I remember arguing that to Walt and Bill, and I think I successfully moved Suppan to guys to consider. Because he wasn't the sexiest guy in the world.... He was just, kind of, Mr. Consistency."

But while Luhnow participated in meetings through normal channels on Suppan, a pitcher the Cardinals ultimately signed, his direct link to DeWitt manifested itself that winter as well, in another key move the Cardinals made.

"The other one was the Drew trade, because I was kind of involved on the sidelines on that almost," Luhnow said. "Bill was asking me, 'What's your opinion on things?' Separate to—not in front of Walt. It was almost like a double check.

"So I do remember the first [Drew] trade proposal, looking back on Drew was [exciting] in my opinion—because Drew was a spectacular producer. Now, injury-prone and all of that, but I had this feeling like we're giving up a lot. And Atlanta, we knew Atlanta was interested, but they really needed him. And so I remember telling Bill that I didn't think we were getting enough back from that original proposal. So the deal didn't happen. Whether or not Bill killed the deal or Walt also agreed, I don't know, but that was my opinion. And at the winter meetings, I remember Bill calling me and saying, 'What do you think we need to do to get in addition to'—'cause we were getting Ray King and Marquis—'in addition to those to guys?' I said, 'Well, to be honest, well, I think we need a legitimate prospect on top of those two guys to make this deal fair.'

"And so I went and researched a lot of prospects stuff. I read as much as I could. I read our own reports, but I read all the prospect reports...going onto blogs. Everything. And I really felt like [Adam] Wainwright was the guy. 'Cause he had fallen off a little bit. He'd been their number one prospect. Still is in the top five but had fallen off. Had a bad year. And I remember, that's the guy I recommended to Walt." Other members of the front office, including special assistant Bob Gebhard and DeWitt, pushed for Wainwright as well.

Wainwright, ultimately, came to St. Louis in that deal. Four top-three Cy Young Award finishes later, he's been one of the most important pitchers in Cardinals history.

But there's a lot more to unpack here than just the addition of a signature starting pitcher. As Luhnow put it, "I felt like, wow, this is unbelievable. A guy like me who was selling jeans six months ago—three months ago—is not only participating in this but potentially even having an impact in the major league trades. That's crazy. This is fantasy come alive. This is every fantasy GM's dream."

As for Jocketty, if he hadn't realized before that the hiring of Jeff had fundamentally altered the front-office power structure, he certainly did now, with Luhnow weighing in on Walt's major moves. And the effect on the Cardinals was nothing less than seismic.

Mozeliak, the assistant general manager, quickly took a position as essentially a moderate figure within the front office, a role he'd occupy for almost five years.

Ultimately, though he considered walking away once the factions grew so bitter, some advice he received helped him navigate how he thought about all the changes. He understood the necessity of altering the way the Cardinals evaluated talent—as he put it, "I always felt like the old world was just too subjective. Almost too random in the sense of, there has to be a way to make smarter decisions."

But that didn't make it any easier to see longtime friends angry and afraid, and his mentor Jocketty undermined.

"So Mark Lamping was our president at the time," Mozeliak recalled. "He and I were driving down to Springfield to discuss the Double-A franchise, and so obviously it's a three-and-a-half-hour drive. We've got a lot of stuff to talk about. And I've always looked at Mark as someone that I could get trusted advice from if I needed it. So we're driving down and I'm venting to him about where we are from a baseball side of things—and bear in mind, we had just gone to the World Series in '04, won 105 games.

"So it was—within that time period between '04 and '05 and that off-season, but, I was, like, what is this? This is tough, man. People just don't get along. It's, if you're seen going to lunch with Jeff, you're an enemy. It was just a really awkward period.

"And so the best advice I ever got, though, was from Mark. And he said, 'Mo. In the end, you work for Bill and that's where your loyalty has to go. And try not to worry about picking sides internally here. Just do your job, and if you do that, everything will be fine.' So, I mean, I actually thought at one point of just leaving here. It was getting so tense and it was very stressful."

But though DeWitt understood the inherent risks in this overhaul, he didn't plan to back away from the Luhnow revolution over some hurt feelings.

"Well, I told the other people that this was not threatening to anybody," DeWitt told me. "It was some independent work and it was a way for us to develop tools to help make the best decisions. And that's the way it was positioned.

"He certainly wasn't universally accepted. That's been pretty well documented. Anytime you make a change in an organization that's different from the direction that it's been headed—and especially one that had a lot of success—I mean, you're going to get pushback. I did get pushback, but I wasn't going to change because I knew in the end that it was something that had to be done."

So, with a 2004 draft to prepare for, and an international scouting department to build up from almost nothing, Luhnow received more than just the title DeWitt had decades before in Cincinnati.

"I told Jeff, 'Look, I'm going to give you resources. Whatever you need,'" DeWitt said. "So he hired some smart guys, and also from the outside. And they went about their business in doing that."

But the core group of statistical analysts that would ultimately power the recommendation and implementation of changes across the Cardinal universe didn't yet exist in 2004. Instead, Luhnow began to move on two fronts, seeing success far more quickly on one than the other: preparation for the 2004 draft, and the overhaul of the team's international scouting program.

"I really treated baseball operations like a McKinsey engagement," Luhnow said. "So I took each area and said, 'Okay. I'm going to study what's going on in the industry. I'm going to study what we're doing internally. I'm going to interview people. I'm going to interview everybody from the guy that runs it to the people at the line level and figure out what we can do.' Make recommendations across each area.

"The first area that was really, really easy for me to do that well was the international area because St. Louis had basically completely gotten out of international. The Venezuela Academy had shut down. The Dominican

Academy had finished playing in '03 and then they no longer played after that, so that, kind of, shut down. I did a trip with [Mozeliak] in January to the Caribbean series in Santo Domingo. He showed me where the old academy was. I met people. I interviewed a lot of people. I called a lot of people.

"And in my work I discovered a couple things. One is that not every club is successful [in Latin America]. But those that are come in at a significant advantage. And to not have a presence there is a disadvantage. The feeling was there was so much need for money to go into major league payroll as we were getting close to a ninety-, hundred-win team and the players were expensive, that anywhere you could shave that wasn't as productive could contribute to that. So they shaved international. The whole budget for international was like less than a hundred thousand dollars. May have been less than fifty thousand dollars the year I got there. Included two part-time scouts, who were not signing players. It just was not a good situation.

"So that was a pretty easy recommendation. And when I did come back with it, [I] presented it to Walt, presented it to Bill. There wasn't anybody running international so they basically said, 'Why don't you take it? Because you speak Spanish. You've been there. You like it. You have a passion for it. So take it.' So that was my first kind of real baseball responsibility besides being 'stat guy.'"

In this way, Luhnow took ownership of an area without coming into direct conflict with Walt Jocketty—after all, the budget was coming out of an additional expenditure from DeWitt, so no department lost anything. If the Cardinals found some additional players, great. If not, it wasn't as if Luhnow would be in the way of what many in the front office viewed as the real business of running a baseball team.

"We had an academy built in Dominican and we had no academy," Luhnow said. "We start from scratch. I interviewed architects, we got an academy. In less than a year, all of a sudden we were operating one of the nicest academies in the Dominican on a shoestring budget. Well, then people were, like, 'Oh, okay. That makes sense, right? I'm glad we have that now.'"

Where it became more difficult to reconcile two dramatically different ways of operating was in the draft room. And the results weren't pretty in that first draft, in the summer of 2004, after Luhnow signed on, or, as long-time Cardinals beat writer Derrick Goold described it to me, "the notorious 2004 draft."

"Oh, it was the '04 draft," DeWitt recalled. "That was a bad draft."

Worth noting here: it was DeWitt who brought up the 2004 draft, as he and I sat with Mozeliak in St. Louis a few hours before the 2014 draft began. The Cardinals, from DeWitt on down, never hesitated to discuss or even to broach the struggles they've endured, the mistakes they've made. If anything, it was getting them to talk about success that would prove more difficult throughout our scores of hours of interviews and time together.

The 2004 draft, though, was not one of those successes.

I would say that we had not fully developed and integrated what we were looking to do," DeWitt explained. "And there was maybe a mind-set in the draft that we were leaning toward more developed players. College players, which wasn't the intent, but since everyone really [didn't understand that], I don't think we were on the same page at that point. Would you agree with that?"

Mozeliak responded, "Well, I ran the draft. So I remember quite well. But it was the inability to really integrate any proven commodity."

Understand that in any major league draft, the players selected come from two pools: high school players, those who have finished their senior year in high school; and college players, those who have finished their junior or senior year in school (or are an equivalent age). Luhnow had gathered significant data about college players but not high school players.

"I got exposed a little bit to the '04 draft, and then Mo allowed me to, basically, participate in the room," Luhnow said. "I was in the back of the room. I was listening to scouts present. I was watching the whole process, and whenever it came to a college player, I had some data that I was able to help present.

Luhnow Enters

"I think that there were people in that room that felt like because I was hired and because I was there and because it was coming from Bill DeWitt, their interpretation of *Moneyball* meant drafting college players and not drafting any high school players, which is completely wrong. But that was the simplistic interpretation, and so I think scouts all pushed up their college players and pushed down their high school players, and I think as a result of that we ended up with all college players and it was a terrible draft."

Let's put this in a bit of context: A big room at Busch Stadium is filled with scouts, the scouting director at the time in Mozeliak, General Manager Jocketty, owner DeWitt, and Luhnow. He's not only a senior hire by the owner himself, at that time he's also undertaken a comprehensive review of the scouting department, determining what is working, what needs to change.

So some scouts moved college guys up in an effort to more closely hew to what they thought Luhnow wanted. Others wouldn't change a thing despite what Luhnow presented.

All the scouts were greeted with surprises on the big board a few times when they did nothing more than go use the restroom.

"So you pick a magnet for a player and you have the scouts talk about him, and five scouts will talk about him, and I would give a comment about the player's percentile," Luhnow said. "This guy's in the ninety-second percentile in terms of offense in [NCAA] Division I. And that really wouldn't move the magnet. All it would do is—I mean, occasionally when the scouts would leave the room and it was just Mo, a smaller group [of us]—we would move a couple magnets based off of—'Okay, well, this guy's got really good performance and this guy's got crappy performance, so let's flip these guys.' So there was some magnet flipping."

The process, as fragmented as it was, led to the Cardinals' choosing Boston College righty Chris Lambert over a player they'd ranked similarly, high school pitcher Phil Hughes.

"I think what the mistake that I made is when Mo asked—during the draft there were like six of us at the table and we were debating between Hughes and Lambert," Luhnow said. "And we actually had Hughes ranked above him. I had not seen either player so I just read both the reports on him and I did vote for Lambert because I figured he's probably a safer bet because he had survived three years of college and the reports were roughly equal. In retrospect, the right thing to do was go with the player that we liked the most because neither should have gotten a bump from their performance. And Hughes had a higher upside based on the scouting love."

Lambert won a total of one major league game, in 33 innings, none of them logged in a Cardinals uniform. The Cardinals traded him in 2007 for Mike Maroth, a middling pitcher better known for his work as a meteorologist, at the end of his (baseball, not weather-forecasting) career. Hughes won 16 games in 2014, the third time he'd reached that plateau in his career, and signed a long-term extension with the Minnesota Twins.

The 2004 Cardinals draft produced, ultimately, four major leaguers, but none of them made a significant impact at that level. None of the four earned even one Win Above Replacement in their entire careers.

But even that analysis requires hindsight unavailable to the Cardinals at the time. What's remarkable is how Luhnow, Mozeliak, and DeWitt all told me they not only recognize the failures of the 2004 draft now, they all recognized it at the time.

But DeWitt, unlike many owners in that situation, didn't back away from the process he'd begun by hiring Luhnow the year before. He didn't banish Mozeliak to the outer reaches of the organization or let him go after he oversaw the draft debacle.

Mozeliak got a promotion, to assistant GM. Luhnow, who'd scouted informally in the lead-up to the 2004 draft, seeing some of the potential first-rounders, received another title: scouting director. And armed with that portfolio, along with his international responsibilities, he went about building out his team within the front office. No longer would he be going about making these changes alone.

Bill DeWitt trusted process over the initial results and recognized that remaking an entire organization would take time. If the tradition-bound members of the Cardinals' front office thought Jeff Luhnow had an atypical background, the brain trust he ultimately formed didn't change anybody's mind. The McKinsey executive hired a guy from NASA and Lockheed Martin, a guy from Brown and Lehman Brothers, and a cartoonist.

I remember Paul DePodesta sent me an e-mail saying, "Keep at it." Something like "NASA meets baseball." That's what we need.

—Sig Mejdal

So a couple months later, I just went to New York and was there for a couple years as an investment banker. I'm glad I did that job because I realized that's something I absolutely never would want to do.

—Dan Kantrovitz

My initial involvement was highly unlikely and serendipitous—by first profession, I'm an artist.

—Mike Witte

If you attempted to create the ideal twenty-first-century front-office experience, training, and temperament for the rebuild of the St. Louis Cardinals, you'd probably end up with Dan Kantrovitz.

First, the young boy needs to fall in love with the game. So a 1978 birthday to parents who were season-ticket holders at old Busch Stadium isn't a bad place to start.

"I was four years old," Kantrovitz recalled in a September 2014 interview. "I went into the stadium club with my dad to look around. I'm not supposed to remember that, I know, but I think I remember it, the '82 Series. And every one, obviously, after that as well.

"I grew up in St. Louis. I grew up in a little suburb about twenty minutes from downtown, and I grew up watching Tommy Herr and Ozzie [Smith] and Terry [Pendleton] manning the infield. My parents had season tickets. That's what I remember most about my childhood. The AstroTurf, Whitey Herzog, and the Cardinals."

That tradition of baseball success in St. Louis first drew Kantrovitz to the game. Now, it's too simplistic to ascribe front-office acumen to someone just because he saw Ozzie Smith backflips all summer long, and a few Octobers, from Section 166. John Mozeliak became perhaps the most successful general manager in Cardinals history, and he fell for the game at Shea Stadium in the 1970s, of all places.

Still, it's impossible to miss the continuity inherent in players that George Kissell helped develop maturing into major leaguers who fostered Dan Kantrovitz's love of baseball.

But the analytical skills that ultimately allowed Kantrovitz to move quickly to the top of the baseball profession wouldn't manifest themselves in childhood—though Kantrovitz acknowledged his mother, Barbara, who works in commercial real estate, and his father, David, who worked in the insurance business, kept stats on him as early as age ten and, according to Kantrovitz, "were into the performance analysis back then. They're both into this."

Kantrovitz, though, grew up playing baseball. He hoped his future would be on the field and went to Brown University, where he graduated with a degree in organizational behavior—a combination program of economics, engineering, and psychology—all while hitting .417/.490/.620 his senior year.

But the ultimate ceiling of Kantrovitz's on-field career also came at Brown.

"I had in a practice, a rundown, a collision with another player," Kantrovitz recalled. "It was a harmless type of thing. It wasn't anything vicious. But my shoulder popped and that's when I tore my labrum. And I had a surgery in college to try to get past it. Because I thought, maybe, I could have a future in baseball. It's what I wanted to do and that was kind of a Band-Aid approach and got me on the field for my senior year. But I was kind of throwing sidearm.

"I built some arm strength, but I couldn't—I mean, there was something really wrong at that time. I was still getting interest from some of the teams, 'cause I could hit a little bit—but knowing in the back of my mind that [my career] was going to likely come to an end. I was like every other kid who studies economics advancement in college, you apply for those banking-consultant jobs. And so I did that at the same time and was hoping I got drafted. And fortunately I did."

The St. Louis Cardinals drafted Kantrovitz, taking him in the twenty-fifth round of the 2001 draft. I asked Kantrovitz if his own injury protocols as scouting director for the Cardinals from 2012 to 2014—put into place to maximize the number of healthy bodies in the draft class—would have prevented him from drafting himself.

"Wow... tough question," Kantrovitz wrote in a December 2014 e-mail. "Since we don't spend much time reviewing medical records of senior signs [$1k bonus guys], if I [or the player] was playing all year long, we would have to assume he was healthy... so, yes. It would have been too improbable/painful for a player to have been able to play an entire season at SS with a torn labrum."

Kantrovitz ought to know—he's the one who did it. Being drafted meant the future scouting director of the Cardinals had an internship in how the Cardinals develop players. Kantrovitz played as Kissell coached. He played with a catcher named Yadier Molina, a pitcher named Rick Ankiel, who walked 1.8 per nine and *struck out 16.2 per nine*, and got into a game at Johnson City—even collected a professional hit—before he and the Cardinals agreed that the only way he'd have a chance to make it through their system would be to repair the labrum with major surgery.

But the surgery didn't work. Kantrovitz remembered drills in the spring of 2002, along with the other young Cardinals shortstops. One after another, fielding grounders, firing them across the diamond, the bullets out of young arms with a future. And then his throws, well short, never too hot for the first baseman to handle.

"And then they said, 'Hey. You know the writing's on the wall,'" Kantrovitz recalled. "You know, 'This isn't going to work out for you.' And, I mean, I knew it, but I had to have somebody else force me out of it. I would have stayed there forever. But that's kind of how the transition came about."

So Kantrovitz's on-field career was over, though the experience allowed him to know intimately the vocabulary and thinking that went into the on-field playing and scouting—one of the two languages he'd need to speak as scouting director.

Instead of coaching next, however, Kantrovitz's path deviated from that of generations of Cardinals prospects who didn't reach the major leagues. He didn't head back to Johnson City. He was off to Wall Street.

"I called the guys at Lehman Brothers, and the investment banking division said—he was offering me a job in college, so I asked if that was something that I could pursue again.... They said sure. So a couple months later, I just went to New York and was there for a couple years as an investment banker. I'm glad I did that job because I realized that's something I absolutely never would want to do."

The job served two purposes for Kantrovitz. While he understood that spending hundred-hour weeks in investment banking wouldn't suit him, he realized that he had the capacity for working that kind of schedule, provided it was in a job he truly loved.

The extent to which the baseball front-office world differed a decade ago from today can be summed up in how Kantrovitz marketed himself, through cold calls and e-mails.

"I was marketing the fact that I played baseball," Kantrovitz said. "I didn't think anyone would care that I learned every macro on Excel and that I crunched numbers.... But I guess that turned out to be something that people started to value at that time."

That process may seem fast in retrospect—Kantrovitz took less than a decade to essentially scale the profession within multiple front offices. But no greater evidence may exist of how different front offices were at the time than the year-plus Kantrovitz spent essentially unemployed, pursuing a baseball job. Any baseball job. Kantrovitz relocated to Seattle to work, for no pay, with Ron Antinoja, doing something called Tendu analysis, which is to say, determining from past performance what individual player tendencies would be going forward. While that didn't immediately lead to a job in baseball—Kantrovitz and Antinoja met during spring training with several teams, including the Cardinals, in 2003, 2004, and a few teams bought their software—it did attract the attention of Bob Bowman, a senior executive with Major League Baseball.

"Bob Bowman and MLBAM expressed a lot of interest in the technology and potentially purchasing it... or just trying to replicate it," Kantrovitz said. (MLB would eventually team up with Antinoja in 2007.)[1]

By the middle of 2004, Kantrovitz was e-mailing with Mariners manager Bob Melvin about strategy, but had little tangible to show for his decision eighteen months earlier to leave Lehman Brothers. He and his college sweetheart, Brenna, a lawyer, had gotten engaged weeks earlier and were busy trying to plan a life together. Then he got a call from John Mozeliak.

"[He] said we do have this assistant job in the scouting department open and you're going to get exposed to a lot of things, but maybe it's not what you're making as an investment banker," Kantrovitz said. "I said, 'Well, whatever it is, it's more than I'm making now. I have nothing.' I jumped at it immediately. Now it was a job in baseball, it was a job with the Cardinals.... I would have paid him to do it."

If it took a long time for baseball to notice Dan Kantrovitz, it didn't take nearly as long for Jeff Luhnow to recognize that the new hire was perfect for his gang of baseball revolutionaries.

"So at the time, that was when I interviewed with Jeff, Mo, and Walt," Kantrovitz said. "And there was a lot of change going on in the office. A month in my time there, Jeff said, 'I need you working for me.' I said, 'Yes, sir.' So from that point on for the next four years, I worked under Jeff pretty much directly. And didn't really realize how lucky I was. Getting exposure and literally responsibility on everything from major league pitching mechanics to the stats. The international stuff. The scouting. It was not your typical assistant job, which [was due] to Jeff. That's the kind of guy he is. He'll give people a lot of runway. And he had a ton of responsibilities that I think he needed to delegate, but it was awesome to get that kind of exposure. And during that time, I was working with Sig."

That would be Sig Mejdal, who took the untrod path from NASA's Fatigue Countermeasures Group, where he served as biomathematician, to the St. Louis Cardinals.

Decades before Mejdal made the jump to a baseball front office, though, he was an OG sabermetrician. Maybe not Travis Hoke OG, Rickey's hire to chart base and out efficiency back in 1914, but well ahead of his time.

"So I grew up in San Jose, California," Mejdal told me in an October 2014 interview. "I played six years of Little League baseball, but I was reading Bill James before he had a publisher. I was in the Society for American Baseball Research in grade school. So I was always fascinated with baseball numbers, and that didn't go away as I got older. I think most every project that I had in high school or college I would twist it to be baseball related.

"I remember asking the teacher in third grade how to do fractions because I wanted to see how many home runs my Hank Aaron card would have over 162 games," Mejdal said. "He's hit five homers in twenty-three games. And I remember asking the teacher how to do this. And she asked why I was asking this, and when I told her, I remember her laughing. On the way to my master's thesis, it was on valuing, instead of estate valuing—[it was] baseball players. So, it was throughout, really."

Mejdal graduated from UC Davis in 1989 and went to work for Lockheed Martin. But he'd volunteer for graveyard shifts so he could spend more time playing with baseball numbers. He'd try to retrofit the spacecraft modeling for baseball instead. On he went, to AltaVista, then to NASA. It wasn't like Kantrovitz's experience, a work life despised.

"I enjoyed my work, but there was no confusing—it was work," Mejdal said. "I enjoyed when I was done with work more than I was at work. But in baseball, now, that's not the case.

"When *Moneyball* came out, I started looking for a [baseball] job, but I did not have the foresight to imagine that a team would be interested in somebody who didn't play baseball. I just had myself boxed in my mind as an outsider. I would always remain that."

It's important to understand the differences between Kantrovitz and Mejdal because what follows comes directly from the personalities and goals of the two men and has everything to do with the roles they played in remaking the Cardinals. Kantrovitz, the crossover figure, fit in easily in any room, whether among scouts or analysts. His long-term goal was to earn a spot as a general manager or director of baseball operations for a major league team.

Mejdal has no such designs on that kind of job. He's extremely well liked by those who know him. But it's apparent in any conversation with him that he's operating at a different intellectual speed, and conversation with most others is the mental equivalent of coasting for him. Nothing in how he interacts with people is condescending—that's just the reality of the world relative to Sig Mejdal.

Put simply, a significant part of Kantrovitz's brainpower is spent on the political/social capital required to survive and advance in the baseball world. It's the skill set that's served John Mozeliak so well. Mejdal, though, is a pure analyst. While I'd like to live in a world where, purely for the entertainment, I could watch Mejdal interact regularly with the media, it's fair to say that Mejdal has no appetite for that.

"All of the interactions with the press," Mejdal said. "All the drama. Yeah. None of that interests me, nor do I think I would be exceptionally good at it. You've got to have a thick skin to be a GM and—I'm trying my best to have thick skin as an analyst and I need thicker skin. So I think I would lose my stomach lining if I were GM."

This should not be confused with Mejdal's desire to get into baseball, nor did it limit the scope of those efforts.

"I did the résumés. The cover letters. The follow-up with phone calls, and I started creating these unsolicited reports. Teaser reports, so if they hired me, [they'd see] how I could complement their existing processes. And I was as respectful as could be. I got virtually no returns. No interest.

"But I kept at it. I ended up dedicating, like, one or two full days a week with doing this research. Sending these reports. Following up. I went to the winter meetings uninvited and stood in the lobby for three days waiting for somebody who looked important to walk from the elevator to the front door so I could give them this ridiculous brochure I made on why he needed to hire me. So, yeah, I did a ton of stuff."

For months, it seemed a waste of time. He did get that polite e-mail from Paul DePodesta. Rick Hahn, later to become general manager for the Chicago White Sox (and briefly a candidate for Cardinals GM in 2007),[2] encouraged him at the winter meetings. David Forst of the Oakland Athletics did as well. So the outlines of the new thinking in baseball were faintly visible, though precisely how quickly and completely they'd come to remake the industry wasn't apparent just yet.

Once again, though, Mozeliak acted as a facilitator. One of Mejdal's brochures landed on Mozeliak's desk, and he passed it along to Luhnow.

"I just got an e-mail from Jeff saying he was interested in it and wanted to talk to me," Mejdal recalled. "And we talked and met in person in St. Louis. I met Walt and Mo and Jeff.... And then I met again in person with him in December of '04 in the winter meetings in Anaheim. And then he hired me soon afterwards. My first day was opening day of 2005.

"It was a wonderful feeling. I remember buying a one-way ticket to St. Louis and how bizarre that sounded as I was leaving my beloved California. And, yeah, it felt like I was starting this wonderful adventure."

As the 2005 season dawned for the Cardinals, Luhnow, Kantrovitz, and

Luhnow Enters

Mejdal set out to discover what they thought could be improved about the St. Louis Cardinals. Everything was on the table.

"The group doing data analysis was Sig, Jeff, and I—it was a three-man shop," Kantrovitz said. "And it's funny because—Sig had this way of saying things in a perspective like nobody else. He would always start off his sentences with 'Imagine...' And I'm going to paraphrase him. And it was 'Imagine...' because people would ask, 'Oh, you guys—you guys are doing really neat stuff.' Well, he would say, 'Imagine somebody who's not really been doing *anything*.' So I was just coming into the draft with a ranked spreadsheet, which, at that point, was a lot. And that's not saying anything against the Cardinals. That's just what most of baseball was in at that point.

"And so whether it was international scouting, whether it was player development pitching mechanics, whether it was draft statistics, I mean, there were so many frontiers to work on. It was really exciting. I mean, it was amazing, frankly."

Change was coming to the St. Louis Cardinals. And if the work Luhnow did as a consultant wasn't concerning enough to those in the status quo, once he had control over the draft and international operations, he couldn't be ignored. DeWitt wasn't about to let that happen, anyhow.

Luhnow's work didn't stop there, though. Everything was fair game. Early in spring 2005, some longtime Cardinals—manager Tony La Russa and pitching coach Dave Duncan—found that out.

"So I remember this meeting we had," Kantrovitz said. "I remember it because I was really nervous because it was when Jeff told me to present to Tony, Dunc, and Walt our theory of pitching mechanics.

"And so, that meeting, Bill stood up and gave the introduction to it, which he never does. At least rarely. And he said, 'You know what?' And this was, for me, the genesis of the whole movement. And he said, based on his time with the Reds—the team was doing well. They were winning World Series. But he saw that they were getting complacent.

"And he wasn't going to let that happen with us. And his introduction was basically saying, 'Hey, Dunc, Tony. Don't kill Dan and Jeff for proposing some of these things that seem wild and outlandish,' because that's what he wants.

"He wanted that change, at least, to be discussed. And that's really, for me, the genesis of it, was that first meeting that we [now] have all the time. It's normal. But it was just questioning what we currently do. Bringing up new ways of doing things. And it was Bill's vision. To say, I don't want to see this happen, what he says happened with the Reds. He didn't want the same thing to happen.

"I think people maybe underestimated his baseball acumen in that sense. And that was driving everything we did. He brought in Jeff, and it gave us a lot of ability to do some pretty cool and creative things, even if they didn't work."

One person who didn't need to be convinced to listen to new ideas: George Kissell, who'd been with the Cardinals since Branch Rickey, who'd hired Travis Hoke, the Jeff Luhnow of 1914.

"George Kissell, the first time I met him, was at the winter meetings, that same Drew winter meetings where he was being presented with a lifetime achievement award," Luhnow said. "And as I sat at the table—met him, his wife was there—and I heard stories about him, and I thought, 'Oh my God, this is, like, a Hall of Famer sitting right in front of me. This guy's amazing.' The next time I met him was at spring training that year. He didn't know who I was. I was kind of intimidated by him because of hearing all these great things about him. He came up to me and starting asking me questions and I thought, 'This is the oddest thing in the world. This is the guy that knows everything and I don't know anything, and he's asking me questions.'

"He asked me about my background. He was asking what I saw today on the field. He wanted to know what I thought. And I started to ask him questions and he said, 'I learn something new every day. It doesn't matter who it's from. It doesn't have to be someone that's gotten more experience who knows more. I learn something every day.' And I thought, 'That's amazing that this guy is such an important part of this organization and that's the attitude that he has.'"

Let's not sugarcoat it—Cardinals tradition was, at times, used like a bat against Luhnow's ideas. But not by Kissell. And not by those who tapped into what has made the Cardinals most successful, when they've succeeded, for nearly a hundred years.

"I think from Rickey to Kissell to [DeWitt] Senior to Junior, there's some thread through those guys that really allows for innovation in a game that isn't necessarily known to innovate," Luhnow said.

Precisely how necessary it was to have an owner urging longtime baseball men to listen couldn't be any clearer than in the hiring of Mike Witte. Witte and DeWitt had attended the same high school, and Witte was a classmate of Drew Baur's, an original investor when DeWitt purchased the team.

When Witte came to the Cardinals, his baseball résumé was as follows: (1) he'd collaborated with Tug McGraw, the relief pitcher for the Mets and the Phillies, on McGraw's *Scroogie* comic, and (2) he owned a lot of videocassettes of old pitchers. Now, of course, he's a consultant to a number of major league teams. But it took the Cardinals to give his ideas a chance.

"It started with Mike Witte, a cartoon illustrator from Princeton," Kantrovitz remembered. "I remember when I picked him up from the airport for his first meeting with our staff down in Jupiter, and he literally packed close to a thousand VHS tapes of old-time pitchers that he had studied. He was kind of like a brilliant mad scientist.

"Bill turned us on to him. What started out as a favor [by meeting with him] became the genesis for our focus on classic mechanics."

While Witte put together some of the intellectual underpinnings for what would ultimately lead to wholesale changes in how the Cardinals trained their pitchers, Mejdal was hard at work determining how to configure the team's process for evaluating players in the draft. Now armed with data on both college and high school pitchers, Mejdal had approximately two months to put those together from his first day on the job in April 2005 to the June 2005 draft.

"I was the only one doing this and so there was going to be models for everything, but I reported to Jeff because Jeff was responsible for the draft and he was the biggest customer of this [work]. It wasn't the others. So with the drafts, whatever, eight or ten weeks away after my first day, that's were my energies went.

"I was the one creating the models. But Jeff was aware of the steps throughout. And so was Dan. But at that time I was the analyst doing the modeling, the database work."

That doesn't mean Mejdal was certain his methods would work. After all, even the best processes don't always yield expected results. In a room full of skeptics, after the debacle of 2004, Mejdal and the rest of the group worried about what that might mean for the analytics team.

"I remember it well," Mejdal said of his apprehension that spring. "Like—the analysis we had done, that I had done, in those two months were showing that you can increase the output of the draft in a very significant way. I think I'm as insecure as anybody when it comes to standing up in a room filled with expertise with a contradictory position when you have not analyzed every imaginable interaction and their attributes. And, frankly, in those two months, we had good reason to believe that we could have wonderful results. But there was still a giant insecurity because there simply hadn't been enough time to throw rocks from every angle at the model."

Ultimately, 2005 saw the Cardinals incorporate analytics into their decision making—but it was a far cry from where the team ultimately arrived, which was making analytics the primary decision driver, with scouting a key component of those overall values on each amateur player. Still, the forward progress is clear, with the 2005 Cardinals draft yielding eight major league players, twice as many as the 2004 draft, and guys such as Colby Rasmus in the first round and Jaime García in the twenty-second round enjoying sustained major league success.

"The difference between '04 and '05 was twofold," Mozeliak said. "One is, obviously we had more confidence in our analytical strategy for the draft.

But we also ramped up that department with personnel and went to a more traditional structure."

The draft could have been even better, though. The Cardinals could have taken Jed Lowrie.

"The model loved Jed Lowrie," Mejdal recalled, "who was this undersized—he was playing second base—undersized second baseman at Stanford who was not—he was well liked by the scouts but not nearly as much as with the model. And I had made my arguments that Jed Lowrie was a better pick with our thirtieth pick than Tyler Greene. And I remember having this sort of sick feeling, like, what if we actually take him because of my work and he fails? So this would be a wonderful anecdote for people that talk to and point to how we [in analytics] have little to add. Because, I was insecure with an undersized player from such an elite school and just [lacked] the confidence that he was as good a bet as the more athletic Tyler Greene."

Greene reached the major leagues, but collected only 746 plate appearances over five seasons while accumulating a career WAR of -0.6 through 2014. Lowrie, meanwhile, reached the major leagues in 2008 and has been a solid starter at shortstop throughout his career, with only injuries holding him back. With 8.4 career WAR already through 2014, Lowrie signed a three-year, $22 million contract with the Astros prior to the 2015 season.

So though it may seem as if the Cardinals remade themselves quickly—to go from no analytics team in the fall of 2003 to essentially a full analytics operation in every level of team operations in less than a decade is remarkably quick for any company, let alone one in the tradition-bound game of baseball, let alone in a hypertraditional structure within baseball such as the St. Louis Cardinals—to Mejdal it still felt slow.

"Jeff was very smart and he brought this in very gradually," Mejdal said. "To me it was frustratingly gradually, but perhaps looking back on it, it was the optimal way of implementing this change. So, no, we didn't pick Jed Lowrie, and, no, we didn't do much in '05 with the model."

Encapsulating the challenge of Luhnow's job is that what Mejdal saw as a slow, subtle difference felt jarring in the more traditional corners of the Cardinals' front office.

"Sig was in the room. Sig was vocal and I was trying to adjust as much as I felt comfortable adjusting given the audience," Luhnow said. "And what happens is you end up with players in this order. And then this scout will vehemently argue that this guy needs to move up, and this guy's scout believes he's probably too high because he's more of a performance guy than a scout guy so he's not going to argue. So then you've got to sit there and the room is kind of expecting you to move that guy up and you have to determine what [to do]—pick your battles, right? And a lot of it comes out of how you massage the conversation in the room and how much time you give each player and all of that. One thing you don't want to do—and this happened the year before—was have the scouts leave the room. And then when they come back in, the order's changed and they didn't have anything to do with it. That did not go over well.

"You have to make everybody feel like their input is valued, but you have to avoid double counting and that's what happens. Because that player's already up there because the scout loves him. So if you allow that scout and his voice to push him up even higher, you're damaging your total output. No question about it."

Put simply, scouts arguing passionately for their own guys wasn't just a different way of drafting from what Luhnow was recommending, and now implementing. It was an impediment to it, once that scouting enthusiasm had already been incorporated into a player's overall grade.

The resulting turmoil meant that John Mozeliak had two jobs. He was the assistant general manager, with a hand in virtually every area of Cardinals operations, very much the Walt Jocketty–trained executive. But Mozeliak was simultaneously among the most receptive members of the front office to the ideas of Luhnow, Mejdal, and Kantrovitz.

"It ate up a lot of time just because we were a fractured company," Mozeliak said. "But I still had my day-to-day job, which was as assistant GM, which was paying attention to waivers. Obviously contract negotiations. Obviously all employee contracts went through my office at that time. Consulted with all the department heads on their annual planning and all that. So that part of the job was very consistent. Very normal."

Meanwhile, the Cardinals moved to implement some of the ideas Mike Witte first brought to their attention. And while Kantrovitz and Luhnow "baseball-ized" the draft ideas that Mejdal came up with, as Kantrovitz put it, they had someone with a long history in the major leagues to do the same on the pitching-mechanics side, someone recommended by Witte. Fortunately for the Cardinals, he was ready to ditch the things he'd been teaching for decades, realizing that he'd been doing more harm than good. Brent Strom, you see, had a pitching-mechanics epiphany of his own.

> *I did nothing to offend anybody. It was just the message. They didn't like the message because what happened—being a traditional game, they didn't like the fact that there may be a different thought process about how to go about things.*
>
> —Brent Strom

The first man to have Tommy John surgery, as you probably know, was Tommy John.

The second was Brent Strom. He calls himself "the Buzz Aldrin of Tommy John surgery."

"I came to spring training in ['78 with the Padres], my arm was bothering me," Strom told Evan Drellich of the *Houston Chronicle* in March 2014. "I tried to medicate it with the hot stuff that you put on your arm and cortisone shots. Actually, I was in Yuma, Arizona. I left about nine o'clock one night and met a doctor at midnight in San Diego to get a cortisone shot without the club knowing, came back, tried to [pitch]. I was hanging on by my fingernails and was released at the end of spring training.

"Trying to see what I can do to make this club, I get released the last day of spring training, I contact—somehow I get in touch with Dr. [Robert] Kerlan, who is alive at the time.... Jobe worked under Kerlan. So then I go out to LA and they look at it, they do the testing, they decide to try the Tommy John surgery again... it was within weeks they wanted to do the surgery. I was a free agent.

"They were looking for another candidate [for the surgery], I think. Obviously, I was at wit's end, desperation time, they performed the surgery. I remembered they tried to take [the tendon] out my left wrist, I still have the scar right here [but they needed to look elsewhere for a tendon]—so they took it out of my left leg. I came back and pitched at the Triple-A level and won [ten] games that next year with Houston....

"It's probably a good thing it's called Tommy John surgery and not Brent Strom surgery. Tommy John wins 288 and I win 22. So it depends on which surgery you get, I guess.

"It's one of the reasons I'm so adamant about the mechanics, we have a better understanding now of why this happens. So we try and do things to help eliminate that. Now medical [advancements] allow Tommy John surgeries—I hate to use the word *routine*—but it's a lot easier to work on an elbow with this than it is a shoulder. Shoulders are more difficult."

So for Strom, keeping pitchers healthy was personal. He remembered when his career ended. He remembered why, what it felt like. And he'd spent a career trying to keep guys from the same fate. He'd joined the Los Angeles Dodgers as Triple-A pitching coach the year after his playing career ended in 1982. And he'd spent most of the subsequent two decades as a pitching instructor at both the minor and major league levels—in Houston, he was the pitching coach for Terry Collins in 1996, and with Tony Muser's Royals in 2000–2001. And he was working as a minor league pitching instructor with the Montreal Expos in 2004, about to give a speech at a pitching clinic in Seattle.

A man named Paul Nyman spoke just ahead of him, and Strom realized he'd been going about his profession all wrong for twenty years.

"Probably the biggest influence that I've had is a gentleman named Paul Nyman, who's out of Connecticut," Strom told me in a September 2014 interview, sitting in the visiting dugout at Citi Field. "And this is an engineer who, when I was doing a clinic one time and I had my eureka moment and he spoke ahead of me. I mean, it was like an eye-opener. To understand that momentum is important. That how the body moves through space and how you can re-create tension and a little tension at the right time. These kind of things. Because before that, I was a dude that would lift the leg, lean balance. Do all this stuff. I was one of the culprits. And I never intentionally hurt anybody, but I know I did."

Added Strom in a January 2014 e-mail, "With my philosophy in mind I then sat back and listened to this engineer show me a whole new way to look at how we throw, how the body moves and so much more. In essence it created a thirst for additional information.... The rest is history as they say. One thing for sure... as I write this, I am still finding out new [things]. I have always realized... 'I don't know what I don't know.'"

The resulting shift in philosophy created several problems for Strom. One was that he suddenly found himself teaching differently from the way that had gotten him hired by the Expos and other teams in the first place. It was also different from what his fellow coaches were teaching.

Ultimately, it cost him his job. The Nationals (after the Expos moved to Washington) let Strom go on the last day of spring training, 2006. He thought he would catch on elsewhere, but it didn't happen. He spent the summer at home with his wife, Carrie, in Tucson, Arizona.

"When I'm home, for the last seventeen years, I take care of my [family]," Strom said. "I have my ninety-seven-year-old mother-in-law living with us, I have a seventy-two-year-old sister-in-law that lives with us. I have three bulldogs. That's my family. So I'm taking care of a lot of people in that regard."

Eventually, Strom decided to take his new ideas directly to teams. The Cardinals needed someone who was thinking along the lines of Witte to implement the ideas Strom had come to through Nyman's work. So when Strom gave his presentation to Luhnow, Mejdal, and Kantrovitz, he'd found precisely the organization where his new way of looking at things was an asset for hiring him, rather than a liability. When I asked him whether he'd have been hired by the Cardinals if not for the Nyman epiphany, he said, "No, I don't think so."

"And so eventually they hired me that year. They brought me down to the instructional league. Just kind of talked to a few people. And I had dinner with Bill and Jeff and showed them what I thought I could do, in terms of injury prevention and increasing velocity and developing pitchers. And they apparently liked what I had to offer, and then they offered me a job as a mechanics coach on the pitching side."

This represented a further incursion of the Luhnow changes into what had been a tradition-bound Cardinals operation. Exactly how poorly that was received finally revealed itself to Strom in the person of Mark DeJohn, who you might remember as George Kissell's self-described adopted son.

"Well, I remember coming in as an outsider," Strom recalled. "And I remember Mark DeJohn, who I became very close with—I remember one day in St. Lucie where the Mets were training. We were in instructional league. It was spring training or something and I'm working with the guy, and Mark is kind of watching me from the side. He called me over the side. He makes this comment. He says, 'You know what? You're a pretty good guy!' He says, 'You're not the asshole that everybody tells me you are.' And so I looked at him and I said, 'I really don't know how to take that.' And he said, 'Yeah. You're a hell of a guy, man. You're fun. You're funny. You like the same music I do. Why doesn't everybody think this about [you]?' I didn't know what they thought of me. But obviously I was not thought of very highly.

"But I think what happened is, the message was different than what people had heard before. And maybe they didn't like the message. Maybe they didn't like the fact that they may have to rethink what they taught. Which I had to do, too. [Coaches like] Tom House. There was an array of people that as you pick and choose from the fruit that you want to use and create your own idea of what the delivery should be like, the training should be like. That kind of thing. [Coaches like] Eric Cressey. And I'm still doing that today. I mean, I'm changing now. I'll be different tomorrow than I am today, as new information comes forward."

For Strom, working under Dyar Miller and alongside Tim Leveque, the principles are easily explained. In essence, a career of educating young pitchers allowed Strom to maximize the delivery of what became a new set of guidelines.

"I did nothing to offend anybody," Strom said. "It was just the message. They didn't like the message because what happened—being a traditional game, they didn't like the fact that there may be a different thought process about how to go about things. Creating an athletic pitcher. Stop doing long-distance running and do sprints instead because of the energy system in pitching, which is one and a half seconds to throw the ball, you wait twelve seconds, you do it again. You do it fifteen times. You do it nine times a game. Total outburst: six minutes, five seconds. Well then, why go out and run an hour when it's not in the same energy system? You're better off doing explosive-type stuff. Okay?

"Things like that. Long toss to develop arm health. Elevated fastballs, which we're doing now. Strength-training-for-the-arm-type stuff that's a little bit different. Learning how to decelerate correctly. Things like that. And are we on top of things? We still have a ways to go. But the beauty of working with Jeff and working with the group that I have now that I'm fortunate to work with is that they'll listen.

"And the one thing about Jeff, don't be subjective. Be objective. Show them, show me the numbers. Show me the money, so to speak. And with that he'll look at, review it, and give you a chance if he believes in it. So I'm fully appreciative of that, instead of those people blowing you off.

"Because had it not been for Jeff, I think I'd have been gone after the first year. You know, there were people kind of looking at me sideways. What's this guy doing? I had long-toss going. I had the velocity enhancement. I had people being more athletic in their deliveries. And as I told everybody, I like the sinkers as much as anybody, but a pretty good pitcher one day told me—my favorite pitcher, Sandy Koufax—he told me, "The people that throw sinkers are those that cannot throw fastballs."

Meanwhile, as the Cardinals altered their pitching instruction and program, they took another step toward integrating analytics into their drafting—"a big step," according to Mejdal. "I think that as time went on, it was more systematic, but even to this day, there is, in general, two methodologies, and while we combine them into a single number, you can still see the remnants of each methodology. Right up to performance base, that takes some of the scouting attributes, and the other methodology, [which] is completely scouting. And so, the Jed Lowries of the world, for instance, score much higher on the first method than the second. And although we had an overall way of combining them, there was still an anchoring to the conventional method. And it was a gradual de-anchoring to the current method and re-anchoring to the method that combined all the information that took place over the years."

Eleven players from Luhnow's 2006 draft reached the major leagues through the 2014 season, with Tommy Pham the latest one for the Cardinals. But the clearest indication of the huge results the marriage of analytics and scouting could produce might have been the selection of Allen Craig in the eighth round.

"So, thinking back to being a fly on the wall in the draft room when we drafted Allen Craig and that process, I think it was when we were just maybe getting started with analytics integrating into amateur scouting," Kantrovitz said back in our first interview in August 2013. "I remember Sig, who at the time had done some really good work on the analytics side, had identified Allen as one of those guys that, as relative to his peers, had done really well. And then I remember our area scout at the time—once Sig mentioned him, I think our area scout was, like, 'Yeah. You're right. That's the guy—

he can turn around a fastball as well as anybody and hit 'em over the parking garage.'

"And so it was an interesting situation where you saw the marriage of what the stats were saying with what the scouts were saying, too. And then there's a lot of players that fit that profile.... So that's like a perfect storm, you know? It's like everything worked and more. And we also probably got a little lucky."

Though Craig struggled in 2014, getting traded to the Boston Red Sox, he's already been a clear win from that draft, with more than 8 career WAR through 2014, and a career OPS+ of 115. It didn't happen because of just analytics, or just scouting, but both, engineered in a process of Luhnow's creation.

One of the myths perpetrated through a misreading of *Moneyball* was that scouts are somehow unneeded in a system where analytics are used. The idea is a riff on the old idea that technology can come in and replace people, like that Woody Allen joke: "I called my parents: My father was fired. He was technologically unemployed. My father had worked for the same firm for twelve years. They fired him. They replaced him with a tiny gadget, this big, that does everything my father does, only it does it much better. The depressing thing is, my mother ran out and bought one."[3]

In fact, as DeWitt pointed out to me when we spoke in September 2014, Mejdal ran the historical numbers on scouting recommendations, and on an *analytics-only* approach, to see which produced better numbers. The scouts won.

Naturally, Luhnow had no intention of relying on just stats, any more than he'd have relied on scouts alone, absent any measurement of their annual performance.

A pair of changes helped to create friction in the short term, but ultimately married scouting to the Cardinals' new strategy in a comprehensive way.

The comprehensive scouting reviews, administered every fall, compared the value assigned to scouting recommendations to the players' actual performance. So things such as being the guy who recommended a particular player, the type of evaluation a scout could lean on in the past, gave way to every value judgment's mattering. Thanks to a Sig Mejdal innovation, a "shadow draft" he began in St. Louis in 2009 and continued in Houston, even players scouts loved but the Cardinals didn't draft could be used to evaluate that scout.

"It is a small attempt at illustrating to the scouts when they are consistently too optimistic or not," Mejdal told me in a January 2015 e-mail. "The scouts actually come away from each draft with a collection of players that they would have drafted if they were the scouting director. The player was at the top of their pref list, he was available, and the scout wanted to take him. At that point, the scout has done all that he can. That he doesn't get him is just happenstance. So, those players are now assigned to the scout and they will be followed and compared to the expectancy of return for that draft pick. The scout doesn't have to say 'I told you so,' and in time he might see that the guys that he has for each round really don't produce as much as the expectancy for that round."

The system essentially rewards introverted scouts. But the real purpose is making sure scouting done by introverts, which is every bit as valuable as the scouting done by those who pound the table, gets incorporated into overall evaluations just as much.

For Luhnow, the deep review of scout performance dovetailed with what he'd done at every company he'd ever run.

"Human resources is a big part of my background," Luhnow said. "I did a lot of consulting on human resource management with companies. I had started two companies from scratch. It's a big passion of mine so we did everything. Everything. All best practices when it comes to HR. We did evaluations. Did goal setting. Looking at actual output. Understanding that there's a variability in the output. And so I gathered a lot of information, and each scout had a review that was pretty thick. And from that we decided which scouts to let go, which ones to promote.

"That was institutionalized and there were reviews—a lot of these scouts had never really received a review in their entire career, and all of a sudden they were getting a pretty intense review on what they were doing and what the numbers were to back it up and all of that."

The wisdom in this is pretty obvious. We wouldn't determine the effectiveness of a hitter or pitcher based on one epic game. Mark Whiten hit four homers in a game. Bud Smith pitched a no-hitter. Albert Pujols never hit four home runs in a game, and Pedro Martínez never pitched a no-hitter.

The long-term health of a team's farm system isn't necessarily determined by the once-in-a-generation player whom everyone else missed, though that obviously helps. Instead, it's building depth, winning at the margins, and adding more talent every single year. That happens by employing scouts who are slightly better at a difficult game—the ones who can identify a sixth-round talent who can be had in the eighth round, a senior sign who can add value without costing the team a significant signing bonus.

But to really understand how and why scouts were so important in the Luhnow rebuild of the team's draft process, one change stands out: they were asked to dramatically expand their lists.

"Jeff wanted a really big list," Turco, then a Florida-area scout, recalled. "I used to have fifty or so." And previous scouting directors, Turco said, wanted that list even smaller.

"I don't care about everybody," Turco recalled one saying. "I want to know who you like. I don't care about the other guys. Just make sure you have a good feel, and you're right about the guys that you do like. So I was gonna drop my list down from fifty, fifty-five to the forties, maybe thirties. Because, if you're telling me, just give me the guys that you really like—I mean, I don't like 'em all!

"Then Jeff comes along, and my list grew from the fifties to over a hundred. Because he wanted all those names."

For Turco, that was confusing. "I told him, when you have all those names, how do you decipher? How do you really know?" Turco's skepticism was understandable. If the Cardinals were continuing to simply weigh the relative arguments of scouts, an overabundance of potential players for the draft would only inhibit the process.

That wasn't the process Sig Mejdal was building, though. Here's how you know.

"You know, my background is in research," Mejdal said. "I'm a scientist, and so wherever the data comes from, if it has predictive ability, I'm attracted to it, and the reports that the scouts generate provide a tremendous amount of predictive ability. And so we traded processes such that we squeezed every ounce of predictive ability out of the scouts' expertise. And in my opinion, in the first draft, 2005, that was my first experience at the draft, much of the scouts' passion came from their confidence to speak during the draft. And so [there are] different personalities and different desires of the scouts. A different personality is a person who may be more quiet. Different desire is a person who really wants more players. [This] was playing a role in the draft. And neither of those things were related to the player's underlying skills."

This was a concern echoed by Turco, by the way. But Mejdal's solution was radically different:

"And so we created processes that would combine all the scouts' orders into a single overall list. And that was the goal of squeezing every last ounce of predictive abilities from the scouting reports, and not simply relying on the scout who happened to sit closer to the scouting director on draft day. We didn't want to ignore the scout who's perhaps a little less confident to speak up to contradict the area scout or the cross-checker."

But making sure the scouting recommendations aren't skewed was only a part of the reason for such a long list. Ultimately, the rankings used by the Cardinals were a combination of what the scouts who saw a player thought, and what the analytics said a player could be based on regression analysis of that player's high school, college, and/or summer league stats.

Many times, the statistics would highlight a relatively obscure player—or maybe a player whom a scout in a given area didn't ultimately like. But without a scouting report, the Cardinals would have half the needed data to plug into their system to determine the value of a player. They could always go back and get the stats for someone off the radar that one of their scouts liked. The reverse wasn't the case, unless the lists were dramatically expanded.

The personnel in scouting changed, too. Luhnow didn't just use his evaluative tools to understand who was best; he didn't hesitate to move people and find additional scouts who he thought could do better. Luhnow scouts did look somewhat different from the guys who'd been in the department before he arrived.

"As we started to bring in new people, the profiles felt different than the guys who had been there, and I knew that in order to be successful I was going to need to not only retain but motivate and get a lot out of some of the veteran guys. Roger Smith. Mike Roberts. You know, Chuck Fick. Joe Rigoli. Marty Maier. So I put those guys in leadership positions. But as we started to backfill for the area scouts, we started to bring in a new breed of area scout. Which is, typically, someone that is younger, played the game. They all played the game. Had a passion for the game. But also have a appreciation-slash-understanding that things were changing, and they're willing to do things new ways. Incorporate new ways of managing their jobs and managing information."

To find them, though, Luhnow followed a process that differed from the closed system that had dominated scouting hires for years. He used, believe it or not, a computer.

"So this is a funny story, but first time I had an area scout opening, I posted the job on the Internet and Chuck Fick came in and said, 'You've got to be kidding me. You can't find a scout on the Internet. That's the dumbest thing I've ever heard.' I said, 'Maybe not, but we just got 250 résumés and so we're going to go through them all and we're going to pick the best ten and we're going to interview them and we're going to see.'

"And sure enough, the number of scouts that we found on the Internet, they now are not only with the Astros and the Cardinals, they're in other organizations as well. So you can find a scout on the Internet. It's just a way of telling people you have a job opening. In the past in baseball, and this is very common [in all industries], people hire based off of recommendations from people they know. I got an area scout job. 'Oh, I got a guy. A perfect guy. He's…' You know, and that's it. You interview him and you give him the job and that's it. To me, that's ludicrous. And so, we went out and we hired people that we had no connection with.

"And sure enough, there's a lot of people that were recommended still, and we put them in the process. If they end up being the best candidate, then they're the best candidate. But they're going to have to go through the process. So each candidate went through three or four rounds of screening, and in the final rounds they would be interviewed by four or five people.

"And then we'd get together and we'd say, 'Okay, here's the criteria. Who's the best guy?' But there was no litmus test as far as can they run numbers, because we weren't thinking that the area scouts were going to actually do any analysis. That's not why we were hiring them. We got analysis guys at HQ. We wanted guys that could do the job of evaluating with their own eyes, but be aware that they were going to be measured in a certain way. That there's certain ways to doing this job that appear to be best practices. They're going to have to hustle. They're still going to have to travel a ton of miles. And they're going to have to appreciate that when they come to the draft, that their guy may not get drafted because there's another guy that's done a better job in his [playing] career that deserves that spot more."

Yet, despite this attempt to incorporate scouting data in a uniform way, one scout Luhnow hired in 2006, Charlie Gonzalez, would play a vital role in how the Cardinals drafted for years.

"So, I felt like we were not covering Florida properly," Luhnow recalled. "Our area scout lived in Tampa, and he was getting [beaten] in Miami. We needed someone in Miami who understood the Cuban thing. Run with the Cuban scouts. And so I told our area scout, Steve Turco, you've got to hire a

Luhnow Enters

part-time guy. So find a couple guys. It's in the budget. Find a couple guys and go interview them.

"And he goes through this whole process and finds a couple guys and we interviewed them and I remember Charlie—I interviewed him by phone, and Steve Turco told me that Charlie was fluent in Spanish, and so I interviewed him in Spanish. And I wish I had seen Charlie over there on the phone. I'm sure his face was red, and he was mumbling and stuttering. His Spanish wasn't that good.

"And so I got off the phone and I was, like, 'Turc, I got to tell you. This guy's kind of a liar.' I said to Turc, 'This guy's a fraud. I can't believe you want to hire this guy.'

"And he said, 'I've got to tell you, Jeff, I don't think he's a fraud. I think he's actually a good dude and he was so nervous.' Because Turco was there watching him do this interview.

"I said, 'Okay, Turc. It's just a part-time job. That's fine. I'll let you hire him.' And I think it was one of the best decisions we've ever made because he is relentless. There's no question that he pitches his guys harder than anybody, and he also advocates for his guys once they get drafted."

I talked to lots of people about Charlie Gonzalez. The response I got, across the board, when I asked about Gonzalez's background, was "Yeah, what is Charlie's background?"

"Well, I know some stuff about him," Luhnow said. "I don't know how much I can tell you for the book. All I can tell you is when I told him we needed to do a background investigation, he got really, really nervous." (Gonzalez says his nervousness stemmed from a lack of professional playing background.)

Charlie Gonzalez will be sixty-one years old in 2015. He's a bear of a man, ruddy complexion over seemingly constant movement. You cannot watch him, out on a field directing a scouting combine, or in a boardroom discussing the minute details of every player entirely from memory, without understanding that Charlie Gonzalez was born to be a professional scout. Yet he didn't start doing it until he was well into his forties.

"Charlie's incredible," Luhnow said. "He really is incredible. He had a surfer body back in the day because he used to surf a lot."

"I'm not quite sure what Charlie's educational background is, but I can tell you he is brilliant," Kantrovitz told me in a July 2014 e-mail. "He can be Jewish, Latin, an intellectual, a car salesman... whatever is needed in any given situation to relate to a player and family. It's one of those rare cases where I'm not sure if he could get a job outside of baseball, but he is elite at his job in baseball."

Charlie Gonzalez was born in Chicago in 1954. His first baseball game was in the stands at old Comiskey Park with his father, Brice, a public-school teacher.

"Mine was the old White Sox," Gonzalez told me in a December 2014 interview. "Minnie Minoso. Louie Aparicio. Nellie Fox. All those guys. I mean, I love the black Sox hat with the White Sox logo with the little red trim on it.

"Used to hate the Twins and Norm Cash and Rocky Colavito and Harmon Killebrew because I was a die-hard fan. Later on, I really liked the Bull, Greg Luzinski, and—what the hell was his name? Used to wear the big teardrop sunglasses. The big teardrop glasses. Dick Allen."

His second-favorite team, which he developed an interest in after moving to the Miami area as a child, was the St. Louis Cardinals.

"We had some college friends of my dad's that lived in St. Louis, and I remember in the summertime we would go," Gonzalez said. "My parents divorced when I was about twelve, and I remember I went to a game at old Busch. But I really, really, really liked the Cardinals. Again, they were just on the heels of the White Sox, and the White Sox were my team."

Gonzalez played baseball, but he says his real passion as a teen was swimming.

"I went to high school down here [in Florida]," Gonzalez said. "I swam competitively. I mean, you have no idea. Practice in the summer twice a day, you know? Six to eight in the morning. Sometimes three times a day. And then we would do long-distance swimming, work on endurance at night. I was at a very, very, very high level.

"I swam with special coaches. A guy named Wally Spence. I swam basically with a—it boils down to and equates to today's terminology or mindset, it would be like travel ball." (Spence, incidentally, was one of the Spence brothers, who were all inducted into the International Swimming Hall of Fame in 1967.)[4]

"Come ninth grade, I went to an all-boys Catholic school and I immediately made the swimming team as a freshman, and I was still very good, but you know what? My enthusiasm was dwindling because really my heart wasn't in it. I was offered a scholarship to Catholic University. Basically, if I kept my times and everything stayed the same—but I was burnt out, you know? I went to a high school that was about thirty-five miles away. And I would take the bus out there. And after school I would have swimming practice and I would have to take the metro bus all the way back home where I lived."

So as swimming faded, Gonzalez took up surfing.

"I started surfing about when I was about twelve years old. And it definitely became a passion and a love. And deep down inside, that was what I did on a feverish level. Surfing's not real good in South Florida. We would go up the coast all the time to Fort Pierce and Melbourne Beach and stuff like that. And I surfed all the time. I finally gave up swimming and basically through high school—though high school, I surfed. And we would surf everywhere in Florida. I really, really knew sports. I really knew baseball. I would pay attention to baseball and everything. But surfing was my passion."

The idea of working in baseball?

"Not a thought. So I went to Miami-Dade Community College out of high school. Graduated. And I went to junior college and then I went to the University of Florida for a few years, but all of that was really working around surfing. I would go to school. We would take jobs, and me and my friends, we would save our money and we'd go on surf trips.

"We'd go to Puerto Rico. We worked at UPS washing trucks. I basically would go to school and surfed as much as I could. We would take trips in the summertime. I'd spend the whole summer in San Diego one summer. I think it was in '73. I went and saved up money working all year, surfing, going to school. Da da, da da. And we went out and spent the whole summer out there in San Diego, all in Southern California. And then we shot out to Hawaii. I would work in a surf shop. Sanding boards, fixing things, whatever. Kind of a nomadic life.

"So I ended up doing that for a few years in the summertime, when I could. And I would go out to Hawaii in the wintertime. You know, when the waves were—the whole winter season in the North Shore. And I would surf all the places you hear about. I would surf Southside Beach. I'd surfed some pipeline and Hanalei. Go to all these places. And several winters, I would save my money and go back there for the winter as long as I could. And go to Puerto Rico. All those kind of trips where there was good surf. 'Cause like I said, in South Florida, there's surf, but it's not really good surf."

Charlie said this is essentially how most of his twenties passed.

"I think I was twenty-seven years old at that point in time. And I basically had just been surfing and going to school and enjoying life. And I didn't really have a plan, you know? I really did not have a plan at all.

"I found that I would think about it. I thought about law school. I would think about things, you know? But I had a hard time just trying to figure out—in fact, I used to scratch my head. I mean, you talk to some of these kids and they're going, 'Well, what's your major?' And they're, 'I got a major in this. I got a minor in this. And when I'm done with this, I'm going to go to grad school.' And I would just—I would kind of envy them, at the same time thinking, excuse my French, that they're full of shit.

"Like, how are you going to tell me—it sounds like something was bred into them by their parents. Like, 'This is what you're going to do.' I definitely was not one of those guys.

"So I was moving along, da da da, da da. And that was that. Turned out I was about twenty-seven, twenty-eight years old. I started doing just odd jobs for work, investing in stuff. My dad and I would do some things together with some homes, some real estate. Things like that. I got a car dealer's license. I started doing stuff, like, I'd go to auctions and just dabbling in different things."

He didn't lose touch with the game, though. Through it all, getting married, having a son, Dylan, at thirty-one, he said he found himself at University of Miami games, surfing, making a living in a thousand different ways. But Dylan turned out to be Gonzalez's pathway into scouting. He didn't go to scout school. He was a Little League dad.

"He got to be four years old or five and started with the T-ball thing and he really loved it. And my involvement with him, I was a very, very hands-on father.

"And so I coached all of his teams and all that. He was growing up out there in Miami Lakes and some T-ball to whatever the different levels were; the Pony League was the affiliation that we played for. And that started bringing me back more into it through him." Not only that, Gonzalez saw Dylan had a chance to make it.

"He's very tall. He's six foot three now, but he was a tall, rangy kid. Pretty athletic. He could hit. He could pitch. He could play. Catch. He could play short—that type of thing.

"So we started—then that started sprouting, and [I was] coaching the kids. And I started doing that very, very heavily. Kind of like how Jeff—I think Jeff got involved in baseball a lot through his—what's that, those leagues, those fantasy-baseball things?

"Whatever. I never did any of that kind of stuff. But the hands-on coaching and all that, and I really knew a lot about the game as far as technique and things like that. I had a really good eye. So I started coaching the kids when they were young and I never stopped. I coached him from when he was four years old to when he was seventeen years old and he was in high school playing."

By then, though, Gonzalez himself had caught the eye of some scouts in the area. He found himself at baseball games all the time, games Dylan wasn't even playing in.

"Going out there and going to games and watching, knowing personnel was a big thing with me—knowing who were the great players there in South Florida. I loved watching the guy who was supposed to be the guy, you know what I mean? And that completely captivated me.

"You follow them to the play-offs, just as a fan-type thing but a little bit more than that, and watching players. Watching players. Watching games. Watching players. I would just sit and get engrossed in the game and the personnel. The players. And you can tell a lot watching them. Who's a guy that's just got a great body and he's got tools, but he really can't play, [as opposed to] that little, scruffy, five-foot-nine, little left-hander over there who can really play the game?

"I would get the sense of who really can do it and who can't and who's the pretty boy. So I started just doing a lot of that. And then I started helping guys out, kind of like a bird dog, and I knew all the scouts. I knew all the coaches and I would get to so many games that guys started asking me stuff. 'Hey, listen. Are you seeing so-and-so?' or 'Whatever happened in that game there?' Well, da da da, da da. And I would start to break down players at that point in time and talk. And some of the guys that knew—had a clue, they can kind of tell. They'd come to me a little bit more often."

And with an unconventional professional life—"my baseball passion flourished because of the work that I did, I didn't have to be anywhere at nine. You know what I'm saying?"—Gonzalez began to do some part-time scouting work for the San Francisco Giants. Brice had come down from Chicago by then, he and Charlie living together down there, flipping houses and raising Dylan, Gonzalez said.

"I knew every coach. I knew every player. I knew which coach would have trouble. I knew which program was good, which one wasn't. I mean, at this point, I'm really plugged in."

Luhnow Enters

Johnny DiPuglia, now director for international scouting for the Washington Nationals, was then a scout with the Cardinals. He covered an international area, along with some Florida territory as well. He'd ask Gonzalez to cover the Florida area when DiPuglia went overseas and catch him up when he returned.

"So I would bring him up-to-date on everything that was going on here now," Gonzalez said. " 'He gets by here. That kid's hurt. The hell with him. You know, I think he's soft,' whatever. So I did that. And he leaned on me pretty heavily. Pretty heavily. And it was nothing but great for me."

Even still, this far along, Gonzalez didn't imagine baseball could be a career for him. "Yeah. No," Gonzalez said when I asked if he thought this could lead to a full-time job. "I had a fever. Big-time. Big-time. And you want to know something, Howard? I don't think there was ever a point—because, listen. There's not a whole lot of money in scouts. And I had done some things. I'd flipped some homes with my dad and stuff like that. And things are going pretty comfortably. I opened up a business with another guy, a friend of mine, called Sky Shop International. We did that for a while in the Miami free-trade zone. And we would import silk from China. Different stuff like that. Stuff that I had absolutely zero heartfelt passion for. And we would import some motorcycles. He brought in a partner from [China] who was a professor—I think it was Miami, whatever. So that was our connection to China. So we imported some silk. We'd design scarves, you know? And beautiful scarves. Silk scarves. And we had go to Federated. I don't know if you're familiar with Federated stores. So Federated is one of those big giants. We did the scarves. We had to go to Federated. You have to pitch your stuff to them. And you do this and that and then they sign you on an account and then you're set. So we did really well with these scarves. I had them in, like, ninety stores and, you know, it was a joke. Because, I mean, I'm not into that stuff. But, hey. We made some money doing that. Imported some Chinese motorcycles. That kind of stuff.

"So really, it was going pretty good. Money was going pretty good. But my passion, Howard, was always—I couldn't wait to get out to the field and coach my kid. Coach my kid and go to my high school games at night and my junior college games and all of that. I did really well. I was a really, really, really good coach."

This was the man Jeff Luhnow hired. He wasn't the kind of hire you'd customarily expect to find in an analytics-driven department. He isn't even your typical scout. I asked Gonzalez if he thought that gave him an advantage in a field that requires so much reading, ultimately, of people.

"There's no question, Howard, that my background, surfing, traveling," Gonzalez said. "You know, you want to broaden your horizons. You want to become more aware, you know? Grab a couple hundred dollars and hitchhike up the coast. And you're living off that or you plan a trip and you're in—you're in Manzanillo, Mexico, and you got eighty dollars left to your name and you take a job somewhere for a few days. You get to know people. You meet people. You think you're on the run, you know? So, yeah, I've seen a lot. I grew up in a place—I mean, South Florida back then, Howard, it wasn't like living in Columbus, Ohio, you know? Nothing against Columbus, Ohio, but you know what I mean?

"It's more choreographed for you. You either work in a factory or you don't, or you do this or you don't. The rules and all that. So, yes. Part of that really allowed me to get to know people. It allowed me to get to feel people.

"Jeff used to say to me, 'Okay, Charlie, we're in Venezuela.' We'd go there and we'd sit down and talk about a player that might require a million, couple million bucks. And he said, 'Get over there and talk to that agent and feel him out. Come back and tell me, is he full of shit?'

"Travel and all those kind of experiences doesn't do that to everyone. There's people that have been through everything I've been through and they're just kind of narrow-minded. They don't have a real good sense of feel. I'm a pretty perceptive person and I definitely believe that it allows me to think and see things and to feel people out and certainly—I mean, listen. I'll be honest with you. If it was a football scout when I was going, I'd pick up the nuances in football and look for them. Or basketball. You can feel it out. I think that I would probably do well in that as well. And it's just feeling people. Feeling players out. Like I said, you can just see and tell. You can feel it out. Who can play and who can't."

But that Luhnow hired Gonzalez and came to rely on him more in the subsequent years as he discovered the nerves from Gonzalez's initial interview were just part of the epic package that is the Charlie Gonzalez Experience is yet another reminder that the idea of some disconnect between the analytical changes Jeff Luhnow engineered with the Cardinals, and an appreciation of scouting, is an utter myth.

"The Cardinals do a very good job of it," Gonzalez said, back in an October 2014 interview, of the combination approach. "I mean, you see it, everyone's using that model, as I believe they should. And able to still let the scouts be scouts. Chris Correa and Sig Mejdal and those guys who are fantastic at what they do. And let me tell you something. Any old soul like myself or any other scout that comes from the old—well, I never to went to scout school—and says that [analytics doesn't] have something to offer, they're blowing smoke. 'Cause it's very interesting what they come up with. And I believe in a lot of what they say. But the key is to stay in the middle. Let your scouts be scouts. And then utilize that great stuff that those guys bring to the table, and then Dan and the department and overall can employ the both of them."

Or as Luhnow said to me via e-mail in January 2015 when I asked him about this straw-man argument, "The anti-analysis people will often revert to the argument that stats alone aren't optimal, which is of course correct, and nobody as far as I know ever said they were! I certainly haven't!"

So the Cardinals hired Gonzalez and instantly understood they'd made the right hire.

"I remember our first encounter like it was yesterday," Kantrovitz told me in a June 2014 e-mail. "He picked up Jeff and I from our hotel—we must have hired him just months earlier—and after somehow squeezing in four games in one day, Charlie looks at us and says, 'I can make a call and get this lefty to throw a pen... but its like three hours on the other side of the state.' Jeff and I looked at each other, and we knew Charlie was perfect for the job."

Yet, it's worth noting that as Luhnow moved forward on this front, along with his work revamping the team's international program, the grumbling was frequent, both internally and to the press.

Mozeliak's office was where complaints were commonly heard, with the assistant GM serving as therapist—along with assistant GM, a monumental job itself. Luhnow would hear about these complaints, usually in meetings with Jocketty. These complaints wouldn't tend to be about the big ideas—though no one doubts that's what the conflict really turned on.

"A lot came up, and it's not clear to me where it came from necessarily, but there were several times when Walt and I would have a meeting and he would have a list of things that he had heard from people that worked in baseball operations or elsewhere in the organization," Luhnow said. "I'm not sure I want to characterize this necessarily as complaints, but 'Jeff is doing this. Jeff is doing that.' Stuff like—we were trying to get a van for the Dominican Republic, and vans—we were on a very tight budget and buying a new car or a used car in Dominican is very expensive. So we were going to buy a car in St. Louis and have it shipped to the DR, which was going to save us some twenty thousand bucks.

"The guy who was going to give a deal on the car—he was going to give us this car for way under what he could sell it for. All he wanted was a Yadier Molina–signed baseball. So I asked the person who worked for me to go, she's Puerto Rican, to go to down to the clubhouse and get a Yadier Molina ball signed so we could save, like, all of this money on this van. That ended up being on the list [of grievances]. You know, somebody said you're running around getting signatures from ballplayers. So it was stupid things like that. I'm a vice president. I can go ahead and get—I sent Maria in there because Yadier seemed to be fond of her and I figured why not. Plus, it was her area because she's helping out with internationals, her area—to get a ball signed by Yadier. You know, is that all? The guy loved it and gave us a good deal on the van, and the van still runs to this day. But it was stuff like that, that would come back to Walt. People felt like they needed to tattletale on whatever I was doing, question whatever I was doing."

So the struggle had shifted, in terms of where the battles were being fought within the organization. Luhnow was drafting the players he wanted. Great. The question became, would those players get a chance to play?

"I felt like we were doing the right thing and that the integration of scouting and player development was working well," Luhnow said. "But quite frankly, a lot of the advantages we were starting to accumulate in the scouting area were not going to be successful unless the integration to player development was smooth. It wasn't smooth for a few years there. I mean, pitching or hitting aside, it was more about how you manage the pipeline of players and who you give the playing time to, and who you give the promotions to, and who you release in order to get the most output.

"It's raw material coming in. That raw material has now changed. Composition has changed. And so the manufacturing process, if it doesn't adjust, it's going to spit out inferior end products, unless it adjusts. And it had to adjust because a lot—the draft was starting to produce guys like Shane Robinson, who were small. Like Allen Craig, who were slow. They weren't sexy prospects like the ones that we had been trying to get before. There had to be a nurturing and developing of these prospects. Appreciation of why these guys came in and that they need a certain type of development to get there and reinforce the things that made them good in college or that brought them into the draft and allow them to maximize their chance of becoming big leaguers."

After the 2006 season, a year, let's not forget, the Cardinals won the World Series, the team made a change. Bruce Manno, the team's director of player development, was reassigned to pro scouting director, then let go in October 2007. And Jeff Luhnow didn't have to worry whether the new director of player development would view the players he drafted differently. Because the new director of player development was Jeff Luhnow.

"And then it became straightforward because we were promoting the guys, the right guys, and giving the right playing time to the right guys and not releasing guys that had superior track records because they were five feet ten or because they were four point four [seconds down the first base] line instead of four point two," Luhnow said. "You know, making sure that we got the most out of the import, basically."

According to Jocketty, though, it took some work on his part to prevent an outright revolt: "At one point, when I had to address the player-development staff, who were very pro–Bruce Manno at the time, about the change that we were making, I told them, this was a change that was being made. This was the direction the organization was going in. And they needed to all work in a positive way and make it work. And I think it took a little time, but it did work out that way. Some guys ended up leaving, but a lot of guys stayed."

Plenty of George Kissell people stayed. Turco moved to the player-development side. DeJohn kept doing what he'd been doing for more than a decade. But alongside those veterans, those who bought into the new way of operating, were some of Jeff's guys, too.

"It was more about making sure we had the right personnel," Luhnow said. "And there were a lot of good coaches. A lot of good hitting coaches and pitching coaches. But I was making sure that we had the right personnel, which is why I brought Strom in and why I brought Jeff Albert in and guys that appreciated the elements that we were looking for in the recruiting side and could help develop those, enhance those, through the development side and turn them into big leaguers. And Tim Leveque, and all the other guys that we started to bring in who were very nontraditional hires for player development, but who ended up being pretty spectacular baseball people."

But as Luhnow made clear, there wasn't an effort to move away, even a little, from the way George Kissell taught:

"The fundamentals of having to teach someone baseball really have never changed. Like, how you field a ground ball. How you swing. The basic fundamentals of how to throw a pitch. You need experienced teachers to do that, and the Cardinals had plenty of good teachers. The history—when I got there people talked about Hub Kittle and, obviously, George Kissell. There were a lot of really good instructors. And so it wasn't necessarily about anything having to do with they weren't getting the right instructions, just how you manage the player flow through."

Meanwhile, the team's international program began to grow in scope as well. Mozeliak hired Matt Slater in 2007, an excellent baseball executive who became available thanks to the disaster that was Frank McCourt's tenure owning the Los Angeles Dodgers. He and other hires, such as Oz Ocampo, a Columbia MBA who improved the Dominican academy and eventually expanded his work to the rest of the Cardinals' international scouting, broadened the reach of an operation that hadn't really existed just a few years earlier. Slater is particularly good at finding players deep in the talent pool, not simply relying on financial muscle or gut feel to get a few high-profile guys or a lottery ticket. Accordingly, the way the Cardinals found talent on the international market—plenty of it, at varying prices—mirrored their amateur-draft success.

"You've got to take a hybrid approach," Slater explained to me in an October 2014 interview. However, Slater's hybrid approach limits subjectivity, unlike when this phrase is used by some others as an implicit contradiction of the growth of analytics in the game. Slater makes even subjective judgments subject to objective analysis. "We are hugely [reliant upon] our data analysts. We have analysis. We have tremendous young guys here in the office that can crack numbers for us. But they don't just crack performance numbers. They crack the numbers that our scouts are giving us as well. The grades that our scouts put on the player. The makeup forms that come out. The medical. So they're putting that all in and analyzing those numbers. So we really believe in the intuitive nature of this business. We believe that you need to have data-based decisions, while keeping in mind that these players are not decks of cards. They're also human beings that have emotions. And so what the scout brings to the table and what the data brings to the table is all churned together in our final evaluation of a player."

Slater's path to the Cardinals came via the Dodgers, and prior to that the Brewers, who hired him right out of Marquette. Slater had gotten into law school, but turned down the chance to go, preferring instead to go work for Sal Bando's Brewers for $18,000 a year.

But McCourt's tenure in Los Angeles meant a number of front-office members there got demoted or left, and the concept of law school came up again. The Cardinals, though, took a different approach to Slater's interest in the law degree. They saw it as an opportunity to get smarter.

"I found a law school in LA that allowed me to go part-time and was still an ABA-accredited—a really good school, Southwestern Law School. And so, I started then. And right when I started, Mo called me and said, 'Hey, we know what's going on with the Dodgers. We want you to come over here.' And I said, 'I would love to work with you, Mo.' We had known each other coming up through the ranks, as both being assistant directors in scouting and so forth.

"And so I took the job with Mo as special assistant to the GM and told Mo, 'But I'm doing the law school thing.' And he said, 'That's fine. You can stay out in California and do that part-time and do this.' So I did law school part-time. I was full-time special assistant to the GM, flying all over the place. Flying to St. Louis once a month or so or once every two months. And Mo let me do it that way. The people at Southwestern were very accommodating in that they would move finals, they would move deadlines, that I had.

"But I was very attentive. I'd stay on top of things. Stay in touch with professors and so forth. And after four years, I finally got through it and got my law degree. That was at the end of December of 2010 that that occurred. And then three weeks later, my family and I moved to St. Louis."

If that story sounds familiar, it's because Branch Rickey did the exact same thing for Bill DeWitt Sr.

"Tony La Russa knew I was doing it," Slater said. "Very few people knew I was doing it. Mo did for sure, of course. But I didn't want to make it look like, in the industry, that I wasn't focused on my job. But the support that Mo gave me in allowing me to do it was critical, I would say, in getting it done.

"And it makes me a tremendously better executive today having that background. With the contracts we deal with. The negotiations. Just the way I think is completely different. And it was a challenge. My wife feels like I lost something when I finished law school because I loved the challenge of it."

So while the team continued to win on the field—105 wins and a National League pennant in 2004, 100 wins and a trip to the NLCS in 2005, a World Series title in 2006—they were still operating on parallel, often contradictory tracks. Walt Jocketty was building the major league team in a certain way. The minor leagues were increasingly populated with Jeff Luhnow figures, whether players or coaches. Tony La Russa and Dave Duncan operated under different principles as the manager and pitching coach in St. Louis than, say, Brent Strom and Dyar Miller did as pitching coaches in the minor leagues.

Multiple people told me that the decision by DeWitt to let Manno go was essentially an attempt to bring peace within the front office without forcing Jocketty out.

"I told Walt, 'I know you're not happy about Jeff taking over from Bruce [Manno], but if you put me in this role, I don't want to be viewed as being disloyal to you if I do everything in my power to help our farm system [and by extension, Jeff] be successful," Vuch recalled in December 2014 e-mail.

So realistically, DeWitt was going to need to pick one path or the other.

"Walt wasn't really sold on the data," DeWitt said, using data as shorthand for what Luhnow was creating.

Exactly how awkward this could be was exhibited by an experience Brent Strom had, in Jupiter during the spring of 2007, involving Wainwright. Luhnow had suggested years before that the Cardinals acquire Wainwright, now Luhnow had a pitching coach who believed the way Wainwright threw could be improved upon.

"I made a mistake one day of—and I got pulled to the carpet on it—we're out on field four and the Cardinals had a concession stand with a big picture of Adam Wainwright on it," Strom recalled. "And I made a comment to my staff. I said, 'That's the way you should not throw.' I mean, he had a front side here. Had wavering foot plant. The elbow was in a bad position. I was just doing it as an educational [exercise]. Word got back to Mozeliak. And I got called on the carpet for it. Because he had just won nineteen games." Strom paused. "But then again, he also had Tommy John the next year."

> *I think both of us could have done things differently. I think I could have done more in line with what they were trying to do, to work more in conjunction with what they were doing.*
>
> —Walt Jocketty

Imagine you are Walt Jocketty as 2007 dawned.

Your tenure as general manager of the St. Louis Cardinals began in 1995. Your Cardinals went to the NLCS in 1996, then began a streak of success from 2000 to 2006 that included six play-off appearances, two National League pennants, and a World Series championship in just seven years.

This is the kind of success that leads to contract extensions, if not employment for life.

Yet you began the 2007 season fundamentally out of step with your own organization.

Jocketty's thirteenth season as general manager of the Cardinals would be his last. As Jocketty pointed out to me, the scouting director and the head of player development—Luhnow—reported directly to the owner.

"That was definitely a concern," Jocketty said. "That's not usually how clubs operate."

Luhnow Enters

Things had changed within the team's farm system. No longer did the players Luhnow's crew drafted have to worry they'd be buried or released, playing for Manno's farm system. Luhnow oversaw both.

But the desire to properly value baseball players extended well beyond the draft. To have a general manager who wasn't, as DeWitt put it, "sold on the data" created all kinds of limitations on use for this new information.

Then again, it's hard to imagine Jocketty felt particularly limited—he was the general manager for the defending World Series champions, who'd also won 100 games in both 2004 and 2005.

A general manager needs to act quickly in a hypercompetitive marketplace to make sure the value his team puts on a player results in the team's paying appropriately in contract or trade for the player. If the person in charge of those transactions isn't sure about the value, or there's internal discussion, another team can swoop in and get that player instead.

"So then, Jeff's work was—I won't say complete, but we felt pretty good about where we were in terms of valuing players," DeWitt said. "And knowing the value of a walk versus a home run. And what a player's contribution to the team was from a statistical standpoint. Obviously, a lot of other factors as well. And that helped us decide what a player was worth financially. If we were making a deal, were we getting value back for what value we were giving up? That type of thing."

But the working relationship between Luhnow and Jocketty—well, as DeWitt put it, "it got filtered somewhat through me." Jocketty described the analytics as "confined to scouting and player development" at this point.

"It wasn't as enjoyable as it was the first few years," Jocketty put it about his job, though unlike Mozeliak in 2005, Jocketty said he didn't consider leaving even at this point. "Because that's why I wanted to try and make it work if I could. But it was a very uncomfortable situation."

As for the drafts, Jeff Luhnow would have fifty-seven players, according to his own count, which he keeps in a file on his phone, make it to the major leagues through 2014. He expects the total, when all is said and done, will be around sixty-five.

But his first, Chris Pérez, didn't reach the major leagues until 2008. (Pérez was a Charlie Gonzalez find.) So the vital changes Luhnow had put into place for the Cardinals hadn't begun to show themselves on the very field where Jocketty's Cardinals had been winning for years.

The 2007 Cardinals draft, with Luhnow in charge of both drafting and player development, but with tensions at perhaps their highest, yielded thirteen major league players. For comparison, the Yankees got eight; the Cubs, six; the Mets, five. The Cardinals also drafted Oliver Marmol, a shortstop out of College of Charleston, in the sixth round. He ended up on the George Kissell track, the Steve Turco track. Remember? You don't just groom players. You groom coaches and managers.

Still, one member of the analytics team said that Luhnow didn't always follow the recommendations of the system, which still combined scouting with analytics, instead giving the scouts in the room some wins along the way. By then, the system—STOUT—produced a single number, with draft magnets organized around the room in order of preference. So when Luhnow reached down to take a scouting favorite ahead of the system's preferences, the room knew it.

This is where the management took over from the data-driven Luhnow, pumping the brakes on the changeover as he went along. Luhnow, like Jocketty, was working to keep the organization together, though from an opposite direction.

But exactly how to integrate an organization operating within two silos—the products being developed for the major leagues in one, and the major league end point in another—well, it seemed intractable at the time.

"And I thought we had to have everybody in the organization on the same page," DeWitt said of this time. "Because if you have outliers or certain views that 'Oh, this is okay. But maybe it's not really what we should be doing'—it just isn't going to be effective. You devalue what you try to accomplish."

No one, not even the principals, could predict how it would play out.

"No," Mejdal said when I asked him if the ultimate resolution was simply a matter of time. "When I got there, I didn't know how the conflict was going to be resolved. I didn't know the director of player development or the GM of a defending World Series champion would be let go. I had no inclination or no idea that was going to happen, and frankly, my mental energies weren't really spent on that. It was improving the processes and what we did have responsibility for. Which was the draft."

The Cardinals did, finally, slip a bit on the field, following their 2006 World Series title, with a 78-84 record in 2007, missing the play-offs. The Cardinals were only a game out as late as September 7, but that had far more to do with a mediocre NL Central than a quality team in St. Louis. The 2006 team also benefited from a weak NL Central, making the play-offs with an 83-78 record. According to DeWitt, that did make things a bit easier from an external view, and Mozeliak agreed, though he isn't sure the center would have held regardless.

"I do think results matter in terms of how people want to make decisions on personnel," Mozeliak said. "But I sort of get a sense that it didn't matter at that point."

Making the change then didn't insulate them from criticism, however. Far from it.

Here's national baseball writer Bill Madden, who is not what you'd call a friend to the statistical advances made by the game he writes about. It's comical to see how much he got wrong in retrospect, but Madden represents a rear guard in the baseball industry, both then and now, that was outwardly hostile to what Luhnow and others have done to grow the game.

The firing of respected Walt Jocketty as Cardinals GM last Tuesday by team chairman Bill DeWitt was just another example of the growing trend of meddling owners reducing the powers of the general manager and shifting the emphasis of baseball operations to statistical analysis....

...But it was a division DeWitt created when he promoted Jeff Luhnow, one of the new-wave stat practitioners, as head of both player development and scouting. Jocketty viewed that as a usurping of his powers—especially since Luhnow clearly had the chairman's ear—and let it be known to his friends and associates that he was not comfortable with the new arrangement....

On the other hand, a big part of Jocketty's undoing with DeWitt was the failure of the Cardinals' farm system to develop any pitchers in a decade and only two frontline players, catcher Yadier Molina and outfielder Chris Duncan, in recent years.

It will be interesting to see who DeWitt hires as the new GM as he's already stated a preference for someone between the age of 30 and 40 with a player-development background and an understanding of a middle-market operation.

Translation: Someone to work alongside Luhnow and DeWitt. (Cardinal insiders say DeWitt could do a lot worse than assistant GM John Mozeliak, who has been installed as the interim GM.)

On the day Jocketty was fired, Cardinals president Mark Lamping declared, "The best job in baseball just opened." It's doubtful if you'd find any other veteran baseball people who would share that opinion.[5]

The Cardinals had reasons to move on from Jocketty. He realizes that now: "I think both of us could have done things differently. I think I could have done more in line with what they were trying to do, to work more in conjunction with what they were doing."

The products of the Cardinals draft and player development system, under Luhnow, would soon become major leaguers, meaning that an integration in how the club valued them would be vital. You can't spend four years building a system for valuing players, and employ a general manager who doesn't share that view.

However, the organization felt plenty of sadness as well. Not only was Walt Jocketty a general manager for thirteen years, making plenty of friends along the way, but even those who understood the need for a change, even if Jocketty didn't at the time, wished it didn't have to end this way.

"All of that was leading up to the crescendo," Mozeliak said of the change. "It was something that you could see building, and you could anticipate that this could go either direction. But if you were a betting man, you knew where it was headed."

It was headed toward a Cardinals team run by John Mozeliak, who would try to heal a fractured Cardinals organization.

5

HAPPY DAYS ARE HERE AGAIN

I get why the comparison between John Mozeliak and Franklin Delano Roosevelt will strike some of you as funny. I do. The ebullient Roosevelt, with his long cigarette holder and smile built for the editorial cartoon. The professorial Mozeliak, careful with his words and precise with seemingly every movement, as if with every press conference he were teaching a college course on building a baseball team.

Bear with me.

The Democratic Party of 1924 was a combination of old and new thinking, of factions north and south, wet and dry (on the question of Prohibition), progressive and conservative.

Accordingly, Al Smith, the governor of New York, drew plenty, but not sufficient, support to be nominated by the Democratic Party to run for president. The same was true of former secretary of the treasury William Gibbs McAdoo, and Oscar Underwood, senator from Alabama. Ultimately, the Democrats settled on John W. Davis, but he was placeholder, not party leader, and he got slaughtered that fall by Calvin Coolidge. There were real doubts about the future existence of the Democratic Party.

Happy Days Are Here Again

Despite all the fighting, everybody seemed excited about one man: Franklin Roosevelt, who gave the nominating speech for Smith, then succeeded him as governor of New York.

Fast-forward eight years. The country was in a different place. So were the Democrats. Roosevelt united the factions of the party so completely that he won the party's nomination for president on the fourth ballot, then won 472 electoral votes in a general-election destruction of Herbert Hoover.

Roosevelt was the winner, by acclamation, out of the ashes of a massive internal struggle.

So was Mozeliak. The Cardinals were every bit as splintered as those Democrats. Yet, in 2007, those across the philosophical spectrum in and around the Cardinals took a close look at things and decided John Mozeliak should be the next general manager. A man at the center of these struggles not only rose above them to lead the Cardinals, but he's led them to the greatest success in club history. The Cardinals reached the postseason four consecutive seasons from 2011 to 2014. That had never before happened in club history. While more play-off spots are to be had now (more teams, though, too), the Cardinals won at least one postseason series in each of their four play-off bids.

So life's been good in St. Louis under John Mozeliak, who believes the only reason he got the chance was because of his role as peacemaker within the turmoil.

"Well, I think if I wasn't acting in that way, I'm not general manager," Mozeliak put it simply, in one of our October 2014 interviews.

Let's take a step back, though, and look at how Mozeliak got to that point.

He started with baseball young. His earliest memories are from Shea Stadium, sitting next to a man who viewed the game through an analytical lens.

"Well, it starts back with my grandfather on my mother's side," Mozeliak told me. "His name was Thomas Walsh. I was actually born in New Jersey and spent my early years there. I was everywhere. But New Brunswick, Wayne. My father worked for IBM.

"Now again, I was a tiny little fellow. But anyway my grandfather was a big Mets fan. So subsequently, at an early age—probably as early as four—he started taking me to Mets games. And he was one of those guys who always wanted to sit on the third-base side, just right above the dugout. And he understood the game."

For those of you keeping score at home, that means John Mozeliak's first experience with baseball was the 1973 Mets of Tug McGraw and "Ya Gotta Believe!" Many young boys and girls committed themselves to the game of baseball thanks to those Mets. The current Cardinals general manager is one of them. It's a reminder of what a winning team does to galvanize a fan base—one reason why Cardinals fans, who have experienced so many victories through generations, have such close ties to the team.

"And he watched almost through a set of lenses like myself now," Mozeliak continued, remembering his grandfather. "I mean, he was very passionate about what it was. This was not really a social thing just to spend time with your grandkid. He cared.

"And so that was my first exposure to the game of that level, and then subsequently, through the years, it was something I also wanted to play and be a part of that way. But my first real taste of this was through my grandfather and his appreciation for the game. I think what he exposed me to and gave me access to was very unique. And I was very lucky for that.

"He would think about it more strategically. He wasn't going there just to cheer. He liked the nuances of the game of baseball. And as you can imagine, as a child, a lot of times you're going to a game and you're worried about are you getting cotton candy or a hot pretzel. I'm sitting with him and listening to him talk about counts. Whether he should be running, bunting."

But in 1977, the Mets lost a pair of baseball icons, one present, one future. They traded Tom Seaver to the Reds, and John Mozeliak's family moved to Colorado. John was eight years old.

Mozeliak spent the remainder of his childhood without a major league team nearby. He followed the Braves and the Cubs, thanks to superstations, watched the Cardinals and other teams on the NBC *Game of the Week*, but his experience of the game of baseball mostly came through reading about it. The local paper. Box scores. Stats. He played through high school, but that wasn't going to be his entry point into the industry.

"Well, I do think I always have looked at it more from a managerial or management perspective than maybe a true player," Mozeliak said. "I knew I was never going to be a true player, so it was something that for me was sort of easier to think about as far as team building or team organization and the nuances that went into that. That was what I was very curious about."

As Mozeliak entered the workforce, an expansion team arrived in Colorado—the Rockies. Mozeliak got an entry-level job with Colorado. But the Rockies began play in 1993, a decade before *Moneyball*. So the idea that someone with a baseball background limited to high school on the field and field-level seats at Shea Stadium could make a career of it, well, it seemed fanciful.

"And there was a door opened," Mozeliak said. "I entered it. I clearly didn't feel like this was a great career path for someone of my background. In other words, when you look at sort of senior management in major league teams at that time, playing background was something that was still an asset. But as I spent more time with the club, I started to realize, well, maybe there is something I could bring of value, but I didn't know if other people would see it that way.

"When I was with the Rockies, I felt like this is directionally not where I need to be. As in, someone in my early twenties and thinking at some point I want to get married. At some point I want to have a family, and having those types of goals, this business was not going to cater to it. But then, at that point, that's when Walt Jocketty was named the GM of the Cardinals."

Jocketty had been in Colorado before going to the Cardinals in 1995. He offered Mozeliak an opportunity to join him in St. Louis, but Mozeliak wasn't sure he wanted to make the move.

"I did not have a close relationship with him in Colorado. And what I mean by that is, we weren't friends. He knew of me but we weren't interacting on a daily basis.

"But he knew some of the things I was working on for the Rockies and knew that some of those skills might apply to what he might need in St. Louis. So he offered me a position in the scouting department for the St. Louis Cardinals. And at that time, I was obviously excited about the opportunity, but I was also, like, 'Is this going to be one of those things [where] I move to a city I have no familiarity with?' I had just recently gotten married. And would this be a true job with legs or is it going to be something where three years from now, I'm regretting this."

So Mozeliak met with Jocketty. DeWitt was still a year away from even owning the Cardinals. Dan Kantrovitz was in high school. Cardinals pitcher Carlos Martínez was four years old.

But the case Mozeliak made to Jocketty was an interesting forerunner to the ultimate direction of the team.

"When I met with Walt, I said, 'I would love to take this opportunity and do exactly what you need me to do from a computer perspective,'" Mozeliak, the son of an IBM man, told his would-be mentor. "At the time we were just trying to figure a way to capture information and build databases and that kind of stuff, and I was very energized to do that, but I asked him, 'If I were to do this, will I get exposure to more baseball-operations decision making or exposure to understanding how that decision tree works?' And he agreed to do that, and so I had some confidence when I came here that this would be maybe a true career path now.

"But, it did work out," Mozeliak concluded, in more than a bit of an understatement. "Midnineties, to the late nineties, I was getting to sit in meetings. I wasn't really a participant, but I was in meetings listening, watching, and learning."

In the fall of 1998, Mozeliak became Jocketty's scouting director. And Mozeliak realized that baseball wasn't just a diversion from whatever career path he'd ultimately take to support a family. It stood a good chance of being his career. The following July, his first child, Ally, was born.

"We knew that my career trajectory was now pointed in the right direction and for where we were in our lives," Mozeliak recalled of the discussions with his wife, Julie. "I mean, we now have entered our thirties, the year [Ally] was born. If you would do this job and fail, obviously, it could go away. But…"

What Mozeliak left unsaid is that he didn't fail—he became indispensable to Jocketty's operation, plugged in at various levels over the next few seasons. Key to what the Cardinals were doing, and personally important to Jocketty, too.

"My relationship with him grew to where we were very close," Mozeliak said. "As you can imagine, as a scouting director you get to know him. Did that for two years and I was named director of baseball ops, which sort of gave me the view of every department. And then subsequently did that for a couple of years and then was named assistant GM."

Jocketty acknowledged that he was grooming Mozeliak for a future role as a general manager somewhere, which is clear given the kind of experience he gave Mozeliak throughout his tenure.

"What I feel like my skills were getting tested or honed for was negotiating," Mozeliak recalled. "Understanding how to do contracts and get players signed. So at that point, Walt was giving me a lot of exposure to all the zero to threes, which are like pre-arb, which then got me doing a lot of the major league contracts.

"So I was getting a spoonful of helping on all of that. But when you ask about what enables me to do what I do today, I think it's far different. I think it's more about having understanding how to manage. And when I say that, I'm not talking about baseball, I'm talking about people."

This is the part of the job few people seem to understand and is precisely where Mozeliak excelled. The proof came before he even got the job, when he managed to combine both sides of a bitter dispute on Team Mozeliak.

John Mozeliak is in an inherently political job. It is his job to lead, to coerce, to convince. This is what a general manager does. This is what John Mozeliak does exceptionally well. It's made him an excellent GM, and it's the reason he could stay at the center of the Cardinals storm through much of the last decade and make friends from all sides.

"Mo's an expert politician," one Cardinals observer said. "I mean, he's navigated numerous land mines throughout his career and come out on the right end of it because he's very adept at doing that and very intelligent. He's usually a step ahead.

"When it came to where the direction was headed, I think he recognized that. And then he also recognizes how he can keep taking it in that direction. And I try to pick up on some of that political adeptness, when you're dealing with scouts or trying to take your constituency in a direction to make a decision. And Mo is really, really good at that. And I think it's something that he tries to impress upon all of us."

So in the fall of 2007, Mozeliak's constituency was, essentially, everybody within the Cardinals' organization, most of all Bill DeWitt. But while DeWitt named him interim general manager immediately—Mozeliak recalled getting the call from Walt that he'd been let go around 11:00 A.M. on October 3 and being given the temporary job in Bill's office by noon—Mozeliak needed to prove he was broadly acceptable, to Jeff Luhnow and the analytics team, which had grown well beyond the three-man shop, to the old guard that remained in player development and scouting, who wondered what would happen to them without Jocketty to support them. Mozeliak had a manager under him, Tony La Russa, who was a power center unto himself. And he had competition—DeWitt intended to, and did, interview a number of candidates for the job, guys who eventually got shots of their own: Rick Hahn, who'd encouraged Mejdal years earlier and went on to get the GM job with the White Sox. Chris Antonetti, eventually named GM of the Cleveland Indians. They were the kind of candidates who had analytic firepower.

One person who wasn't a candidate, to the surprise of many, was Jeff Luhnow.

"Jeff was a potential GM candidate," DeWitt said. "But really, at that point, he didn't have the major league experience. He didn't have the experience of signing players and all that. He just wasn't quite far enough along. But I think a lot of the media thought that Jeff was going to be the GM. That wasn't in my mind. I talked to Jeff about it, and he was happy with the process and didn't really lobby for the job. What he really loved was the buy-in of the whole organization of what he was trying to accomplish at the player procurement and development level."

Luhnow echoed these sentiments when I asked if he'd made any attempt to get the promotion to general manager:

"No. I had a very frank discussion with Bill, and he didn't think I was ready. I didn't think I was ready. I didn't want it. I had so much in front of me. I was managing this player pipeline that to me it would have been irresponsible to leave that, sort of, as it was still being raised. And the results still hadn't gotten to the point where I felt like we could say that we had been successful. And that was my sole goal. I was hoping that we would hire a GM that would facilitate that now and repeat, and that was my own guidance to Bill on the process."

Hence, Hahn. Hence, Antonetti. Several others were interviewed as well.

"I had a number of candidates I'd talked to, but I needed an interim GM. Mo was the logical choice as assistant GM to become interim GM," DeWitt said. "Then I said, 'Look. You've got a lot of turmoil here. I'm doing this search.' He was a candidate, but not necessarily a leading candidate.

"We need the organization to be led by someone who agrees with what I'm trying to accomplish here. And he said, 'I understand that.' Even as an assistant GM, it was hard for him. Because he would understand Jeff's work, but then had to try to get buy-in throughout the organization, which was difficult."

So there was Mozeliak with less than a month to prove he was the guy.

It helped that nearly everybody, across a spectrum where there'd been massive disagreements on big and small things—from the makeup of and input on which players to draft to how to properly thank someone for helping in the purchase of a truck—all advocated for Mozeliak.

Notice that even Bill Madden, in a column that otherwise rivals Ed Wood's friend the Amazing Criswell for lack of foresight, talked up Mozeliak as a possibility.

So did a far more impressive reader of the present and the future from that time, Bernie Miklasz of the *St. Louis Post-Dispatch*:

> If DeWitt and team President Mark Lamping seek to go outside the organization to hire a new general manager, they'll find plenty of promising candidates. But in assistant GM John Mozeliak, the Cardinals have a perfectly fine candidate, in house. He's a smart baseball man, with good people skills, and has demonstrated an easy rapport with player agents. He also can function smoothly with Jeff Luhnow, the VP of player development. It's important to heal the organizational divide, and Mozeliak can do that.[1]

One reason for the confidence of Miklasz, and ultimately DeWitt himself, was that both Luhnow and Jocketty saw Mozeliak as the right choice.

"First of all, Mo had been with the organization a long time and he had been involved in every element of it," Luhnow said. "And when he was given the opportunity to be interim GM, he treated it as if he were the permanent GM. He organized everything. He got everybody mobilized and really did a nice job. And I think that's ultimately why Bill removed the *interim* and hired him as the GM. And so he had—he had the wrong view if he [had been] behaving as if he wouldn't be there for a long time when he's continued that to this day."

Ultimately, he had Luhnow's support because Luhnow recognized that Mozeliak, despite his personal connection to Jocketty, was an intellectual ally.

"He was there from the beginning," Luhnow said of Mozeliak. "He saw the resistance. He started to recognize the output that was starting to come, and I think he recognized the need to do it and, quite frankly, I think inside of him there was something that he would have wanted way back when but it was difficult to do some of this stuff.

"And it would have been difficult for him to advocate for any sort of substantive change in that environment without the support of Bill DeWitt and at the level he was at. So I think there was part of him that felt a kinship to what was happening and rooting for that. You know, rooting for the change to be successful."

Consider that for a moment. Mozeliak, hired and mentored by Jocketty, managed to make Luhnow feel that Mozeliak was an intellectual stakeholder in the movement that had pushed Jocketty out. This happened in an environment where, as Vuch put it, it seemed as if one side would give you a dirty look if you were caught talking with the other side.

That sense of Mozeliak as ally was reflected throughout the expanding analytics department, not just a three-man shop any longer.

"I remember it was this big surprise to me," Mejdal said of Jocketty's firing. "I mean, Mo had a ton of experience and was quite capable and was more than open to analytics. So I thought that—yeah, Mo is the one who's ready for the position at this time.

"All we ever want is someone with an open mind who's willing to question convention and look to what has taken place and realize [what is possible] to guide them. And Mo was open and curious to this from the beginning. He was always very kind to me. He had more interest in this than anybody that was in the front office, other than Jeff and Dan, of course, when I came. And Vuch. Vuch was great with it, too."

Yet, at the meeting with Bill DeWitt to learn of his dismissal, Walt Jocketty recommended one man to take his place:

"I had recommended Mo. I told them when I was leaving that I thought Mo was ready to take on the position. I know they interviewed a few other people, but they ultimately decided on Mo."

Though he wasn't yet ready to understand why he'd been let go, Jocketty said he recognizes now that Mozeliak could unite the organization in a way he hadn't.

"Well, you'd probably have to ask him that," Jocketty said of Mozeliak's ability to heal the organization's rifts. "But he probably saw the difficulties I was going through. And he was able to make some adjustments. We talked about some of the things we had to do differently, and he made those adjustments."

Or as Luhnow put it, "Well, I think everybody felt good about Mo being there because he had been with the organization long enough to appreciate and have relationships with all the people that had been there, but also had been witnessing and assisting the transformation Bill and I began. So it was an ideal bridge between the two ideologies with the role. I think that's strong here. And there was quite the sigh of relief throughout the organization that we were not going to have to deal with somebody new. This guy understands the Cardinal history, tradition, and that he appreciates the things that are evolving."

DeWitt saw it, too:

"But what he did was, he met with Jeff a lot. Convinced him that he agreed with the approach. And went around to the other people of the organization and said this is the direction we're headed. You better get on the train or you're going to get off the train. And he made it pretty clear that he was all-in on what we were trying to accomplish.

"And Mo was computer literate and he was of an age with the young guys in the business at that time. You know, he got it. He understood what we were trying to do and he agreed with it.

"He didn't put a big sales job on me to be the GM. He knew I was out looking at those individuals with other teams who clearly were what we wanted to have—the data-driven decision-making process."

What's fascinating is that leading the club in this direction—twenty-eight days after Jocketty was let go, Mozeliak got the full-time gig—didn't include some Hollywood moment with Mozeliak, say, taking the mound at Busch

Stadium and delivering an inspired speech. Few could pinpoint precisely how Mozeliak had earned the confidence of people throughout the organization, which likely speaks to how he really did it—through building relationships over years, rather than with a particular moment.

"I thought about the things that I liked about how I was being treated or growing," Mozeliak said about how he treated people once getting the GM job. "I really [tried to incorporate] those observations of having employees that truly enjoy being at work. When I became general manager, we had gotten away from it. We needed to get back to it. And have to have an environment in the office that people want to be a part of and want to come to work."

That didn't mean Mozeliak ran away from making changes, however.

"The important part was clarity and communication of what the front office was going to look like," Mozeliak said. "Because it was certainly going to be different than what a lot of people had become accustomed to knowing.

"Walt was the boss. And I was his right-hand man. I did a lot of the day-to-day duties. I just wanted to create very defined roles for everyone. And also at that time, a little bit of cross-pollination for everyone as well."

But while Mozeliak began to arrange the talent around him according to ability and optimizing performance—something that had taken a backseat to ideology under Jocketty—he had another potentially thorny issue to navigate: his relationship with Cardinals manager Tony La Russa. As Jocketty put it, "Tony was going to run his club the way he was going to run it. He wasn't necessarily going to play who he was told to play." The unhappy tenure of Colby Rasmus in St. Louis, for one, confirms this.

Mozeliak recognized this reality of La Russa, too, and essentially avoided a confrontation there.

"I had the front office piece that I was just trying to make sure everybody understood what they need to do and where we needed to go," Mozeliak said. "And to get that defined and moving. And then, the other part of that was, now, how was I going to work with La Russa in this role? Because

Tony knew me. It wasn't like we were strangers. But he looked at me as someone that held a junior role, and certainly not an equal.

"And now these roles were changing and he was going to have to work with me as we decided how to put this club together. And so I was just trying to walk very gently on that. I wasn't trying to be bold or bullish in any manner. And I wasn't trying to flex muscles to say, 'Look, I'm now the boss.' I was trying to get through this as peacefully and successfully as possible.

"But I mean, Tony at that point had the '06 championship under his belt, so that sort of solidified who he was. And in terms of roster construction or need, he was at a place where he could be vocal."

Instead of attacking La Russa, trying to weaken him, Mozeliak worked on strengthening his relationship with DeWitt.

"Well, I think that's where Bill and my relationship grew a lot," Mozeliak said. "Because rather than me independently make decisions or push an agenda, I would talk to him a lot on, like, how do you handle this? Or, how would you go about doing that? And just, before I did anything, I would always tee it up with him and talk through things. And his relationship with Tony obviously goes back to when he purchased the club.

"And nothing's changed with Bill, right? He was the principal and remained the principal. And so that became, how Bill and I, our relationship, went from where we certainly knew each other and I would imagine had mutual respect, but where it grew to where we started to understand some of the intimacies of decision making and how we think about it."

Mozeliak's strengthening his relationship with DeWitt made sense in a general way—DeWitt owns the club, after all—and in a specific way with La Russa. It also mattered with Luhnow, a subordinate now to Mozeliak, who still had a direct line to the owner. This was less threatening to Mozeliak than it was to Jocketty for any number of reasons—Luhnow and Mozeliak had a similar macro view of the Cardinals, Luhnow and Mozeliak didn't clash personally the way Jocketty and Luhnow did. But to solidify the lines of power, Mozeliak needed to be the one making the final baseball decisions in conjunction with DeWitt, and that wasn't how the Cardinals had been operating for years.

"It was not something I overly fretted about or felt like I needed to change," Mozeliak said. "I sort of thought about it more organically in the sense of, if I'm doing my job, if I'm being responsible to this organization and specifically to Bill, then he should be getting everything he needs from baseball operations from me. If not, there's probably somewhere along the way I'm just falling a little short, and I would imagine if you talked to Bill, he will tell you that his interaction with Jeff after my hiring did—did go down, probably gradually to the point where it became almost more rare.

"Frankly, I feel like it's a confidence thing. I wasn't so insecure where I was worried about what people are running to Bill with."

For Luhnow, the change in management meant he now had the support of the general manager. But remember, Jocketty had essentially ceded to Luhnow the territory he'd been covering anyway. So his ability to continue his projects didn't change much.

"To be honest, not a ton," Luhnow said on how his work changed after Mozeliak took over. "Mo is very aware of everything that's going on in player development and scouting internally. He knew the role of scouting directors very well. He knew player development. And international area—so really, I was just told to take as much off his plate as possible so that he could focus on being a GM, which has so many pressures that nobody really understands until they actually get a chance to do it."

Luhnow's work continued apace with Mejdal, and with additional hires aligned with the new paradigm for the Cardinals. Michael Girsch, who'd been a Luhnow hire in the scouting department after striking up an e-mail friendship with Mozeliak, was promoted to director of baseball development in 2008—a department described by the Cardinals as "a group focused on supporting Baseball Operations via internet applications, analytical models and decision support tools."[2] Over the next six years, Girsch became as important to the integration of analytics into everything the Cardinals did as anyone else.

"On the Girsch and Correa front, what they were able to do was take a square peg and make it round," Mozeliak said in January 2015, who noted at the time that the lack of publicity about them limits the credit they deserve. "They really helped optimize what we were doing."

The three-man shop not only had many more than three men now. The resulting boom allowed Luhnow a freer hand to operate as someone who used the Baseball Development group he'd created like Mozeliak, or any other front office member—a client utilizing their information. It was a freestanding thing now. And eventually, incredibly, at least some of those within it would turn against Luhnow.

On the international side of things, Matt Slater had the Cardinals involved with an ever-increasing number of intriguing players. So in 2008, as another nine eventual major leaguers were drafted by the Cardinals—including the criminally underrated Lance Lynn—guys such as catcher Audry Pérez, who reached the Cardinals in 2013, began filtering through the farm system in greater numbers as well.

"We built an academy in Villa Mella," Slater said. "It was a small academy that we started our operations at. And we were there for about four or five years. And we kind of built the international program at that point."

About two hours north of Villa Mella, that version of the international program found a young outfield prospect named Oscar Taveras. In December 2008, he signed with the Cardinals for $145,000. He was sixteen years old. By the start of the following decade, everyone who saw him came away believing he had a chance to be one of the best hitters in Cardinals history.

Essentially, 2008 was a consolidation year. The draft protocol used the STOUT score, the single value for players, to a greater degree, but not as the fundamental ranking for amateur players.

This actually worked to the team's advantage at times, as in the case of Kevin Siegrist.

"Well, with Kevin Siegrist, you look at that. I wanted the kid in the eighth round," Gonzalez said. "I wanted—I had two hundred grand to give him, and I would have given it to him in a heartbeat.

"And it depends on who's up there, who's pulling the magnets off the board," Gonzalez said of how hard he needs to push for his guys. "Now, let me just say this. I don't want to pump my reputation, but the proof after a while starts to come in the pudding. Dan had the luxury of knowing after a while. I would like to have sat in on a room with Chris Correa and Dan and Sig and some of these guys when they're sitting back—and Girsch—and they're back there chewing the fat with the computers blazing. [And see how often] when Charlie unloads and he says, 'Damn it, this is a gut feel'—what are percentages of when he's right?"

Let's put it this way: it happened often enough that Kantrovitz said to me in an e-mail, "I'll hang my hat on Charlie's senior sign every time."

So the Cardinals drafted Siegrist in the forty-first round, gave him $85,000, and sent him to the Gulf Coast League, then to Mark DeJohn and low-A Batavia in 2009. And then they waited. And waited.

"So we drafted Siegrist, a draft-and-follow, we almost didn't sign him," Luhnow recalled in September 2014. "Charlie kept insisting that this left-hander, that changeup and that body, was eventually going to throw hard, and with that velocity, was going to be really good. And even several years into his development, still hadn't hit any of those marks. [Charlie] just continued to have passion that this was going to come. And lo and behold, you look up last year, and there he is, pumping high nineties in the [2013] World Series."

Siegrist's debut came on June 6, 2013, at Busch Stadium against the Diamondbacks. He struck out four of the six batters he faced over $1\frac{2}{3}$ scoreless innings. Gonzalez got to see it in person—it was also draft night in 2013, and the Cardinals had just taken one of his players, Oscar Mercado, in the first round. Charlie walked out of the draft room, took in the view of the field, and saw Siegrist blowing away Arizona hitters—pitching to Tony Cruz, a catcher the Cardinals had drafted on Gonzalez's recommendation.

But all that was years away in 2008. The Cardinals won 86 games on the field—better than 2007, but still short of the play-offs.

That year also saw the Cardinals lose one of their original three-man shop, in essence because Dan Kantrovitz took the ethos of the DeWitt rebuild—how to make a successful operation more successful—and applied it to his own life.

Kantrovitz had helped create a computer system to streamline the team's amateur scouting operations, Redbirdog. His position within the hierarchy, as a Mozeliak hire who worked directly with Luhnow, was secure.

But Kantrovitz left the Cardinals in late 2008, and not for another job. Kantrovitz went back to school.

"Well, my departure was not one where it was 'I don't like what we're doing here. I'm going to go try something else,'" Kantrovitz recalled. "I—intended—thought that I would go back to the Cardinals after I finished my program." This program was an effort to move beyond his ability to understand the vital role analytics played in the twenty-first-century game, and to become fluent in running the numbers himself, to be someone pushing the analytics even further. To be more Sig, even as he was learning how to be more Mo.

"My curiosity was to learn what we were stumbling upon," Kantrovitz said. "Which I did. And to really not just make some assumptions, but to really figure it out. And we were doing things really well, but that gets to what Sig was saying earlier. That [we were] doing things really well compared to what they were doing before, which wasn't much at all, wasn't hard to do. I wanted to make sure that what I was doing for the long run was sound. And I had such a curiosity [about how to do] that. I felt like I could handle the analytical rigor of what we were doing. And I wanted to train myself in that."

That's not to say the decision was easy, professionally or personally. He and Brenna had a life together in St. Louis.

"So, we were married and I remember telling her that I wanted to go to Harvard and get the master's in statistics because these guys were doing groundbreaking stuff," Kantrovitz recalled. "And she looked at me and said, 'Wow, I know you well enough to think that you're serious.' And then on the other hand, hoped that maybe I wouldn't get in or something." Kantrovitz chuckled. "And I remember getting the envelope, and I said, 'Well, let's just wait to see if I get in.' And then I was one of, like, four kids from the US that got in, and I couldn't turn that down. I was working with a professor doing groundbreaking research in baseball already and who I had a relationship with.

"I ended up flying home, I think, every weekend because she was working as a lawyer. There was no social life at that time and I was just—it was the hardest thing I've ever done.

"The program was probably a little longer than twelve months because I had to do five months of math refreshers before I went. While I was still scouting, I was retaking all the levels of calculus and that sort of thing. And then when I was actually at Harvard, it was just for a school year. I mean, it's a two-school-year thing, like an MBA. But, my wife would have probably not wanted me to come home if I stayed for two full school years."

Brenna welcomed Kantrovitz back, but not to St. Louis. The Cardinals had supported Kantrovitz's decision to go back to school and had even considered tailoring the leave to a specific job for his return. Baseball history offered no precedent for that.

"Baseball's not that industry where you can get an education then guarantee their job when they come back," Luhnow said. "We almost did that for Dan. We almost structured a program to do that. But he really wasn't—it's very outside the normal way of doing things. So we figured we'd take our chances that he would go do that and he'd have a job. We would put him in somewhere when he came back. So I was really proud of him when he got that degree."

This was the St. Louis Cardinals, circa 2008: more like a twenty-first-century tech company than a tradition-bound baseball team, blue blood of the National League.

"Imagine working at Google or Apple today and telling people that you're going to take a year off and directly better yourself for what that job is," Kantrovitz said. "People would be, like, 'Wow. That's amazing.' That was the kind of culture we had then, that was what Jeff fostered. It wasn't odd, is what I'm [saying]. It was more, like, 'Yeah. Right on. Let's get better at this.'"

But if the Cardinals of 2008 weren't the Cardinals of 2002, neither were they the only ones in the marketplace who'd figured out the importance of the work. Remember that whole *Moneyball* crew? The book about Billy Beane's Oakland A's, one that inspired such people as Mejdal, Kantrovitz, Correa, Girsch, and countless others to try to make a career in baseball? They were still around. And they needed someone to run their international department, the area they'd identified, as had the Cardinals, for some of the next advances in scouting. The A's did what Luhnow had considered doing with Kantrovitz. They asked him to tailor his program to get him ready to come take over their international scouting department when he finished. That meant some changes to the analytics side of things, but also "you know, you need to go learn Spanish."

So that's what Kantrovitz did—he says the Spanish was the hardest part, learning the language in intensive Spanish classes with undergraduates. But if *Moneyball* had given the Cardinals many of their best people and ideas, had convinced them to take back the explorer ideal and make it a fundamental part of the Cardinals' identity once again, well, Beane and company extracted a price for serving as inspiration.

So the three-man shop was down to two, but that had less of an impact on what the Cardinals were doing by 2009 than it would have years earlier for two reasons. One was the extent to which Mozeliak had incorporated analytics into his day-to-day operations. Chris Correa, hired in 2007 on the analytics side after Mejdal saw his work at Firstinning.com, described it this way: "When I came on and Tony was the manager, there were basically two customers for our work. It was Mo and it was Jeff."

Some of the fruit from the Luhnow changeover in the farm system began to ripen as well, giving both fans and the major league staff their first glimpses of what kind of players analytics-driven Cardinals drafting could produce. Jess Todd, Clayton Mortensen, and Mitchell Boggs all made appearances for the 2009 Cardinals, while Chris Pérez became an intriguing bullpen option, striking out 11.4 per 9. The Cardinals won 91 games and returned to the postseason, though they were swept in the NLDS by the Los Angeles Dodgers.

The first regular player in the Luhnow drafting era, Colby Rasmus, earned the starting center-field job and held his own as a twenty-two-year-old, with an 89 OPS+ and flashes of far more. That jumped to a 132 OPS+ in 2010, and though conflict with Tony La Russa derailed his Cardinals career, Rasmus was still a regular in 2015 for the Houston Astros.

But there's essentially a five-year lag between any change in drafting and fully reaping its benefits, and the Cardinals were barely four years into the Luhnow draft era. Even then, those changes had been relatively limited at first.

The Cardinals would continue to evolve, altering their processes with an aim on improving. STOUT continued to develop, as did how and when Luhnow integrated it into the final selection process. But 2009 could well be considered Peak Luhnow. It would be the final year Luhnow held both the position of scouting director and director of player development, giving him full control over the pipeline.

No one could fully evaluate at the time what the 2009 draft produced. We, however, have the benefit of five years of hindsight.

So how did he do?

In the first round, the Cardinals took Shelby Miller, who pitched to a 133 ERA+ in his rookie year in 2013, finishing third in the Rookie of the Year balloting. He fell off a bit in 2014, but was still highly regarded enough to be the centerpiece in a December 2014 trade for Jason Heyward.

In the third round, the Cardinals took Joe Kelly, a durable, versatile swingman who won 10 games in 2013, then got traded to the Red Sox in 2014 with Allen Craig to bring back John Lackey.

Two notable things about these pitchers: both of them made the long journey from draft to the major leagues, then helped Cardinals teams into the play-offs. And both were ultimately used by Mozeliak to get precisely the kind of players the Cardinals used to get from other teams, a decade earlier, in salary dumps or via free agency. That was possible for Walt Jocketty in 2003. It wouldn't have been possible for John Mozeliak in 2013—the marketplace had changed. The currency required was no longer currency—not when three subsequent collective bargaining agreements, 2002, 2006, and 2011 each flattened the major league playing field, thanks to revenue sharing, and with a boom in local television money making spenders of nearly every club in baseball.

Young talent had become the coin of the realm. And the Cardinals received plenty of it in 2009.

But wait, there's more. In the fifth round, they took middle infielder Ryan Jackson, who made it to the big leagues.

In the thirteenth round, they took Matt Carpenter. All he's done is post a 125 OPS+ as a rookie third baseman in 2012, improve to a 140 OPS+ in 2013 while learning second base, a new position, for a team that won the National League pennant, then return to third base in 2014 for another Cardinals play-off team, then set a team record for leadoff home runs in a season by August 2015.

In the twenty-first round, the Cardinals took Trevor Rosenthal, out of Cowley County Community College in Kansas. He grabbed the team's closer job in 2013, carrying them to the 2013 World Series on the strength of nine scoreless appearances over three series, then followed up with a more difficult 2014 that still included a 111 ERA+, 45 saves, and a 11.1 K/9 strikeout rate, before a return to form in 2015.

In the twenty-third round, they took Matt Adams, who hit 17 home runs and posted a 129 OPS+ in 2013, then a solid 115 OPS+ in 2014 as the regular first baseman. At the very least, the Cardinals have the strong half of a first-base platoon in Adams, if not more.

Bonus major leaguer: twenty-fourth-round Keith Butler, who made brief appearances in 2013 and 2014. Though he had Tommy John surgery in 2014, he's also a pitcher with a 2.22 ERA and 11.2 K/9 over six minor league seasons, and it's far from certain his ability to help a major league team is at an end.

But let's stick with that five-year window. Just five years and four months after the St. Louis Cardinals drafted their 2009 crop, the Cardinals entered Game 4 of the NLDS leading the Los Angeles Dodgers, two games to one. A win would mean a berth in the NLCS for the fourth consecutive season. A loss would mean having to fly back for a deciding Game 5 against Zack Greinke. And they'd need to beat Clayton Kershaw, the best pitcher in 2014, to do it.

The Cardinals started Shelby Miller, who pitched well into the sixth inning. (He was relieved by Seth Maness, an eleventh-round pick by the Cardinals in 2011, then Marco Gonzales, first-rounder in 2013.)

But enough about other Cardinals drafts. This is the 2009 draft's moment.

In the seventh inning, trailing 2–0, the Cardinals placed two men on ahead of Matt Adams. Remember, Adams had struggled throughout his career against lefties—through 2014, his OPS against them was just .553, nearly 300 points lower than his robust .851 mark against righties. Kershaw is the toughest lefty of them all. Adams fell behind 0-1. Then Kershaw left one of his trademark curveballs up, and the bearish Adams launched it into the right-field bull pen, gloriously making a half-pirouette as he neared the first-base bag and the ball cleared the fence. "Big Matt Adams, jumping in the air with sheer delight," Vin Scully described it.

Trevor Rosenthal came on in the ninth to record the save and send the Cardinals to the NLCS.

No, Matt Carpenter didn't play a big part in that Game 4 win. But that was the only game in the series where he didn't homer, and he finished with a 1.537 OPS against the Dodgers.

And speaking of key 2014 contributors, let's not forget Carlos Martínez, who came to the Cardinals officially in 2010, but was courted throughout 2009 thanks to the existence and maturation of the team's effort in the Dominican Republic.

Martínez had signed with the Boston Red Sox in 2009, but the contract was voided because of a discrepancy between Martínez's identity and the one he used when he signed the contract.

So the Cardinals needed to do more than figure out how much money they wanted to bet on a young pitcher, always a deeply speculative enterprise. They needed to find out first why Martínez's first contract had been voided.

"Mo gave me a call," Slater remembered. "It was in May [2009]. And I already knew, obviously, we were in on this hotshot young kid. He used to be in the Red Sox system, who is now a free agent. He became a free agent because of a name discrepancy.

"And one of the advantages we had with Carlos is Moises Rodriguez, our international operations director, used to work for MLB. So he had a lot of contacts, knew the rules, and looked into this case. And it was determined that Carlos did not have a birth-date discrepancy, which is the main reason why players down there did [get contracts voided]. He had a last-name discrepancy. Because he was raised by his grandma and his aunt and was going by their last name instead of his mom's last name."

Having Rodriguez directing operations—to determine, for instance, that Martínez wasn't secretly twenty-four—allowed the Cardinals to continue forward with their evaluation knowing that they didn't have to worry about discounting any eventual valuation because of the voided Red Sox deal. They could also clear the red tape, thanks to a significant presence in the country.

"Also, when it came to signing him, there was some governmental protocol we had to get through," Slater said. "With getting Carlos out of the country, because he had registered for a visa under the other last name of Matias. Carlos Matias was the name he was going by when this was all going on. And Moises and Aaron [Rodriguez], who's our assistant in the Dominican, were able to work with the Dominican government to get through those issues. Whereas some other teams maybe had a little harder time with doing it."

So Mozeliak called Slater, still in California finishing up his law degree, and asked him to fly down to the Dominican with Dyar Miller, the minor league pitching coordinator, to see and evaluate Martínez.

"He met me at the Miami airport, and Dyar and I flew down and we worked out Carlos at our academy in Villa Mella, the original academy we had," Slater said. "Carlos came in and it was an incredible display of fluid arm action. I remember—I looked through my notes after you e-mailed the other day, and eleven of his first twelve pitches were fastballs for strikes that were at least ninety-five miles an hour. And this was a seventeen-year-old kid at the time. And you just don't see that very often."

But Matt Slater needed to go back to his bosses, to Mozeliak and DeWitt, and tell him how much money he thought the Cardinals should commit to Martínez, echoing Rodriguez's enthusiasm. To a person, not just to an arm action.

"All of us, what we do is—we need to be careful with makeup and character," Slater said. "So our scouts down there have told me about Carlos and where he came from. He came from a very poor background where he grew up in Santiago in Puerto Plata, the port of Dominicans. But Dyar and I wanted to get to know him ourselves. So after the workout, Dyar and I went for, probably, a twenty- to thirty-minute walk with Carlos by ourselves around the outside of our complex. And [I remember] speaking with him in our broken Spanish and his very, very limited English at that time, trying to get to know him better. He told us his favorite player was Pedro Martínez. I'll never forget that." (Probably because few pitchers since Pedro have looked more like him on the mound.)

"He told us what pitches he wanted to use and so forth. And everything he dreamed about being was on the mound and pitching in the big leagues. So it was just—it was more of just trying to get his intentions. Because we did have questions. He was a very flashy kind of kid. And sometimes you worry what the flash means. So we need to really get down inside and get to know him better. And here's a—a sixty-five-year-old, longtime, crusty, old pitching coach and a young scout from the US walking up to a seventeen-year-old Dominican kid, trying to get to know each other."

Imagine a therapist tasked with getting to know a patient in a single, fifty-minute session. Slater had half that much time to determine whether to pay Carlos Martínez $1.5 million. This is yet another challenge in scouting. Mistakes will be made. Having the smartest possible people available to evaluate in the time teams get with young players is paramount.

"I think that walk, to me, is what solidified my call later that day on the phone with Mo and Mr. DeWitt. I remember saying, yes. We should give a guy a million and a half dollars."

Slater looks right. Martínez rocketed through the farm system, became the Cardinals' bridge from starters to Rosenthal in 2013, and held his own as a starter in 2014 once given the chance. In 2015, he made the All-Star Game, and through August had been the Cardinals' best pitcher.

One bull-pen session. One walk. And Slater had to make that call, though he never gets the chance without the team's presence in the country in the first place.

"You have to be somewhat of a gunslinger," Slater said, "in that the percentage of data you're using to make your decisions compared to the intuitive nature of things may be a different ratio. And with Carlos, certainly, it was what we saw that day, what our scouts had seen the month or so leading up to that. And also that walk convinced Dyar and I that this guy has something inside of him that's going to really push him to get to the big leagues.

And maybe it was his background. That he came from such a rough upbringing that he would fight through it.

"And there was some worries about his flashiness and his flair. And you still see that now in his game. But we kind of saw that as something that may be a positive. So it may make him an even better pitcher."

And Baseball America *wasn't rating Jon Jay and Dan Descalso and Allen Craig. Those guys were top of their prospects. It's a lot of high-floor, no-ceiling guys is what they kept saying. We ended winning the championship. So pretty good high floor.*

—Jeff Luhnow

The hiring of Jeff Luhnow came at the conclusion of a whirlwind month, an e-mail from Bill DeWitt's son-in-law to a few meetings to a memo announcing it all. That project, as 2010 dawned, was entering its seventh year. The project continued, to be sure. But neither internally, nor externally, was there any consensus that it was working.

The skeptics weren't simply those who opposed analytics.

Baseball Prospectus ranked the thirty organizations. On March 8, 2010, Kevin Goldstein ranked the Cardinals...thirtieth:

Why They Are Here: Their recent drafts aren't awful per se, but they're certainly boring and lacking as far as star power. The graduation of a few prospects and the trading away of even more (which happens when you are a perennial contender) leaves the system almost solely riding on the hopes for Shelby Miller's right arm.

Where They Will Be Next Year: Either here, or darn close to here. Their first-round pick doesn't come until the 25th selection, so there's no star power coming from there either, not unless someone falls into their lap. If Miller collapses for some reason, there's nobody here worthy of top-prospect recognition.[3]

To be fair to Goldstein—one of the best writers on the minor leagues before getting hired in 2012 by the Houston Astros...and Jeff Luhnow—he wasn't so much criticizing the Cardinals' overall development of minor league talent as what was left—note the point about trading, "which happens when you are a perennial contender." From that perspective, the new pipeline was working quite well.

As *Baseball America Prospect Handbook, 2010* noted, "The Cardinals rushed RHPs Clayton Mortensen (1s) and Jess Todd (2), then used them in deals for Holliday and Mark DeRosa...3B/1B Brett Wallace (1) would be the best prospect in the system if the Cardinals hadn't used him and OF Shane Peterson (2) in a trade for Matt Holliday."[4]

If that sounds like the Cardinals traded a ton of talent to get Matt Holliday, you're right. But a few things about that: They targeted Holliday for nearly eighteen months before acquiring him. This happened in a multitude of ways, from scouting him first with the Colorado Rockies, then with the Oakland Athletics, who acquired him in November 2008. Mozeliak and DeWitt met and discussed what it would probably take to keep him once he hit free agency, and they created room in future budget years for a player they hadn't yet acquired.

Holliday was something the organization hadn't developed—a right-handed, power-hitting left fielder to put in the middle of the lineup with Albert Pujols and absolutely terrify opposing pitchers. Holliday would be in high demand, and by some of the smartest teams, too—note that it was the Athletics who first pried him loose from the Rockies.

But money alone wasn't going to give the Cardinals a chance to trade for him. Again: the paradigm had changed.

Why that mattered so significantly, according to DeWitt, was how much more success the Cardinals have with retaining free agents once they play in St. Louis, as opposed to luring them to the Cardinals when they hit the market, unfamiliar with the experience.

"We actually talked to Colorado about dealing for him before the A's made the trade," DeWitt said.

Happy Days Are Here Again

"We had a lot of intel on Matt that he was a great team guy in addition to being a good player. He was in the right point in his career. We haven't been successful in getting free agents who weren't already here. Once they hit free agency, they know about the Cardinals and they know it's a great place to play, but that process is so hard. You get a lot of advice when you're a player in free agency. Players have told us it's not pleasant. You travel all over the place. You talk to a number of teams. And players, generally, who go that route, gravitate to the highest bid. And we just haven't had success in being the highest bidder for premium players. Sure, we've signed free agents, but they haven't necessarily been premium players. They've been more complementary players. They're not all-star players.

"Unless they've been with us. And once they're here and they understand the environment, I've never heard a player say, 'You know what? When I get to free agency, I'm going to look around and decide to go somewhere else.' They always say, 'I want to stay here. Let's try and make it happen.' They just wanted to be treated fairly. And we've really had a lot of success with that." DeWitt mentioned the signings of Jim Edmonds, Mark McGwire, Darryl Kile, Scott Rolen, and Matt Holliday off the top of his head, and there were many others.

The approach also requires discipline, which means avoiding an overpay relative to what the team has determined a player is worth. Without the analytic firepower to confidently run an estimate for a player going forward, Mozeliak and DeWitt would instead have been making their best guesses, as much of baseball did for nearly the entirety of the sport's existence.

"Because every team has their limits, whether it's the Yankees and Red Sox or the smallest-payroll team," DeWitt said. "They feel like for a given need, they can pay so much. Another team might feel they can pay more for that need if they have a higher payroll or if maybe they have some young players and they just feel like they need to get that last piece. So it's what we feel a player's worth to us. What we can afford to pay him and still have a team. I've said many times to players when they negotiate, 'I'm better than so-and-so, why can't I get paid what they're making?'—because we can't have a team if that happens. We've got these arbitration-eligible players coming up, and we don't want to put all our eggs in one basket and then gamble that we can fill with cheaper players.

"So, if we have someone who can fill the need internally and it's a younger player—we know we'll always have needs. And you've got two resources. You're got financial resources and player resources. We'd rather use financial resources in this era than player resources."

Notably, the Cardinals spent both on Holliday, first dealing Mortensen, Peterson, and Wallace, then retaining him that winter, after he experienced St. Louis, for seven years for $120 million.

How were they so sure?

"Well, I mean, first—the first question is, is this a replaceable asset?" Mozeliak said of the thinking in paying big for a free agent. "And if the answer is yes, then you have to define how. If the answer's no, that obviously puts a priority on trying to find a way to get it done.

"The season before we traded for him, which was '09, the winter of '08 to '09, we had the scouts looking at Matt Holliday with the Rockies. He subsequently got traded to Oakland. So when he was in Oakland, he was someone that we had a lot of interest in, and the thought process there was to get him here. And then we felt like if he was here, he would enjoy it and want to stay here. And ultimately, that's what happened."

One of those scouts was Slater, who dug deep into Holliday's profile to get a full sense of the person they'd potentially be investing in. Meanwhile, those on the analytics side put together an estimate of what the Cardinals could expect in production from Holliday on the field as he pushed deeper into his thirties.

"We talked about him leading into that year," Slater recalled of the winter of 2008–9. "And then come June, I specifically remember being on the phone with Mo at my son's Little League tournament and—the offense needs a lift and why don't we revisit Holliday. So then at one point, Mo said, 'Okay, make sure you see him.' And the A's played a series at Dodger Stadium that year that I went and saw him. And the one thing I remember is that, even though he wasn't hitting all that much for the A's—maybe not the great numbers he was, if you recall—the ball was coming off the bat. The power being displayed in BP was what I always remembered. I think he was just not in a great [hitting] environment there. That's why he wasn't producing at all." Playing in the pitcher-friendly Oakland Coliseum, Holliday's OPS+ was 120, down from his career mark of 136.

"And the thing with Holliday, as you know, we re-signed him to a big deal after we had him for half a season. What I recall from seeing him then was his work ethic. His being the first one out of the dugout and—early in the BP and so forth. And that's a key for a good scout, going to games early, are notes on little things like that. That can make a difference.

"And Mo will tell you—we're not a team that signs free agents from other organizations to big contracts. But we do give big contracts to our own players who become free agents. Yadi, Holliday, Wainwright before he did, and so forth. But that's because we feel like we know these players very well. And what do we know about them that makes us give out these contracts is the fact that they have a certain work ethic that tells us that they're going to make team performance better or at least maintain effort throughout a long-term deal. And I think that's something that Holliday showed to us. He was going to be someone who kept his body in shape. Was going to be giving us the effort that we would need to make a long-term commitment to him."

Holliday, through August 2015, is nearly six years into his seven-year deal. His career OPS+ is 136. With the Cardinals, over that time, it's actually better, 143. And he's been durable as well, averaging 147 games per season, though that number will come down following an injury-filled 2015.

That's an absolutely critical way that Mozeliak incorporated analytics into the Cardinals' full operation—these decisions were made with a full complement of information on hand. This is scouting, this is statistical builds, this is psychology.

The Cardinals are quick to tell you that they haven't invented something new, something that will leave the rest of baseball behind. But what the Cardinals are doing, at all times, is trying to make sure they are using every bit of information available to them, integrating it as quickly as possible into decisions that often have to be made with blinding speed, and to constantly be asking themselves how to get even better at that entire process.

One way Mozeliak thought they could get better was to separate the decisions of the scouting department from player development. So Mozeliak put John Vuch, with longtime development executive Gary LaRocque, atop PD. Luhnow would now be overseeing the draft alone.

"The reason for that was that I felt like having one person doing that meant there just weren't enough controls or filters on it," Mozeliak said in one of our October 2014 interviews. "Because I think scouting directors, they're not necessarily calibrated on the players that they're drafting and signing. They want to see them succeed. I think it's an imbalance on decision making.

"Well, we were doing an okay job. What was happening was—I don't think we were being honest on when it was time to maybe let a player go. And at some point you need clarity. That's sort of the nature of our business. And when you're convinced, in terms of who you're picking and you want to see them succeed, you have that inherent bias. And that's just a hard thing to get over.

"I think it's more like your personal investment and you want to see it [proven] right. Human nature. It's almost like watching the play-offs right now, right? And you see that manager. You know it's time to get the starter out, yet he tries to get another out. And guess what? He didn't get the out.

"And that's sort of what happens with farm directors, if they're the scouting directors. You're always hoping to get more than maybe you're going to get. And I just felt that having that clarity in our front office ended up helping make better decisions."

The pairing of Vuch, a lifelong Cardinals fan and front office member who worked his way up from a runner in the late 1970s while he was still in high school, with LaRocque, a cerebral former player and manager who'd taught high school math in the gap year between the end of his playing career and the start of his coaching career, turned out to be effective.

While it was the 1982 Cardinals who lured Dan Kantrovitz into a life of baseball, Bob Gibson's 1968 Cardinals captured Vuch.

"I was born and raised in STL, and like almost everyone in the area was a huge Cardinals fan," Vuch told me in a December 2014 e-mail. "One of my first memories was my father taking me out of school as a five-year-old in 1st grade to see the Cardinals play in the 1968 World Series. As much as I'd like to say I got to see Bob Gibson strike out 17 in G1, unfortunately it was a 13–1 Game Six loss. From that point on, [I] was a huge Cardinals fan."

Vuch actually transferred schools, to the University of Missouri–St. Louis, to be available for the team year-round through college.

"The runner duties were pretty basic—we primarily just worked on game days and we'd take tickets and cash from the main ticket office out to the ticket windows throughout the stadium, would take phone messages down to the clubhouse, would run off stats for the media relations department, escort groups down to the field for pregame ceremonies and pretty much anything else they needed us to do.

"I graduated from college in January of 1985, and of course was hoping to get on full-time with the team after graduation, but back then there were probably no more than 30 or so full-time front office employees, so it was a little tougher to find an open position. Of course, after paying for my college education, my parents were wanting me to 'get a real job,' but since the team was doing so well in '85, I wanted to hang around until the end of the year in case we made it to the World Series, so we agreed that if I didn't get anything full-time by the end of the year, that I would then get more serious about finding a job outside of the game. As fate would have it, in August of '85, Dave Edmonds [who was Stan Musial's son-in-law] mentioned to me that he was leaving his role in the sales department, so I spoke with Joe Cunningham (Sales Director) and expressed my interest. He knew me from my work with taking the groups on the field, and also from running other errands for him, and agreed to hire me for the role. He knew that while I was doing fine with sales, my true interest was on the baseball side of things. He was close with Lee Thomas, who was the Farm Director at the time, and Lee mentioned that he had a young lady [Madeleine Clever] working in an administrative role for him, who felt like her ceiling was limited on the baseball side and was looking to get into sales or marketing. So just prior to the 1988 season, she moved to the sales department, and I moved into her role as a Player Development Assistant—or as I would later tell people, I was 'traded for a secretary to be named later.'"

Within a few years, the Cardinals GM had Vuch working up arbitration cases. He recalled a desire to incorporate statistics long before the Cardinals ultimately did, which helps to explain why the Strat-O-Matic–playing Vuch, who discovered Bill James in college (and still has the 1983–88 abstracts on his office bookshelf), was so in sync with the Luhnow changeover.

"For a long time, I was the closest thing we had to an analytic department—at one point my title was something like Manager of Baseball Information, so I was all for us ramping up the statistical side of things, as I thought we underutilized the stats in our decision making process," Vuch wrote. "For example, one of the things they would have me do each year was project what an appropriate offer would be for free agents, and when I gave them my projection for Tino Martinez, they thought I was crazy for saying that he shouldn't get more than two years and shouldn't get more than $5MM/year because 'he hit 34 HR's last year.' I pointed out that he was 32 or 33 years old and that 22 of those 34 HR's came at home as a LH hitter playing in Yankee Stadium, and that you shouldn't expect nearly that level of production playing 81 games in Busch Stadium. Unfortunately, we ended up giving him 3 years times $7 MM and his production ended up dropping off to about what you would have gotten if you took out his Yankee Stadium numbers from his last year in NY."

As for LaRocque, his experience as both a player and a coach prepared him for the almost familial obligations when it comes to developing and promoting within the farm system. A Hartford, Connecticut, product, LaRocque stayed local for school at the University of Hartford. The Brewers drafted him as a shortstop.

"And I'm a fourteenth-rounder, senior sign," LaRocque recalled when we chatted in a June 2014 interview. "I'm a college kid. There's not a big negotiation going on here. And they said—I'll never forget, because [Brewers scout] Dick Bogard, at the end of the conversation, he said, 'Now we got your contract.' And they put the contract out and I said, 'Well, Mr. Bogard, don't guys in a draft normally get some kind of bonus? Even five hundred dollars?'

"And he said, 'Well, they do. But not in your case.' End of negotiations. So I signed the contract right away."

LaRocque played a few years in the minor leagues, OPS maxing at .697 in A-ball, though he did steal 27 bases in 34 attempts. But he said of himself, "Looking back now with my scouting background, I was a Double-A player. I didn't have enough bat to carry me to anything higher."

So LaRocque went home to East Windsor, Connecticut, taught mathematics at the local high school, and coached the baseball team. He'd been told by several people he should get into coaching.

"I decided I wanted to go from being an old player, twenty-four, twenty-five, to being a young coach," LaRocque said. "In February of '79, I had written a note to the Dodgers vice president Bill Schweppe, a minor league man that's in charge of their system. So he called me back and said, 'We have an opening.' This is in February. Spring training's coming. He said, 'We've got an opening in Clinton in the Midwest league for a coach.' Keep in mind, back then you have one manager and coaches were just starting into systems. And I'm saying to myself, 'This is an opportunity. This is the Dodgers. I'm twenty-six years old, whatever. I got to take this.' But I said to him, 'I'm sorry, Mr. Schweppe. I can't do it.' I said that I made a commitment here. I'm coaching a baseball team in the spring. I can't do it. He said, 'Well, I'm awfully sorry,' and I thought that was it. I get a call, April first, when camps breaks.

And he said, 'Gary. Bill Schweppe. We still have that opening in Clinton. We haven't named anybody.' And I said, 'Well, Mr. Schweppe, I can't do it, you know? I'm coaching this baseball team. I'll be done in June. I made a commitment to the school. I can't do it.'

"So the year's up. He calls me. I thought for sure that I'd lost him. He called me in June and he said, 'We have two openings. One in Clinton. Clinton still. And Lethbridge in the Pioneer League rookie league. We need a coach there, too.' He said, 'Can you make it?' So I said, 'I'll be there in two days.' He said, 'Where do you want to go?' I said, 'I want to go to Lethbridge. I want to start at the bottom and work my way up.'

"He said, 'You got it.'

"Five years later, Bill Schweppe said to me in the car one day, we were riding to go grab a bite to eat. It was '83. I was doing the Gulf Coast League. We were talking about the old times. I said, 'Why did you keep calling me back? I know you have hundreds of guys that will qualify. I had not coached. I had only played three years, two and a half years. Why did you call me back?' He said, 'I only called you back for one reason. You said something to me that made a difference,' he said. 'You said, 'I cannot leave the high school. I won't break my commitment. That's the kind of people we want here.'"

LaRocque stayed for years, coaching, then managing in Vero Beach, another Dodger affiliate at a complex built by, yes, Branch Rickey. Then San Antonio, Double-A. Then on to scouting, with an eye toward eventually making his way to the front office.

"That's when I started to really realize I'd broadened my base," LaRocque said. "I've got to use it to give back. And I've always cherished the idea of leading. Of management. I mean, to this day, I see how Mo handles things and I watch and I listen to how he does it. And I thought, 'Okay, I'm going to make this my life.' And I thought, 'How do you want to do it?' And so in the early nineties, I thought, 'I want to be in the front office and manage that way.'"

Eventually, LaRocque got a gig as scouting director for the New York

Mets before the Cardinals brought him over first to scout major league teams, then to work as an adviser to Vuch. In 2011, LaRocque took the reins as senior adviser in player development, before getting named director of PD in November 2012.

Notably, neither LaRocque nor Vuch had any conflict with the changes implemented by Luhnow, nor any issue with the Kissell way of developing players. Once again, the idea that a constant questioning and attempt to improve methods was a departure from Kissell's teachings proved to be a fallacy.

LaRocque and Vuch, in conjunction with longtime Kissell disciple and Cardinals minor league manager Mike Shildt, worked at revising the manual to most effectively instruct young Cardinals players and managers throughout the system.

Still, the Cardinals missed the play-offs in 2010, though they finished with 86 wins, and their Pythagorean expectation of 91-71 means they likely underachieved. Rasmus looked as if he'd taken the step toward becoming a star, with a 132 OPS+ in center field at just twenty-three years old. Jon Jay, a discovery of Charlie Gonzalez's down in Florida, posted a 113 OPS+ in his first extended big league look. Allen Craig surfaced at the major league level, as did Daniel Descalso.

But the 2010 Cardinals finished second in the NL Central to Walt Jocketty's Cincinnati Reds. While Jocketty now understands what the Cardinals were doing, those who wished to strangle analytics in the bassinet used Jocketty's Reds beating Mozeliak's Cardinals as some kind of referendum on it.

You might know Murray Chass as the *New York Times* reporter who did groundbreaking work at the paper on labor issues in Major League Baseball. You might know Chass as the guy who, for some unexplainable reason, refused to call himself a blogger when he left the paper and began a blog at MurrayChass.com. You might know him as the guy who continues to oppose Mike Piazza's bid for entry to the Hall of Fame based on having seen

Piazza with "bacne," something Chass seems to think proves definitively that Piazza used steroids, and something that, when I interviewed a half dozen dermatologists to ascertain this after Chass's crusade began, turns out to do nothing of the sort.

A consistent theme in Chass's work, like that of Madden, is a dismissal of anything that smacks of analytics. Accordingly, with the Cardinals finishing five games behind the Reds, here's what Chass had to say on his...blog.

A Jocketty Jeer for DeWitt's Cardinals

Walt Jocketty has too much class, is too much of a gentleman to thumb his nose, stick out his tongue and say to the St. Louis Cardinals and their principal owner, Bill DeWitt Jr., "na na na na na." So I'll do it for him: Na na na na na.

DeWitt deserves this rude treatment because three years ago, only a year after his Jocketty-built team won the World Series, he fired Jocketty. Now Jocketty's new team, Cincinnati, is on the brink of dethroning the Cardinals as National League Central champions....

"It was philosophy, the direction they wanted to take the organization, how they put their team together," Jocketty said. "I didn't necessarily go along with the thinking. We had a pretty good organization in place. I was given the right to run the organization the way I thought it should be, and I think people would say we had done the right job in scouting and player development and had the right people, quality people, to run it."

...Jocketty was probably the most notable victim of the modern-day baseball war between evaluation and analysis. It mattered not to DeWitt that Jocketty's belief in player evaluation had worked extremely well for the Cardinals. The owner was seduced by others in the organization into believing that statistical analysis was the way to go....

Has Jocketty made any changes in his method of operation since becoming the Reds' general manager? "No, not really," he said but acknowledged that "you have to use a certain amount of statistics."[5]

It's fascinating to hear Jocketty, three years after the fact, yet to fully embrace the direction of the sport. Jocketty had come to feel differently by the time we talked.

But it's also notable that as late as the end of the 2010 season, it was still possible to make a case that the Jeff Luhnow reboot had been something short of vital, or even successful.

That all changed in 2011.

It wasn't just that the Cardinals won another World Series, though that kind of victory, in Mozeliak's fourth full year as general manager, validated both his overall work with the major league team and the altered focus of the organization as a whole after Luhnow's hiring.

But the particulars of with whom and how the Cardinals won impressed even those most reluctant to accept the changing baseball landscape.

"I don't remember getting much kudos from the work in the draft until the 2011 World Series," Mejdal said. "In the play-offs, when I think Craig and Jay and Descalso were needed and they hit the ground running. And then, there was a—'Wow. These guys are useful.' I remember La Russa saying once that he was impressed with how these guys were ready to play. That they hit the ground running."

Mejdal experienced something similar the night the Cardinals beat the Brewers in the NLCS to advance to the World Series. At the celebration dinner, shortstop Ryan Theriot came up to Mejdal, Luhnow, and others at the table, specifically to talk about the young players making a difference in St. Louis.

"'These guys are great,'" Mejdal remembered Theriot saying. "'They came up. They filled holes. And they didn't just fill the holes, they were valuable major leaguers.' I took great pride in that. That was wonderful to hear. You can imagine, after year after year, you guys are drafting, whatever, low—high-floor, low-ceiling, complementary players. And having that database saying, no such thing. You know? To actually begin to hear and see the results on a play-off stage and then, certainly, the World Series. You can imagine how rewarding that whole aspect was."

Luhnow remembered La Russa saying to him, "If I'd known you were going to send me so many guys who can throw ninety-five-plus, I wouldn't have been so hard on you for so long!"

While the 2011 champions were, without question, driven by such players as Yadier Molina and Albert Pujols, those two had been stars in St. Louis for years. The difference between the earlier Molina/Pujols teams and this one, for the most part, came from player development, not to mention the team-high 151 OPS+ from Holliday, who couldn't have been acquired without the topflight prospects the Cardinals gave up in the trade.

Colby Rasmus began the year as the center fielder, but by year's end the man in center was Charlie Gonzalez's find, Jon Jay. Allen Craig started in right field for much of the 2011 World Series and homered in three different games. Lance Lynn pitched in relief throughout the series, too.

Game 3 was a fine example of how important the Luhnow products were in making the 2011 Cardinals into champions. Craig homered. Jay started. Daniel Descalso came on as a pinch runner and scored. Fernando Salas, who'd signed as an international free agent, came on in relief for an ineffective Kyle Lohse. Lynn got the win. Mitchell Boggs, from Luhnow's first draft in 2005, pitched the ninth.

Oh, and Pujols homered three times, too. Cardinals, 16–7.

But this team, while not quite the full manifestation of the new approach to drafting and developing, relied on those players to put them over the top. Four of the top eleven hitters, via WAR, came through the system. Jaime García, a twenty-second-round pick back in 2005, became the team's second-best starter. Jason Motte, a catcher the Cardinals converted to pitching in 2006, took hold of the closer's job late in the 2011 season.

Motte took the ball from Lynn, who'd pitched the eighth. When Motte induced the Rangers' David Murphy to hit a fly ball to left field, where Allen

Craig caught it, there was no denying two things: The Cardinals were world champions. And the leadership of John Mozeliak, the revolution of Jeff Luhnow, and the counterintuitive approach implemented by Bill DeWitt Jr. had brought them there.

6

AFTER HE'S GONE

Even if the world at large didn't fully realize just how completely the baseball industry had changed by 2011, many of those inside the sport absolutely did.

One was Jim Crane, who bought the Houston Astros in May 2011 for $680 million. His goal, once he decided what kind of baseball team he wanted, was straightforward: he wanted the St. Louis Cardinals.

The Cardinals had a general manager, John Mozeliak. But they also had an executive who'd been with them for eight years, had experience running international, had run player development, was running an enormously successful scouting department.

If 2007 was too soon for Jeff Luhnow to ascend to general manager, by 2011 he was, if anything, overqualified.

"By '11, I felt like the work had resulted in something tangible, which is contribution to a championship," Luhnow said. "The '06 was a great feeling, too, because Suppan and Weaver, I'd [advocated for] signing a few guys that had helped. This one was so much more meaningful because players that I saw as amateurs sitting in the stands were now playing.

"It was incredibly satisfying, and so when the opportunity came up, I had to just [try it]," Luhnow said. "It was easier, too, because we had a great group of people in St. Louis that were doing an incredible job for decades. So it felt good that that was a good time for me to start off new."

Remember, Luhnow was a turnaround guy at heart. But not only had the Cardinals implemented so many of his ideas, of Sig Mejdal's innovations, then built on them with the next generation of analytic talent in Correa, Girsch, and others, they'd seen the results on the field as well.

Luhnow also believes the varied areas he'd immersed himself in while with the Cardinals—part of Mozeliak's strategy to have all of his specialists with significant knowledge of other areas as well—made a difference in both the perception and the reality of his baseball profile.

"Yeah, I think had I not gotten involved in the different areas of scouting and player development, international—had I just come in as the manager/consultant side—you know, numbers guy—and never expanded beyond, there would have been zero chance that we would be successful," Luhnow said of his Cardinals tenure.

I asked him if he meant that in terms of actual strategies, or in his credibility within the Cardinals along with the rest of baseball.

"In terms of methods and in terms of acceptance," Luhnow said. "Because by really, truly appreciating what happens in the field—where the scout goes, where the coach goes, what it's like to scout in Venezuela—like truly be able to do that firsthand and appreciate all of that, it made me change the way I thought about things. And it's also allowed for some street credibility. You're not going to be considered a baseball guy by the industry. You know, not like playing the game for their whole lives, or those who coached. But, I think people who were on the fence appreciated the fact that I was sitting there with a radar gun while getting on that plane, flying to Timbuktu, scouting a sixteen-year-old kid. I started making the rounds in a foreign system and going everywhere. It allowed them to consider you more than then. That's where it changed."

Mozeliak said he didn't much doubt that Luhnow, eventually, wanted to be a general manager. DeWitt agreed, saying, "I thought he'd get a GM opportunity." But to DeWitt, that it didn't happen until after 2011 was key in allowing the Cardinals to continue progressing as an organization.

"Well, you never like to lose someone who's doing a really good job," DeWitt said. "But Jeff was scouting director, and he was given an opportunity to move up, and that's just the way it is. We were far enough along with the people and the understanding throughout the system. If he had left earlier because of the turmoil or something, that would have been a different story. Because we weren't far enough along. But by the time he'd left, we were deep with people who had the knowledge to continue what had been developed. Dan [Kantrovitz] had worked there. And Mike Girsch understood the whole model and had been part of it and knew what we were looking to do. He was all-in on it and helped a lot. Also Chris Correa, so we were pretty deep."

That depth became a bit shallower, though, with Sig Mejdal leaving as well and joining Luhnow in Houston. The decision was not easy for Mejdal, who had a strong working relationship with Mozeliak, and, as Mejdal put it, "There's something scary when leaving the World Series champion St. Louis Cardinals, who had arguably the strongest player development system with an owner that I had a wonderful relationship with. I was leaving about as much job security as you can have in baseball. And I was going to the team with the least major league skill and the least minor league skill. With an owner I didn't know. I had never met. With, certainly, a whole lot less security."

Yet, to be part of an organization headed by Luhnow struck Mejdal as an opportunity to see his work more fully implemented than even in St. Louis.

"Some of the other analysts [working for other teams] would talk to me, and they would, frankly, be jealous of the amount of Jeff's willingness to use this," Mejdal recalled. "And not only his willingness to use this, his willingness to share that he's using this with others. And that makes the job so much more rewarding when the work you actually do is implemented in a seemingly close to optimal way. And so, with Jeff gone, of course my concern was who was going to be the next scouting director and would they implement it anything like this. And so there was question of whether my current job would be as exciting. But then I imagined Jeff going to the Astros and creating it closer to what he created in the scouting department in St. Louis and imagining what an exciting organization that could be."

Mejdal became the director of decision sciences for the Astros. That position didn't previous exist in Houston, or on any other team in baseball.

"When I heard that Jeff was hired by the Astros, I was hoping that I would be able to go with him as he is such a good manager. He was my biggest supporter, and there was an uncertainty in what things would be like in the Cardinals after he left. This industry has the somewhat strange rule that in order to talk to another team, your current employer has to give permission for that to take place. I had spoken with Jeff in general terms over the years of what we could do if he were ever GM, but since his hire, I had no contact with him. Was he going to bring me over? Had he asked and Mo said no? Finally, Mo called me into his office and said that Jeff had asked to speak to me and that he was going to grant that permission. Phew. At that point, I knew I was going to be an Astro. There was excitement but at the same time I felt terrible about leaving Bill and Mo. They both were always very supportive of me. Mo had spoken to me and gone to lunch with me at a time when just doing that could cause issues amongst others in the organization, and Bill DeWitt—I can't say enough about him—he took a chance on me and treated me so well for so long. I thanked Mo for all that he had done during that meeting, and I called Bill and did the same."

So the Cardinals found themselves without two of their three-man shop. The third, Kantrovitz, was in Oakland.

"Mo and I put the full-court press on him to come back to the Cardinals because Jeff was looking to hire people, too, at that time," DeWitt said. "And also, Billy Beane didn't want to lose Dan."

Suddenly, the would-be baseball executive who couldn't get hired for more than a year less than a decade prior had three teams who wanted him, not because of his playing background, but because of his facility with the new paradigm. That's 10 percent of the industry, pretty significant validation for Kantrovitz's decision to go back to school.

"Dan was just somebody that I'd known a long time," Mozeliak said. "Brought him into the game. Hell, drafted him. Released him. Hired him. There's a guy I just felt like would understand exactly what we're needing to do. And when you talk about succession plan, that just shows you I didn't have one for that position. Because I felt like we had to go outside and fill it, and he was the one guy who I felt would be ideal. And luckily, we did get him. And at that time, Jeff brought him in and offered him, I think, the farm director job."

Mozeliak was right.

"I left, I thought of him, and so did Mo. And Mo beat me," Luhnow said. "I brought him to the holiday dinner and Jim Crane, Franci Crane, and—he got the full-court press. You've got to remember, he's from St. Louis. They had home [field] advantage. And he got drafted by the Cardinals and he had a lot of relationships over there. The only relationship he had in Houston, really, was me. I think I made it tough on him and I probably earned him a few extra thousand dollars, but..."

Luhnow trailed off. Ultimately, Kantrovitz went home and took over as scouting director beginning in 2012. And even though it meant Luhnow couldn't have him in Houston, that wasn't entirely a bitter pill for Luhnow, either.

"I was so happy—getting Dan to work for the Astros was the goal," Luhnow said. "But it was a great compromise that he was going to go work for the Cardinals and go do stuff that I had been doing there. 'Cause when you're a guy who puts so much into it in ten years, you want someone to take it to the next level. To build on it. To improve it and not just go backwards. And I had good confidence that he was the right guy for the job. So I was very happy that he was the one that was going to continue that tradition. Because he was there when all of that started. He watched it evolve and I knew he had the skills to not only continue it, but improve it. Which is what he's done."

After He's Gone

You could hear the struggle in his voice as Kantrovitz thought back to that time, choosing between three innovating employers.

"It was a pretty complicated decision. Because number one, we loved Oakland. I loved working for Billy and David [Forst]. Those guys were amazing and Farhan [Zaidi]. I mean, they're as smart as it gets. So, it wasn't a foregone conclusion that I was going to leave there. But, just the opportunity, you know? I worked under Jeff. He was the scouting director. Deep down, that's kind of what I wanted to do all along. And when he was doing it, he was great at it. But once he moved on to bigger and better things, that was kind of my dream job."

And so began a pair of great evolutions.

In Houston, Luhnow and Mejdal began to build out an organization that didn't need to conform to any vast, long-held traditions. If the Astros weren't an expansion team, they were about as close as an established team could be, with an imminent move from the National League Central to the American League West, and an owner ready to let Luhnow tear down completely and remake the club as he saw fit.

And Kantrovitz had an opportunity to take the Cardinals in directions he'd imagined as well. Both he and Luhnow made it clear that despite mutual respect, their draft boards would not look quite the same.

"But what I wanted to do—working under Jeff for so long, and he had such success," Kantrovitz said. "But there were some things that I thought I would do a little differently. And would hope to do even, maybe, better from a fairly different perspective."

As if Kantrovitz wasn't under enough pressure already, replacing Luhnow in a role where he'd had so much success developing talent that brought a World Series championship to St. Louis, Kantrovitz also had to justify, in many minds, replacing a legend.

Albert Pujols, promoted to the Cardinals in 2001, posted an OPS+ of 157 as a twenty-one-year-old; .329/.403/.610, with 37 home runs. Then he did that again, more or less, for the next ten years. The Cardinals had previously employed one hitter, ever, who had enjoyed that much success: Stan Musial. Pujols, through age thirty-one, posted an OPS+ of 170. Musial, through age thirty-one, checked in just above him, at 172.

Musial is the iconic Cardinal. But Pujols looked as if he would equal Musial, with a second world championship in 2011 (including that 3-home-run Game 3). That is, if he stayed in St. Louis. I flew into town just after the World Series, and I asked my shuttle driver from the airport how she was doing.

"Okay," she answered. "Just worrying about Albert staying."

Pujols didn't stay. The Angels offered him $254 million over ten years. The Cardinals thought that was too much to pay for anybody's age thirty-two-to-forty-one seasons, even the great Albert Pujols.

Fun fact: Musial, over those ten seasons, posted a 147 OPS+, averaging 138 games per season. Pujols, through August 2015, has put up an OPS+ of 129 over nearly four seasons in Anaheim while averaging 142 games per season. So far, it looks as if Musial's record of achievement is safe.

And the same is true of the Cardinals, who were not safe in the world of public opinion at the time for letting Pujols go. All they received in return were a pair of compensatory picks—a first-rounder from the Angels and a sandwich pick, which comes between the first and second rounds. It would be up to Kantrovitz, a few months after getting hired, to make those picks.

"It would be insincere to say I didn't feel a ton of pressure in that first draft, or really any of the 3 drafts, for that matter," Kantrovitz recalled in a January 2015 e-mail. "Obviously a lot of attention was being paid to the extra picks we had in the 2012 draft. And, unlike previous years, there was the new wrinkle of being subject to a 'cap.' And while extra picks were a huge bonus, it also added a new layer of complexity that had not been part of the calculus previously. But, any way you spin it, it was no doubt a huge opportunity for the organization and one everybody was excited to tackle."

What followed is basically unprecedented in baseball history: the payoff of letting Albert Pujols leave became clear in record time. Normally, in such a situation, here's your best-case scenario: A prime player leaves for a long-term, new contract. The very performance that got him that new contract seldom disappears overnight. And the compensatory draft picks, even when they turn out well, take years to make the climb through a team's minor league system.

"In terms of realizing the gravity of the Pujols decision, I knew that history was not on our side when looking at the odds of cashing in on a comp pick," Kantrovitz recalled. "And I certainly didn't expect we would get as quick a return as we did."

But before the Cardinals even made their picks on June 4, 2012, one factor already made the call by DeWitt and Mozeliak not to match the Pujols offer from the Angels look prophetic: Pujols himself. His numbers had dropped a bit in 2011, in his final season for the Cardinals. His OPS dropped below 1.000 for the first time since 2002, and his OPS+ of 148 was the lowest of his career, if not dramatically below a few other seasons.

But despite a still-excellent 138 OPS+ for the Angels in 2012, much of that production came in the second half of the season. He failed to homer in April, and on the day Kantrovitz made the two compensatory picks, Pujols had an OPS of .694.

Still, a declining Pujols was only part of the equation. The players Kantrovitz drafted, particularly Michael Wacha, took a very fast track to the major leagues.

"While we had him high on the list from day 1—it's not like he all of a sudden became a good pitcher," Kantrovitz said in a January 2015 e-mail. "But, I will say that his first couple outings were not against good competition. As a result, he didn't need to use his changeup or breaking ball much, if at all, and it was tough to get a thorough scouting evaluation. Then, I remember one of our national cross-checkers, Jamal Strong, texting me while watching Wacha against Pepperdine, a good hitting team. And, Jamal, who played in the big leagues, said it was the best changeup he had ever seen. I'll never forget that."

They sent Wacha to Steve Turco in the Gulf Coast League. He didn't stay long, with 5 innings, 1 walk, 7 strikeouts. To challenge him further, they moved him up to high-A Palm Beach, skipping two levels. That didn't prove to be much of a problem for Wacha: 8 innings, 1 walk, 16 strikeouts, no runs allowed. On to Springfield and the Double-A threshold that proves difficult for many pitching prospects: 8 innings, 1 run, 3 walks, 17 strikeouts.

Across three levels, Wacha posted an ERA of 0.86. Walk rate was 1.7/9. Strikeout rate 17.1/9.

Pujols struggled to even stay on the field in 2013, playing in just 99 games, while his OPS+ dropped to 116. And by May 2013, less than a year after getting drafted, Wacha was in the big leagues. He threw 7 innings against the Royals, allowing just 1 run, didn't walk a batter, and struck out 6.

"The day Wacha got called up—you know, the first big leaguer technically that got called up from a draft when I was scouting director—Jeff was the first person to e-mail me saying, 'Nice work. Only forty more to catch me,'" Kantrovitz told me in October 2014. "So it's definitely something that I won't forget, that e-mail. And I'm going to e-mail him once I get to forty-one so I can tell him—I got you."

Nor was this an anomaly for Wacha: he finished the 2013 regular season with a 135 ERA+, 2.6 walks per nine, 9 strikeouts per nine. He went out and won Game 4 of the NLDS against the Pirates, pitching into the eighth, before Carlos Martínez and Trevor Rosenthal closed out a 2–1 win.

And in the NLCS, Wacha twice outpitched the Los Angeles ace, Clayton Kershaw. In both Game 2 and Game 6, both times surrounded by a red wall of sound at Busch Stadium, Wacha didn't give up a run. In Game 2, that was vital, in a 1–0 win. In Game 6, his teammates picked him up offensively. Wacha gave the ball to Martínez, who turned it over to Rosenthal—two draft picks and an international signing. At the end of the game, a 9–0 win, the Cardinals were National League champions. And Michael Wacha was the NLCS MVP.

"It's funny because I ran into his agent at the playoffs in L.A. and we got on the topic of Wacha and he asked me what I was thinking as Wacha was falling in the draft," Kantrovitz recalled in a January 2015 e-mail. "I said I was thinking, 'Holy shit, what do other teams know that we don't?' According to our performance metrics and scouting opinions, there were only a few higher-ranked players… and it didn't seem plausible to me that he would get to 19 without some sort of issue… him being hurt, a signability issue, or something similar."

Meanwhile, Stephen Piscotty has made steady progress through the Cardinals' system, debuting in 2015 and posting an OPS+ of 132 over his first 72 plate appearances with the Cardinals through August 2015. "Piscotty was actually a pick that was not consistent with our system, if you can believe that," Kantrovitz said. "He was more of a 'subjective' pick, more of just listening to our scouts. When that 3rd pick rolled around, we had just taken a 'performer' in Ramsey with our 2nd pick and I didn't want to miss the opportunity to get a high ceiling hitter like Piscotty. I looked at Roger Smith, our nat'l cross-checker and asked him what he thought [pointing to Piscotty's magnet], and Roger in his deep Georgia accent said, 'You betta f@#%$@#'n believe it.' Then, I looked at our area scout, Matt Swanson, and asked him, and he actually said he'd prefer Carson Kelly. I didn't think that was a bad thought but at that point, we also figured Kelly was sliding and would likely be around later."

The Cardinals got both Piscotty and Kelly that year. By the beginning of 2015, Piscotty had ascended to the third spot in *Baseball America*'s Cardinals prospects.[1] Then Kantrovitz in 2014, with a pair of first-round picks in 2013, went out and got even more topflight pitching, taking Marco Gonzales and Rob Kaminsky. Gonzales, Steve Turco explained to me back in May 2014, was on "the Wacha Plan." Sure enough, he debuted in June, and by October was one of Matheny's trusted relievers.

"As I suspect is a lot more rare than I even realize, we identified Marco as a top target in our preseason scouting meetings," Kantrovitz said. "Somebody with a chance of getting to our pick who already had a lot of 'scout love' coming into the year. Marco checked a lot of boxes. He had the performance, so the model liked him. He had stuff, so the scouts liked him. And he had the top mechanics grade in the class. As long as he didn't lay an egg his junior year and somebody completely unexpected didn't fall, Marco would be in consideration for our pick. In fact, he was probably the top pitcher on my personal pref list. Realizing that he could be in play for us, I explicitly told our area scout not to contact his agent. In fact, during the draft, Mo and I went into his office to call Marco's agent somewhere in the teens...just a few picks before ours. And the first thing out of his mouth was, 'Shit, I didn't think the Cardinals were interested!' I smiled. He also said there was interest in the top ten from more than one team and we got lucky he fell...that also made me smile."

As for Kaminsky, the high school product out of Montvale, New Jersey, held his own with Turco in the Gulf Coast League after getting picked in 2013.

"I remember meeting our area scout, Sean Moran, to go watch Rob pitch," Kantrovitz said. "It was an incredibly efficient outing, and afterwards I remember talking with Sean and it was clear how much he liked Rob and wanted us to draft him. Agreeing with Sean and having complete trust in his evaluation ability, we agreed the best strategy was to downplay our interest and not sound any alarm bells."

In 2014, Kaminsky pitched in full-season ball with Class-A Peoria, a jump of two levels, and his 1.88 ERA proved he was certainly ready for the challenge. Pushed another level to high-A Palm Beach, Kaminsky posted an ERA of 2.09 over 17 starts, before the Cardinals traded him to Cleveland for Brandon Moss, a straight one-for-one deal for a hitter the big club needed.

"For a starting pitcher, best season in my 11 years with the Chiefs," Peoria Chiefs play-by-play man Nathan Baliva told me about Kaminsky in January 2015. "Number 2 SP ERA/Avg against, and #5 Whip in franchise history."

The final reason Cardinals fans rested easier about the loss of Pujols, a generational talent, was simple: the heir apparent was coming.

After He's Gone

That $145,000 spent on acquiring Oscar Taveras by the international department quickly turned into one of the best investments by any team. Taveras held his own as a seventeen-year-old in the Dominican Summer League in 2009. But in 2010, the numbers began to look a lot like those of another great young hitter whom the Cardinals had once developed: Albert Pujols.

Taveras went to low-A Johnson City, and hit .322/.362/.485. He got promoted to Quad Cities in the Midwest League, a pitchers' circuit, but not for those facing Taveras: .386/.444/.584, in his age-nineteen season.

By the spring of 2012, the torch even had a physical manifestation, with a bat that Pujols gave to Taveras, one that Taveras put aside as a memento. He did too much damage to his bats to use it more than once.

"The fact that he almost hit .400 kind of had my attention," Matheny told Derrick Goold back in the spring of 2012. "You play a full season and you hit .380, I don't care if it's T-ball, you've done something pretty special. To see a nineteen-year-old that is doing things that he's been able to do … it's legitimate."

Taveras hadn't gotten to major league camp yet, but Goold reported Matheny kept requesting him personally for Cardinals major league spring games.[2]

Pujols had only spent one season in the minors. Surely, Taveras would be in St. Louis soon as well. The Cardinals would have their draft picks and their franchise bat. He was the third-best prospect in baseball, according to *Baseball America* in 2013. A foot injury limited him to 47 games in 2013. That kind of thing sends prospects farther down the list. Some questions also arose about how hard he worked on the rest of his game, one reason he didn't get promoted as readily as Pujols.

"There's no reason you can't work as hard on your baserunning and work as hard on your defense as you work on your hitting," Vuch recalled saying to Taveras back in 2012, from that same Derrick Goold profile of Taveras. "You appeal to his pride.… The goal is not just to be a good hitter. He has the potential to be a really good player. We're not doing our job if we can't extract everything out of him."

And yet. He entered 2014 at... third in all of baseball, according to *Baseball America*.

"I will remember the lengthy interview for a long time, where I sat, where he did... The bat given him," Goold recalled in a January 2015 conversation. "It was clear he'd be a special hitter. Question was dedication to other parts of the game. Kid had crazy obvious talent."

"You always have this feeling that he's half a level ahead of where he's playing," Luhnow said in 2012. "You get the feeling he's the best player on the field when he comes up to bat. He's the guy you want to watch. He's the guy who sells tickets in the future."

Or as Taveras recalled Pujols saying to him, "I'm looking forward to seeing good things from you."

2014

March 23, Jupiter, Florida

Ask every one of the hundreds of Cardinals prospects what they're thinking about as spring training days dwindle to a few, and it's where they'll be going for the summer, and what level they want to reach by the fall.

"I have to prove I can get lefties out in Peoria," Joe Scanio told me as we stood at the nerve center of the George Kissell complex, a group of six fields surrounding a small tower that holds a restroom. There's no shade here. The fans are elsewhere. Later that day, the Cardinals in major league camp will play on the main field at Roger Dean Stadium.

Scanio was a sixteenth-round draft pick in 2012, Dan Kantrovitz's first season as scouting director. He isn't a top prospect—he's a minor league reliever and was from the moment he started playing in Batavia, where he was old for the league. Just a fastball and a breaking ball.

But this is what the Cardinals do: they make sure every prospect of theirs knows precisely what is expected of him. I encountered this, over and over, whenever I spoke to one of their players. Nothing is left unsaid so that players will know what they do well, what they need to work on, how they progress.

"I pitched at that level last year," Scanio told me. "I know I can do it."

Lefties posted a .795 OPS against Scanio in 2013. A broken wrist held him back in 2014, but across three levels, he lowered the lefty OPS against him to .590.

The activity was constant across four fields, every player equipped with his information, every player desperately hoping to show enough to get the choice assignment, one step closer to the major leagues.

On a fifth field, outfielder Devante Lacy is facing Nick Frey. The Cardinals took Lacy in the twenty-fourth round in 2013, Frey in the thirty-third round. Paul Davis, minor league pitching coach/coordinator of pitching analytics, supervises. It's what Brent Strom used to do, but Strom went off to Houston to work for Jeff Luhnow, promoted to the major league side.

Davis is guiding Frey, but Lacy and Frey took the opportunity to debrief each other as they left the field. The conversation isn't just vertical in Cardinals camp.

"That two-seamer, I thought I was right on it, then it dropped," Lacy told Frey.

"Yeah, I was leaving some of those up, but down, they can't hit those," Frey responded.

Lacy's rehabbing a hamate injury. Frey's rehabbing from Tommy John surgery.

"Eventually, we'll be a bunch of guys pushing each other," Lacy told me as we walked toward the minor league clubhouse. "For now, we're all trying to work together. He tells me what I'm doing wrong, I tell him what he's doing wrong."

And of course: "I'm hoping to be at State College in June," Lacy tells me. "It's in God's hands."

This happens with the most promising prospects, too. The two first-rounders from the 2013 draft were Marco Gonzales and Rob Kaminsky, a college pitcher with a changeup scouts compared to Johan Santana's, and a high school hurler with a plus curveball to go with his MLB-ready fastball.

Get them together, and what do you think happened in the spring of 2014? Gonzales taught Kaminsky the changeup. Kaminsky taught Gonzales the curveball. Then they both went out and excelled.

As for promotion, Lacy didn't have it quite right. It wasn't God so much as a chess game played by Gary LaRocque, in conjunction with the rest of the front office, though LaRocque is given a free hand to use his decades of expertise to make the final call on where everybody begins.

"We, in our structure, look at each roster and we try to set certain parameters," LaRocque told me in a July interview. "You know, they're not hard caps, but they certainly are benchmarks. And if a player gets to that and takes himself above the level of the league, then we consider how to move him, when to move him [up]. It's more of a timing issue. We've done that throughout our system. We have a series of benchmarks. A lot of that's driven just by my own initial conversation way back in April following spring training."

That's even communicated to Corey Baker, who by any benchmark is at the very edges of the Cardinals system.

It didn't matter that Baker was selected in the forty-ninth round back in 2011, a round that no longer exists in the MLB draft—the total was dropped to forty rounds in 2012. Or that Baker was a senior sign, getting a bonus of not much more than LaRocque did all those years ago.

Baker didn't even think he'd get drafted. He'd been a mideighties fastball guy at Clarkstown South High School in the northwest suburbs of New York City, then an upper-eighties fastball guy at the University of Pittsburgh.

"Yeah, I was back home," Baker recalled in a June 2014 interview. "I was back in Rockland County. And, you know, it was the forty-ninth round.

"So I obviously know I wasn't going in the first day. I obviously knew I wasn't going early in that second day. But I was watching on the computer. I had teammates go. We had two guys from Pitt go in the seventh round, and watching a bunch of guys that I had played with. So I was just watching on my computer. I didn't get drafted the second day. I was, like, no big deal. Tomorrow you have [rounds] thirty-one through fifty, you know? Maybe I'll get drafted tomorrow. And I was watching on my computer and around round thirty-five, I stopped watching. I was like, man, this is terrible. I see all these guys getting drafted. Why am I not getting picked? And I stopped watching. And I was home. Me and my mom and my brother were at home and my dad was working. And I remember I turned it off, and I had just, like, had enough. And I called my girlfriend, who was in Florida at the time, and I was just, like, 'Well, I guess I'm not getting drafted. Time to start figuring out some other stuff.'"

Baker has alternatives. He was a history major at Pitt, minor in political science. He'd interned in both Pittsburgh's and University of Central Florida's Sports Information Departments, the latter to be closer to his longtime girlfriend, Jenna, an up-and-coming industrial engineer at Disney.

"And I was sitting on my front porch for a while. And in my head I was, like, 'All right,' you know? 'It's probably the fortieth round by now. It's got to be the forty-fifth round by now. All right. It's over. I might as well go check and just see if anyone else I know got picked.' And I walk inside and the forty-ninth round was still going on, and I was, like, all right, I guess I'll watch. And then about thirty seconds later, it was the Cardinals' pick and they took me. And I called my dad right away, and me and my mom and my brother were there. We were all excited about it. So it went from a pretty low time for me to wow, you know? I didn't get drafted. It just came and went. And then it was awesome 'cause I found out it wasn't over and I got picked.

"And then I had to leave in, like, three days, but my girlfriend flew up from Florida to spend the time with me and my family. And it was a lot of joy but it was also sobering. Now it's time to get back to work 'cause I'm starting from the bottom again."

This is the year ahead for hundreds of Cardinals prospects. The team needs to figure out how to keep them focused, get their needs met within the financially restrictive confines of Major League Baseball's guidelines on minor league salary, per diem, and other logistical difficulties that come with long bus trips and daily games. The staff need to make sure they're connecting with their players as people—these guys, for the most part, haven't been away from home very often, and certainly not for months and months at a time.

"I think Gary was there all these times when we were up there," Baker recalled, also noting the continuity with both his manager at several stops, Dann Bilardello, and pitching coach, Ace Adams. "And they all told us the same thing, that it's an exciting time and we belong there and that they took us for a reason, and it's exciting and it's time for us to embrace the competition of professional baseball and enjoy the Cardinals. And they all stress the amount of pride they had in the Cardinals organization and that we are obviously extremely fortunate to be a part of it."

The Cardinals' seventh-round pick in 2013, Chris Rivera, had experienced some of the travel, playing USA Baseball in high school. But he was being separated from his longtime girlfriend, Angie, and the two of them had to figure out how to make it work while a continent separated them, and Rivera's time was spent on baseball fields by day and buses by night.

"I've been dating the same girl for four years, so being with her every day at school and then after school on the weekends was every day," Rivera told me. "So coming here was a little different, not seeing her every day."

Now?

"She came out for a week and then that's about it. So that's a little hard. And then not knowing where we're going to go in about two weeks is a little different, too, because she's not going to know. And I would like for her to come out and see me, but then again, I don't know.

"People—they don't know how much of a grind it is. They think you make all this money and they think you get an endless amount of money. And that's not the truth at all."

Rivera is hoping he'll get to State College. But that season doesn't begin until June. In the meantime, Rivera remains with Turco in the Gulf Coast League.

And even for loved ones who have been through the grind, have seen how hard it is, there's still a transition from the off-season.

"He's there, but he's not there," one of the wives told me as we sat on the silver bleachers radiating the heat of the March Florida sun. "Like we don't have a real conversation for six months. Just a different lifestyle."

Her husband is on the mound, facing some of the more advanced hitters. I hear her grunt with every pitch, as if she were delivering them.

"Sixty-five pitches. He's done." She's been keeping the pitch count in her head. "Today, he'll really dissect it, then he's done. But you should see his iPad. He has a scouting report on everyone he's ever faced, from rookie ball to the majors. You know, 'This guy can't handle oh-and-two changeups.' He's really smart."

Smart will only get you so far. You've got to execute. And even then, it may not be enough, not with so many other guys around trying for the same finite number of jobs.

Against some lower-level guys, a bright kid named Sam Tuivailala cannot find his changeup.

Minor league pitching coach Ace Adams, ahead of coaching at Palm Beach in 2014, looked on with minor league pitching coordinator Tim Leveque, a Brent Strom disciple.

"Best pitch!" Adams shouts to Tuivailala. Leveque told me later Tuivailala's best pitch is "a fastball he keeps down in the zone."

Tuivailala was twenty-one in the spring of 2014. The Cardinals drafted him in the third round back in 2010 out of high school, not knowing whether he'd ultimately hit or pitch for them.

"There were more than half the clubs that saw him as a pitcher, but we were one of the clubs that saw him as a position player," Luhnow told me about the thinking behind taking Tuivailala. "Our area scout believed that he would be a successful position player. We wanted the talent here respected, and it's much easier to go from being a position player to a pitcher than the other way around, so if you make him a pitcher, you're never going to find out if he's a position player."

But after Tuivailala struggled to hit with Turco in the Gulf Coast League—a .591 OPS in 2010 after signing, and a .661 OPS repeating the league in 2011—he was ready to make the switch to the mound.

"When a player first comes to you, very first year of pro ball, it's very easy to find flaws," Turco, who once resisted a switch to the mound himself, told me in May 2014. "So you can try and tell them what they need to do to succeed there, right then. Or you can let them fail, and then when they do, they're going to be far more receptive to change."

Accordingly, the Cardinals will not shift a player from pitching to hitting, or vice versa, without a full buy-in from the player. One such player, Rowan Wick, decided to stick with hitting after a 2013 season with power at Johnson City—10 home runs in 241 plate appearances, a .464 slugging percentage—but difficulty making contact as well, striking out nearly 30 percent of the time. The Cardinals moved Wick from catcher to right field, but Wick wasn't ready to give up on hitting, though Turco said he thought Wick might throw harder than Tuivailala did. Wick returned to the Gulf Coast League ahead of a summer assignment to State College and told me he had his eye on full-season Peoria.

Meanwhile, Tuivailala hit 95 miles per hour with his fastball once he transitioned, but control eluded him. He struck out 23 in 13 innings with Johnson City in 2012, short-season A-ball. But he walked 13 as well. The next year, in full-season A-ball Peoria, no one could hit him very well. The strikeouts were absurd—50 in 35⅓, 12.7/9. But the walks stayed high, 5.1/9. He hit four batters. His ERA of 5.35 was extremely high, considering all the strikeouts and that no one homered off him all season.

So that's where Tuivailala found himself in the spring of 2014.

"I still feel like a position player trying to pitch," Tuivailala told me when we sat on the bleachers and talked after his outing, Tuivailala still in uniform. "That's what needs to change."

Leveque told him, the two of them standing just outside the makeshift dugouts surrounded in chain link, "Oh and oh, oh and one, you can't be afraid to throw that curveball. It's not just for you to throw it in safe counts, one and two. And that changeup, you might be able to get some quicker outs, pitching inside."

Leveque doesn't know which of his pitchers will figure it all out. The point isn't that the Cardinals identify those guys, though obviously more attention is given to the high-profile prospects. Everybody comes away from the spring knowing what needs to happen.

"We'll use last year as a baseline," Leveque told me in the shadow of the Kissell plaque on that March day. They'll send Tuivailala to high-A ball, to Palm Beach. Put another way, he'll stay right in Jupiter. "Guys are cheating on Tui's fastball, which sits ninety-five. Look, he's a converted guy, so it's more about progress than a specific benchmark."

The same is true for the guy hitting on a separate field, taking his cuts ahead of the highest-level minor league intrasquad game. It's that man again, the one Albert Pujols cited, the one John Mozeliak called "the most prolific hitter I've seen in this organization since Albert."[3]

When Taveras steps into the batter's box, helmet a bit loose on his head, he has a casual, jaunty air. Meanwhile, the world snaps to attention. Before his turn to bat, other hitters were preparing, coaches chatting, players examining their bats, playing catch. Taveras enters the box: coaches look up or gather. Several come from other fields. Red Schoendienst makes sure his golf cart is parked directly behind Taveras's BP session, Mark DeJohn joining him in the two-seater. His teammates all watch.

The unstated understanding is that we're all watching something you don't often see. Keith Butler, a pitcher, Tommy Pham, an outfielder, James Ramsey, the team's 2012 first-round pick—all stand just beyond the black mini-structure set up for BP, taking a view from the third-base side to enjoy

Taveras's left-handed swing. Each drive impresses. The sound, as the baseball cliché goes, is different off his bat. I heard that sound twice last spring—off the bat of José Abreu of the White Sox, out in Arizona, ahead of Abreu's 2014 of terrorizing American League pitchers and winning the AL Rookie of the Year.

The other time I heard it was when Oscar Taveras hit the ball.

"Yeah!" Ramsey says as Taveras drives one over the right-center-field fence. Taveras turns and acknowledges Ramsey's enthusiasm, smiling, with a slight nod. Another ball clears the fence in right field, and another, Taveras like a red-and-white barber pole in perfect rhythm, twisting upon himself in that pristine Cardinals uniform.

"Nice," grunts Schoendienst, impressed when Taveras takes his next turn in BP and decides to go opposite field for a while, sending the ball on screaming journeys up the gap between what everyone can imagine are helpless left and center fielders on July days at Busch Stadium, and maybe October nights, too. Schoendienst knows a little something about great hitting—the Hall of Famer in his own right also roomed with a guy named Stan Musial. Schoendienst sticks around until the end of the Taveras BP. He doesn't look away for a moment.

Later that afternoon, Taveras comes up during the intrasquad game. Turco gives him some perfunctory advice. He smiles, about to enter the place where he knows precisely what to do, the batter's box. Instructions for everything else is what Oscar Taveras seems to need, but not hitting a baseball.

He taps the bat against the grass as he approaches the box, the weights dropping to the earth. Taveras seems to know how much he looks like a ballplayer. The world turns—both dugouts focused on him in a way they hadn't been on the hitter just moments earlier. Coaches from other fields turn to watch. So do players in dugouts across the dirt path, all around the Kissell complex.

Earlier, Taveras had struck out, but didn't lose his smile, tossing his helmet nonchalantly to the side and heading out onto the field. This time, his final at bat of the day, he gets ahead in the count, 2-0. The pitcher, bowing to the inevitable, throws him a fastball. Another rope, this one right at the shortstop for an out.

He stops a few steps toward first base. He thinks a moment, looks up into the sky, and breaks back into a huge smile. Coming off the field, he throws an arm around James Ramsey. It's just one of many line drives, he seems to think. There are so many more to come.

April 7, St. Louis, Missouri

Opening Day came to St. Louis, and so did a thoroughly unwelcoming rainstorm that threatened to cancel festivities altogether.

Bill DeWitt Jr. and his son, Bill DeWitt III, are monitoring the action from their offices inside Busch Stadium. The elder DeWitt makes a call, about three hours prior to game time, which revealed conditions had not yet deteriorated to the point the Budweiser Clydesdales would be forced to cancel their jaunt around the warning track to the familiar organ music theme and fifty thousand clapping fans.

While the horses were ultimately rained out, DeWitt made his way down to the field for the opening ceremonies. Cardinals Hall of Famers stood in their red jackets. Other dignitaries, such as Mike Shannon (who'd be inducted in August), were on hand to shake hands as each player was introduced, over that organ music, standing in front of World Series trophies the team had won.

"I like to head down when the Clydesdales march," DeWitt had told me. "I like to see as much of the game as I can, in the seats outside. Usually, the weather's better than this."

This is what a city looks like when no one since 1902 has reached the age of twenty-five without seeing a World Series parade. Thousands gathered ahead of time, lining up not merely to enter Busch Stadium and greet their defending National League pennant-winning heroes. They gathered by the thousands to enter Ballpark Village, a collection of restaurants and bars, highlighted by the St. Louis Cardinals Hall of Fame, to entertain those who are enthralled by the industry that is the Cardinals.

You'll find Rickey there, and Musial, and Kissell—the Cardinals museum has a Kissell manual from 1969—and everyone who came after. Kissell himself was inducted in August 2015. You'll even find the Browns there, the team that almost owned this city, and even Eddie Gaedel, the three-foot-seven-inch man Bill Veeck hired to bat for the Browns in 1951, wearing little Bill DeWitt Jr.'s Browns uniform.

Out they came, those products of the Jeff Luhnow and Dan Kantrovitz drafts, the next chapter in Cardinals history about to be written—"Number 26, Trevor Rosenthal!" Rosenthal, huge grin on his face, shaking hands with Whitey Herzog. During the 2013 play-offs, Bob Gibson had given Rosenthal some tips that he refused to share with the media.

"Number 19, Jon Jay!" A Charlie Gonzalez special, Jay regained the center-field job in 2014, hit .303/.372/.378, and his on-base percentage topped .400 in a second half that seemed to find Jay in the middle of nearly every Cardinals win.

"Number 31, Lance Lynn!" Lynn leaped out of the back of a blue pickup truck, embarking on a 200-inning season with a 2.74 ERA, quietly elite once again.

"Number 33, Daniel Descalso!" The third-round pick from 2007 shared an alma mater with Sig Mejdal. Descalso shook hands with Tony La Russa, a Mejdal skeptic. Descalso and La Russa won a World Series together thanks to a system Mejdal helped build.

"Number 40, Shelby Miller!" An excited Fredbird points at Miller, who had another 10 wins in him in 2014.

"Number 44, Carlos Martínez!" Still just twenty-two, Martínez tantalized fans with the kind of stuff that led Matt Slater to tell his bosses to throw $1.5 million at a teenaged kid he'd just spent a few minutes watching. By 2015, he wouldn't be wearing number 44 anymore, for a tragic reason.

The wind whipped through the stadium. The game wouldn't start for another forty-five minutes. The red, white, and blue bunting that signifies important baseball moments—Opening Day, the postseason—shuddered along the right-field wall. The stands, though, were filled already.

The cheers got even louder for that pitcher Luhnow pushed for more than a decade ago, men and women in red ponchos roaring as the public-address announcer said, "Number 50, Adam Wainwright!" The veteran hurler waved to the crowd with a wide smile.

Even the lesser 2014 contributors came mostly from the farm—Joe Kelly, traded to Boston with Allen Craig, Shane Robinson, Pete Kozma, Kevin Siegrist, Tony Cruz, Seth Maness, Keith Butler—so many players the Cardinals drafted and developed.

And the roars, still louder, for the starting lineup, teeming with home-grown talent: "Number 13, the third baseman, Matt Carpenter!" Carpenter gives the crowd a businesslike wave, all focus, even amid the cheering. "Number 21, the first baseman, Allen Craig!" Craig jumps gingerly out of a white pickup, his movements still limited after a 2013 foot injury. "Number 32, the first baseman, Matt Adams!" The big man is noticeably trimmer and takes that extra second to soak in the handshakes, lingering with Red Schoendienst.

Of course, another level for Yadier Molina, warming up the starting pitcher. And perhaps the crowd at its loudest, not for Molina, but for the Kantrovitz pick and Pujols compensation: "Warming up in the bull pen, Number 52, Michael Wacha!"

Wacha pitched six solid innings. Martínez, Siegrist, and Rosenthal finished it off. Molina drove in three with a booming double in the first. Craig added an RBI single. Adams had two hits. Wong contributed a walk and a single. Carpenter, leading off, reached three times.

The soaked fans went home happy. The Cardinals won.

"It's a lot of fun pitching in front of your home crowd, forty-thousand-plus fans," Wacha told us, standing in front of his locker, when it was over. "I don't know who wouldn't thrive off those kind of situations."

The next morning, as I prepared to leave St. Louis, a man in his fifties rolled his suitcase toward the hotel elevator. He held one item apart—a stark white Cardinals Willie McGee jersey. It belonged to his wife, and he'd been asked to take particular care of it. "This is how she wants me to carry it," he told me. Treating it as a holy item, he lifted it carefully away from his suitcase and body as we entered the parking garage. On the hook it went in the back of his SUV. The couple had come in from Illinois for the home opener, stayed over, and would drive home the next day. The last I saw of them was their license plate, an Illinois personalized GOKARDS.

May 24, Jupiter, Florida

Late May in Jupiter is no place for the player who only suspects he wants the major league dream.

Your clothes stick to your body the moment you step outside. Those Cardinals minor leaguers who aren't in full-season ball are playing at the Kissell complex, awaiting assignments to Johnson City or State College. Otherwise, it's Jupiter for the season, and the Gulf Coast League Cardinals.

But they don't have the same experience back at the Kissell complex the high-A minor leaguers do at Roger Dean Stadium, visible from the six back fields. There's no shade. The one bathroom is augmented by a Porta Potti, labeled ALL STAR, which leads one to wonder about the Porta Potti that didn't make the team. It's not even 10:00 A.M. yet, and there's Ramon "Smoky" Ortiz, with a weighted bat, teaching the handful of switch-hitters that old drill of Kissell's I found written down on Ginny's stationery.

Running this team is Steve Turco, in his thirty-fifth year in organized ball. He's not looking to reach the major leagues. He's just carrying on Kissell's work. We sat and talked about it all on a scalding day in late May, but he never once took his focus off the field while we chatted. Every single play was an opportunity to teach.

"See what we did there, it was not right, either," Turco said, breaking off from his own train of thought, not unkindly, just observing something he'd need to bring up with his youngest charges. "They played that sure double, and it wasn't a sure double, it was cut off in the gap. We had nobody at second base. Actually, the shortstop should have been there. The second baseman went out to get the throw. Rivera looked to second because that's where the play was."

No one had any question about Chris Rivera's baseball IQ. Like George Kissell, a Cardinals minor league infielder signed in 1940, Steve Turco, a Cardinals minor league infielder signed in 1979, and Ollie Marmol, a Cardinals minor league infielder signed in 2007, Chris Rivera clearly had a future in coaching. But Dan Kantrovitz took him in the seventh round of the 2013 draft hoping for more than an eventual heir apparent to Kissell.

"He was alongside the top high school players on every draft board," Kantrovitz recalled. "He slipped to the second round, and my guess is all assumed he was unsignable. Because of his relationship with [Cardinals scout Michael Garciaparra], he texted him in the sixth round and said he wanted to forgo his commitment to Fullerton. After hearing that, we did not hesitate.

"He runs the largest scout-ball setup in SoCal," Kantrovitz said of Garciaparra. "Some people in baseball view that as a negative in that it can take some time away from scouting. Frankly, that is a big reason *why* I hired him. In addition to being an excellent evaluator, his relationships and knowledge of high school players is as good as it gets. And, I guarantee you, Chris Rivera was not texting the same information to twenty-nine other clubs as he was to Gar during the draft."

Rivera stayed with Turco in the Gulf Coast League and put up an .820 OPS in June, a .722 in July, and then cratered—a .456 OPS in August. As Turco pointed out, he'd done this while learning a new position—the first-round pick Oscar Mercado took over at shortstop, so Turco had Rivera move to second. But Rivera believed he could do better.

"It really frustrated me because I was starting out hot," Rivera told me after the morning game on May 24, as we walked toward the minor league clubhouse. "Really hot. I was just hitting the ball. Hit. Took a couple home runs the beginning of the year. And so—and then leveling off, I just—I don't know. I mean, mentally, it was okay 'cause I've learned to become mentally strong with that. My dad has taught me that over the years. So just physically, you want to get that hit so it's frustrating not getting your hit. But coming into this year, I have a lot of confidence going up to the plate. I feel like I was hitting the ball a lot better. Driving the ball with power into the gaps. So I feel a lot better this year."

Turco also had Rowan Wick with him. It had been a rough spring for Wick, who wasn't yet showing Turco or the rest of the Cardinals decision makers that he'd been right to keep pursuing the major leagues as a position player.

"I believe I'm going to State College," Wick said as we traveled that same path from the field to the minor league clubhouse. "And—I mean, I'd like to finish in Peoria by the end of the season. I was hoping to break spring training in Peoria. I did well last year in Johnson City so I was hoping to just jump to Peoria right away, but there's a lot of outfielders in the Cardinals organization obviously, so..."

It was true—I'd had a scout from a rival team tell me back in March that he'd trade his team's major league outfield for the Cardinals' Triple-A outfield of Oscar Taveras, Stephen Piscotty, and Randal Grichuk. Tommy Pham, who hit .324 and eventually earned a big league look, couldn't break into that Triple-A starting outfield. James Ramsey, the first-round pick from 2012, was stuck at Double-A, despite an OPS above .900, because of the talent glut.

Wick grew up in the Vancouver area, and he saw himself similarly to how his supporters in PD did.

"I definitely think that's the kind of player that I am," Wick said, referring to his strong Johnson City numbers in 2013. "Hit for power and play in the corner with a solid arm. I have power potential."

Or as Kantrovitz put it, encapsulating the Wick conundrum, "Wick is polarizing. He has a legit fallback on the mound if his bat does not play at higher levels. And obviously you don't want to wait too long to make the switch. But his power is rare, and I'm a strong advocate of being patient with his bat. I'm still betting on the bat, and him being a high-K guy with twenty-five-plus bombs. But as hard as it is to believe if you haven't seen it, which you have, his arm might end up being his carry tool."

Wick, a Canadian native, had to figure it out without his family nearby, or even in the same country. "My parents were down here for spring training, and I haven't seen my sister since, like, February," he said.

But at this point, with short-season assignments coming, Wick had a simple task: he needed to hunt strikes, as Turco put it. It was up to Turco and Wick to figure out if he could do that. When I asked Wick if he thought he'd made any progress, his response was telling:

"I don't know." He went off to lunch.

Meanwhile, Corey Baker was not in Palm Beach, where he'd started the season. The Cardinals promoted him to Double-A, a place he'd struggled in limited opportunity in 2013. Baker arrived in the professional ranks with a delivery that needed refinement, and primarily a fastball and changeup—the changeup, he believes, is what got him drafted at all. He remembers an early conference between Ace Adams and the pitchers.

"He spoke that to the group. He spoke to moving off the rubber. Momentum. Getting some tilt. Getting that angle on the ball in your body. So that was definitely mentioned. And I'm sure he definitely worked with guys, and I'm sure when Brent Strom at the time, my pitching coordinator, came around, he worked with guys at it. For me, personally, I don't think that's something that was a big issue for me. I think it was more the momentum and working on that front side."

And shades of Mike Witte, Adams brought his pitchers in to see old video of Greg Maddux, of Mariano Rivera, of Justin Verlander.

"And obviously not that we have to repeat that, because everyone's different, but just what's in their delivery that you think is necessary and they think could help everyone. I remember Maddux, and I had a side view of him and how far his body is away from the rubber when he lets go of the ball. And that's going to create a huge advantage for you."

But take it from someone who made five trips up to Double-A from Single-A by the end of the 2014 season—the continuity in the Cardinals system mattered.

"I've been promoted a bunch in my career, and the transition from level to level was always really easy because of that single-mind-set way of 'Hey, this is how we're doing things,'" Baker said. "It's the same at every level. This is how they do it in the big leagues. And when you get promoted from low-A to high-A or high-A to Double-A, you're not facing the added challenge of trying to learn a new system or anything like that. It's all in place. You're done it in spring training. You've done it ever since you've been with the Cardinals, so that makes success probably that much easier. Even though I'm with a new team, everything's exactly the same. So that continuity probably has led to success with guys just being able to focus on a game, because there's not all that added outside stuff they need to figure out."

Baker says this kind of focus helps players fight through the difficulties of a minor league season. Again, the role Cardinals coaches and managers play in reinforcing these ideas is notable.

"You probably see some guys struggle with that and you struggle with that," Baker said. "And really, the only way for me to kind of combat it was, once you're on the field—I mean, the field's the same and you're there to play baseball. It's tough. It's hard on everyone to travel. It's tough. The sleep situations are tough. Everything is tough. And physically, there's nothing you can do about it. You just kind of just stay focused mentally. Kind of remembering why you're there... give one hundred percent of what you have that day. That's something that Dann Bilardello always says to us. They understand that coming off the bus, you might not feel at your best every single day, but it's giving one hundred percent of what you have that day and just working through it and understanding everyone's going through it at the same time, and it's just something that you need to adjust to. And if you're going to keep playing, it's something that you're going to have to learn to deal with."

Baker made what turned out to be a brief trip to Double-A Springfield, returning to Palm Beach after just a few weeks. Bilardello and Adams were there to talk him through it.

"I mean, the initial talk with Dann was that there's two ways to go about, and the first one is be pissed off and let it get to you and not do well and stop working hard," Baker told me when we spoke in mid-June 2014. "Or the second way is, don't let it get the best of you and get doing what you do and earn your way back up there, and that's really it. There's two ways to go about it, and obviously the latter is what you want to do. It's what I plan to do. It's what I did last year when I got sent back down here." Baker had the advantage of a support system at home, too.

"You know, my parents still think—they obviously want me to keep playing. They've seen the success I've had and seen me from T-ball now pursuing this goal and pursing this dream. And they've been there forever. And so they want me to keep going, keep playing. And Jenna is the same way. I've been with her since sophomore year of college and she is behind me, and it's obviously a lot tougher for her, me being away for half the year. But she is extremely supportive.

"She has her own career. She's career oriented, goal oriented, and she wants me to be the same way. And I think, obviously, she would like to spend the whole year with me and it's not ideal. That she is behind me and she's also seen the success I have and she believes in me, too. So I get nothing but support from both my family and from Jenna. And I know for a fact that other guys don't have it the same way. I hear guys all the time: 'Oh, my wife wants me to quit.' 'My girlfriend wants me to quit.' And I don't have that situation at all."

Meanwhile, Sam Tuivailala was destroying Florida State League hitters. Baker, despite his frustrations, was clearly happy for a teammate he'd gotten to know in 2014:

"I would say we're definitely opposites. We were in extended together but didn't interact much. He was still a position player at that time, and we were on different extended rosters. He was younger. We only overlapped in Peoria for about a week or two last year. So this year when we both broke in at Palm Beach, I think this was the first time we ever really spent any time together. I mean, he's a great kid. You would never know that he is an up-and-coming prospect and has all this attention on him and stuff like that. He's as humble as it gets. He works as hard as anyone, and as an older guy who's been around, things I try to, that we all try to, teach him—obviously nothing physical. There's nothing physical we can teach him. He's been blessed with that. It's just learning how to pitch certain guys and just the mental part of pitching and taking care of your arm because he's so new to that.

"I think that's one of the great things about the Cardinals, is, yeah, we're all competing with each other to get to the big leagues, but I don't think any of us are going to shy away from helping each other. So I think specifically with him because we know how new he is to pitching, guys will maybe go out of their way and say, 'Hey, this is kind of how we got this guy out' and 'Look at it this way,' or that kind of thing. And just give him little pieces along the way to help him out because, like I said, he's so new to it and he's still learning. I mean, he's learning how to pitch in high-A when, I feel like I've been doing this forever and we're at the same level. So just imparting that on him, a lot of guys just take it upon themselves. Just little things here and there."

It worked. Tuivailala walked 9 in his first 9 innings in 2014. The next 9? He walked just 2 and struck out 13. Ace Adams and I discussed it after the game on May 24, and Adams put it bluntly: "The way he's pitching, I'm not going to have him too much longer."

Tuivailala had simplified: he still threw that fastball, which was now sitting upper nineties, but he was throwing it more for strikes. Crucially, that curveball was getting over as well, around 81, 82 miles per hour.

After a night game Tuivailala stood and chatted with me in the hallway leading to the minor league clubhouse. His entire demeanor had shifted from our conversation back in March.

"I probably trust in it a lot better than the previous year," Tuivailala said of his curveball. "When I get it, I'm not really nervous. I'm not trying to aim it. It's more just grip it and rip it. And I feel a lot more comfortable throwing it now.

"Sometimes if I have a feeling the guy's going to sit on a fastball, I usually tend to just dump it in there and give the guy a different look. And if it's for a strike, I'm feeling pretty comfortable about that at bat, have the batter think about what the next pitch is going to do. And when I throw the first-pitch curveball, if it's for a strike, well, it really makes my fastball a lot better 'cause he hasn't really seen it yet."

As for Florida State League hitters, they were being asked to try to hit two plus pitches that differed in velocity by fifteen, sixteen miles per hour. Tuivailala didn't dispute it when I pointed out that meant they didn't have a chance:

"Yeah. Yeah. So I mean, it's been—it's been really effective for me. It's been working."

For Tuivailala, the tilt of his delivery—preached by Leveque, reinforced by Adams—had been the key that unlocked consistent command, he believed.

"Just, when I'm coming up here," Tuivailala told me, showing me his hands in set position at around his chest, "and right before I just—I tend to tilt a little bit. And that just causes the fastball to get a downward angle. And even my teammates mentioned that so I actually learned a lot from my teammates. And that would allow my curveball, so I can get on top of my curveball from my fingers.

"So it was just a little adjustment. So I mean, after that, I felt really good with it. I felt like my arm wasn't as stressed as before. I'm using my whole body instead of just trying to whip my arm. I mean, they always talked about it in the spring training, you know? It was always mentioned to all the pitchers. Tilt. Tilt will help everyone.

"But every pitcher's different. They mention a lot of little stuff. You just pick what works for you and just keep working on it and then—even when we're doing long toss on flat ground, everyone's messing with a little something. Just trying to get that edge."

I asked him whether he felt different, emotionally, than he had in the spring, when he told me he still felt like a position player pitching at times.

"It definitely feels a lot more normal now. Last year, I felt like a pitcher at the same time, but it was kind of like I feel like a third baseman still up there. But now I'm more in the mentality of a pitcher."

He told me his parents and his sisters—a thirteen-year-old and a nineteen-year-old—would be coming out from California to see him pitch in July. I told him that by July I didn't think they'd be coming to Palm Beach if they wanted to see him pitch.

As I was leaving, I saw Alex Mejia, the Palm Beach shortstop. I'd taken notice of him prior to the game, and even in the game, seeming to know not just where the ball would be hit to him, but what kind of ground ball it was. I mentioned the Kissell ground-ball drill, and Mejia broke into a huge smile, nodding.

And Oscar Taveras, the heir apparent to Pujols, was putting up the same kind of numbers he always had—.325/.373/.524—at Triple-A Memphis. He reached another level, even for him, from the middle of May on: .462 average, with an 1.129 OPS, over the final ten games he played for Memphis.

Then, an opportunity: Matt Adams's calf injury sent him to the disabled list. On Friday night, May 30, Taveras got the call and was scratched from the Memphis lineup.

"I think everybody should be excited; I know he is," Cardinals manager Mike Matheny said that night.[4] "We've been waiting for a while. There've been a lot of people anticipating him getting here, and hopefully we can limit the distractions for him for where he just goes and plays the game."

"There's definitely a high level of anticipation and excitement," Mozeliak said. "When you take the time and you invest heavily in the international market, you're looking to someday maybe get a return like this. I think everybody involved in that is A, proud, and B, excited to see what he can do at the major league level."

But with Taveras, always, the anticipation mixed with concern about how fully he'd embrace his playing responsibilities beyond the batter's box. "He's done a lot of things right for a lot of years to get the excitement level to where it is," Matheny said. "I know the fans have been waiting for this to happen. We'll get a chance to see him, see how he mixes in. Hopefully he jumps on board with what we're trying to do as a club and realizes all he needs to do is his part."

Meanwhile, even while Cardinals across the system battled opponents and one another with a goal of playing in St. Louis, Kantrovitz and his team of scouts met up across the country to provide everyone with even more competition for playing time. The 2014 draft was just twelve days away.

May 25, Jupiter, Florida

Dan Kantrovitz gathered a group of his scouts in a conference room in the office building the St. Louis Cardinals have beyond Roger Dean Stadium's right-field fence. They share the facility with the Marlins, whose offices are along the left-field fence.

The meeting was one of several Kantrovitz would hold over the coming days with his scouts, going through regional preference lists while flying around the country. This was just day one of two in Jupiter. The second day was dedicated to an in-person workout for as many of the prospects as the Cardinals could get to come to Roger Dean Stadium.

Day one started at noon and ran nearly nine hours. Lunch and dinner were skipped—a bag of bagels and a bit of egg salad were passed around at one point.

At the head of the conference table Kantrovitz, in a checked polo shirt and khaki pants, had his computer in front of him, providing him with every bit of intelligence the Cardinals had gathered on every prospect to be discussed that day, the ingredients of STOUT. The prospects had been run through the system statistically—their performances retrofitted to that of others at similar ages, competition levels—and then the mechanics of the pitchers were analyzed. The prospects were given a grade for health, which helped or hurt their stock.

But the scouts, too, were vital in assessing the players' overall grades. As Kantrovitz described the system to me that day, "We're hoping to come away with a single value for each player going into the draft. How many runs do we think this guy will be worth to us?"

Across from Kantrovitz sat Charlie Gonzalez, in a Hawaiian shirt adorned with pineapples, and jeans. He, too, sat in front of a computer, but the machine was off—he was using it to charge his iPhone. Gonzalez himself is a computer, every member of his pref list committed to memory. This is not just names and physical descriptions—it is everything. Each player who came up—and Charlie Gonzalez, per the preferences of the St. Louis Cardinals, had ninety-three people on his pref list, ranked from those he wanted most to those he didn't think highly of at all—became a story for Charlie to tell.

Not that Charlie was alone in this—that's the coin of the realm in scouting, to see a player in snippets, and to piece together not only what you think he is today, but what he will be in two, three, five years.

Joining Dan and Charlie around the table were Joe Almaraz and Jamal Strong, two of the national cross-checkers, Fernando Arango, the Southeast cross-checker, Ty Boyles, who covered the Southeast beyond Charlie's Florida, and Mark Ellenbogen, a local product who'd assisted Charlie.

It was up to Charlie, Ty, and, when they'd seen the players, Fernando, Joe, and Jamal to paint a picture of what they thought would happen if a player got drafted by the Cardinals. They frequently disagreed. They often thought more highly of a player than what the stats on the computer in front of Dan told him, or mechanics said about a player, or medical said about a player. Dan had to speak two languages at once—the analytics and the scouting, and to translate back and forth—to the scouts, who spent the better part of a year working ungodly hours to collect this information, and to determine how to input what his scouts were telling him into STOUT, all in the hope of arriving at one value.

"The plan is to talk about everybody on your list as if we're not going to talk about them again," Kantrovitz said to open the meeting. "'Cause that might be the case. In St. Louis, we're going to get there and probably line up the top fifty to sixty guys. So, I guess, Ty, Charlie, I would figure, talk in depth about everybody except your top two or three guys. And those, we'll still talk about as well, but just know that we're going to touch on them again in St. Louis.

"So, the other thing I want to talk about before we get going—all season long, we operate as very close-knit group and we're considerate of each other's feelings. I'm going to go out of my way, over the next week to ten days, to be very inconsiderate of your feelings in the draft room. I think that's how we're going to have the best draft. We're not going to worry about who's getting what player when. We're not going to worry about somebody having to get a player in the draft room. We'll worry about having the best draft for the Cardinals.

"And, Ty, this is worth emphasizing for you. It's your first draft in St. Louis. Those of you that have been in St. Louis for a few drafts know the deal. But because of our process, our system, which is different than every other team, you're going to walk out of that draft room, hopefully, feeling a little uncomfortable with the picks. If it was intuitive or obvious to all of you what our picks should be, how it should go, then we'd be like everybody else and our process wouldn't be helping us at all. The best drafts happen when you guys are a little uncomfortable with what's going on. And that goes for me as well. It's not obvious how we should weigh performance when we take a player. It's not obvious how we should deduct based on some medical issue. Again, if it were obvious, then everybody would be doing the exact same thing.

"So our list is not going to be a direct reflection of my personal pref list. And we might, along the same lines, Ty, take a player that you have a little bit lower on your list than—and you might be saying, 'Well, wait. I've got this guy higher? Why aren't we considering him? Well, it's because we're weighing Joe's report, Jamal's report, my report. The performance, the medical, the mechanics. So it's natural, normal, for you guys to walk out of that draft room being a little uncomfortable and to be a little perturbed, in some cases, with me. My goal is not to appease all of you guys in the draft room. My goal is to have the best draft and use our process as wisely as I can. And again, if we all walk out of there just a little bit uncomfortable, I think we're going to have the best draft.

"So having said that, I want you guys to, again, talk about these guys—I know you guys have spent a lot of time this year traveling, driving, staying at hotels, going to see them. Talk about them. Take whatever time you need. I'm going to play devil's advocate and ask you questions about them. And pretend that we're not going to talk about them again. Because that might be the case."

No one seemed to mind. As Joe Almaraz put it, "What you said, the key word for me was *you walk out*, 'cause, hey, there's some places you don't get to walk in or out."

"Most teams don't bring everybody into the draft," Kantrovitz agreed. "I can't imagine a scenario where you guys aren't all in there. I can't imagine doing the draft without everybody in there, but like Joe said, I think the majority of teams out there bring very few guys in."

With that, Charlie began to run down his list of players. He'd made a bet with Jamal—Charlie's presentation would last no longer than fifty-five minutes. If Charlie lost, he owed Jamal a steak dinner.

Charlie lost. He spoke starting a bit after noon, stopping only for a five-minute break at three, until five fifteen.

The conversation ran along a pair of tracks, and it's vital to understand both to fully comprehend the task at hand in a major league baseball draft room.

One part is what you'd assume: it's how good is this kid. Can he hit for power? What's his time, home to first? Will his arm keep him at shortstop at higher levels? Or for pitchers: What's his fastball look like? How consistent is his velocity? Does he throw strikes later in games?

But that's only part of the equation. The other thing scouts need to determine about the players they like is, to the last possible dollar if possible, just what it's going to take to sign a kid. They need to do this while the players themselves, if they are staying true to amateur rules, do not employ an agent. Not before getting drafted, not before getting signed, because if a player enlists an agent, but fails to come to terms, he'll have forfeited his amateur status.

It's an insane system. It doesn't help the players at all, and many of them get around it by making deals with "advisers," who are a kind of agent on contingency fee, or flat out hire agents and hope they won't get caught. It might be the only payout they'll ever get from playing baseball. It's the only reasonable thing to do.

For the teams, too, this cloak-and-dagger nonsense is especially problematic since 2012, when Major League Baseball instituted pretty strict slot amounts for each team to pay out in bonuses. Now, a team drafts a player in, say, the third round, only to find out it will cost much more than the team anticipated to sign that player. The team is left with three options: blow through the cap and forfeit a future draft pick; give up on the player and lose that infusion of talent into their system; or sacrifice some other pick made elsewhere in the draft.

So the Cardinals have every scout put a financial value on every player—what the scout believes the Cardinals should spend on him, based solely on talent—and also give as much information as possible on what it will probably cost to get that player.

With every team dealing with their own slot amounts—it varies based on where a team drafts and whether it's forfeited any picks or accumulated extras—the sweet spot of the major league draft is the player who not only provides the most value, but does it at the lowest actual cost. Sign a $2 million player for $2 million, and you received value for your money. Not bad! But sign a $1,000 player worth $2 million, and you not only have that $2 million player, but you can go out and spend almost $2 million of your draft pool on other players.

So Charlie Gonzalez had a pref list ninety-three players long. It didn't mean the guy ranked fiftieth was necessarily worse than the forty-nine above him. It meant something more complex: the guy ranked fiftieth, taking both cost and talent into account, was less likely to provide excess value to the Cardinals than the forty-nine players above him.

Here's an example of what I mean, about a player the Cardinals ultimately didn't draft.

"He's the kid that's—he's a very questionable bat," Gonzalez said. "He may run a six-two-five for us tomorrow. He's got a fifty arm. He'll flash you a fifty-five arm. He can catch it in center field. The bat has never really played for me. My feeling is he's going to be a two-year rookie-ball guy. And I would give him a hundred grand and put him out here and just cross our fingers and hope he hits. I would turn him around to the left and hope that works. And let it be. You know, his feeling is, and he's told me, and we've talked. I've talked to his coach. He said, you know, give baseball a few years and see if he can hit, if that works. If not, he can go and he can run and go to school as a track guy. He's got Olympic-class feet."

But for many players, scouts play well beyond the dual roles of talent evaluator and financial analyst. Psychology comes into play, the way it did for Moises Rodriguez, Matt Slater, and Carlos Martínez. Here's an example of another player the Cardinals ultimately stayed away from.

"He's a left-handed pitcher, slash, you know, right fielder. Definitely, the only interest I have in him is a left-handed pitcher. Six feet. About two hundred pounds. Very loose, elastic. We'll get to the baggage first. Get that out of the way. He had issues and attempted an assault with a baseball bat to one of his roommate's girlfriends was in the dorm. Got arrested. Da da, da da, da da. He's had shoulder surgery already years ago.... Now, the tools... he's got big raw power. He's super, super strong. Reminds me of a bigger Billy Wagner kind of body. But bigger. He's six feet. Maybe six feet one. I didn't touch him last year. He's been up to ninety-four. Didn't touch him. This year, I watched him. I watched the way he handled himself. I stayed in touch with the coaches. I'm very close with the guys over there. He really minded his p's and q's. He's done a lot better and he's pitched well. We saw him the other day. He probably was hitting ninety, ninety-one. He's got a workable curveball. He's got a changeup. He's the Friday-night guy [for his school] ... sixty-nine innings, sixty-two strikeouts, seventeen walks, two point seven RA. Good lefty—and he's got a loose delivery. He's a crazy kid. He also had medication for the ADD type of thing. He's got crazy eyes. But he's a lefty and I wouldn't take him before the tenth round."

Dan returned to the whole assault thing.

"I mean, one thing we have not done, and I can't see us doing, is sending [player development] projects off the field. I mean, if he's a project on the field, it's one thing. You think that was 'He's a good kid. He made a mistake and he's over it?' Or is there something there?"

"As I found out more about that thing with the baseball bat," Gonzalez responded, "his roommate was bringing a girl in that wasn't supposed to be in the room, you know, and he was, like, 'Get her the hell out of here,' you know?"

"He threatened her with a baseball bat?"

"He lifted a bat. Yeah. Listen, Dan. That's our call what we want to do. Those are the facts. It's not like I pounded the table for this guy. I put him in just because I said, you know what? This arm's too good to just leave off my list. You know?"

Kantrovitz asked Gonzalez flat out, "Would you want to put your name on this guy?"

"Well, let's put it like this. I would leave him as, like, the lowest-priority guy out there. There's been a lot of other guys that are better."

The world is filled with people who have trouble accurately diagnosing the people they live with every day. It is part of a scout's job to do this about players they see a handful of times. It's usually not as extreme as this case, but this kind of temperature-taking allows scouts to arrive at opinions—opinions the Cardinals want, need, and are vital to overall scores—about a player's ability to thrive in the difficult world of minor league baseball and claw to the top of it.

But there's so much more. There's scouting of family.

"He's six feet six, two hundred, and he's a baby, okay?" Gonzalez said of one pitcher the Cardinals didn't draft. "He's going to put on thirty pounds more. His dad is six feet five, two hundred thirty, you know? And the thing about him I like about the most? He's aggressive. He thinks he can get anybody out. I love that."

Or: "His mom is in the picture. They're very academic oriented, you know? I think he might come down to two seventy-five or something."

Even the circumstances and attitudes of some parents were taken into account and committed to memory by Gonzalez, who threw them into the scouting reports to add to the picture: "A blue-collar mom, beer-drinking mom." "Parents aren't really baseball people, grasping at pitching gurus." "The mom is gorgeous."

I also heard the following player comps: Steve Cishek, "the Ron Gant dude," "Jeff Kent–looking body," Hunter Pence, and Gomer Pyle.

About two hours in, Charlie got to Darren Seferina.

"He's a second baseman. Lean, small-bodied kid. Quick twitch. Solid average defender. Has a chance to be an above-average defender. Still a little unpolished. Has a superquick left-handed bat. Short to the ball. Tries to hit balls up in the air a little bit. He's hit a home run here and there. Can't, you know, he's going to learn that. He's also from Curaçao. He's a seventy, at times seventy-five runner." Eighty is as high as the scale goes, so that means he's really fast. "Three-six on bunts. Four point oh five down the line. Four-two on turns. Really, really good first-to-third. Really like this kid. He's an electric player. I wish he was a little bit bigger, but he's bigger than a lot of guys that play in the big leagues that are probably as big as Omar Vizquel.... I like this guy quite a bit. And I think he's going to turn into a really good ballplayer."

Clearly, the computer showed Kantrovitz something because his response was "Okay, well, I want to spend some time talking about this guy."

Arango didn't have as much money on Seferina:

"My biggest concern about him, this guy's not very physical. And he can run. He's got good hands. His arm—his double-play turns are not that great. A guy small, to me, has to be physical, you know?... This kid has got some authority.... Now this guy is a seventy runner. At some point—I understand that. And he hits his ground balls and line drives here and there. [Another prospect] can drive the ball. Okay? And he's got a plus arm."

What followed was a colloquy designed to figure out how strong Darren Seferina would eventually become.

DAN: Do you think this guy can drive the gaps?
FERNANDO: He's going to need some more strength. That's the thing, you know?
CHARLIE: Well, I mean—
JOE: Is he big-boned or is he just—is he big-boned?
FERNANDO: He's just thin. Just thin.
CHARLIE: He's about five feet ten and a half and he's lean. But he's well-leaned muscled and he's young. He's going to get a little bit stronger.
JOE: Does he have a good arm?
CHARLIE: He has plenty of arm for second base. He's a second baseman.
FERNANDO: Forty-five [out of eighty] arm at best.

At this point, Charlie returns to the weaver-of-dreams role, what every scout in that room did at some point: made himself into Don Draper giving the Kodak Carousel pitch.

"You know, he had a really good year. He hit .402. He had 164 at bats; .402. On base, .482. Slugging, .494. And he stole thirty-two bags. Okay? He's a top-of-the-order guy and he can get things nutty out there when gets on the bases. Now, can he drive a ball? Listen. He's not real strong, but to win the game, you got a guy throwing a ninety-two or a ninety-five and he took a ninety-four-mile-an-hour fastball and went oppo with it over the shortstop's head. He doesn't back down and I got the money on him that I have, and every bit of that I leave on him. He's another guy that says, Dan...he would like to get a little more than the hundred thousand bucks. Maybe two hundred or something like that. I think it's a little bit of a smoke screen. And we can get him for around the hundred or a hundred whatever. He's got an agent. He has no problems going back to school next year at Miami Dade. He even said to me, he goes, 'Well, if I go to school, I can get a little stronger and come back.' And I think he's completely right. I mean, too bad he's not going to be here [tomorrow]. He's in the World Series right now."

"We've got a guy from California watching him right now in the World Series," Kantrovitz replied. "So we'll get a report on him in his final games."

The consensus, Gonzalez included, was that Seferina didn't have the arm for shortstop.

"Everything else is there," Gonzalez continued. "The hands are good enough. The range is good enough. But he doesn't have the arm. He's perfectly suited for two places. Second base and center field. But I think this guy can stay on the dirt at second base. I know he can. I've seen him do too much there."

The question then turns to how long they can wait and still get him.

"Well, if we're interested in this guy, and not without me getting any new information that I should get plenty more before the draft, I would say we wouldn't have to take him before the fifth, you know? Start talking about him at the fifth. And I would say between the fifth and the ninth round."

On the other hand, Kantrovitz appeared unmoved by the enthusiasm from Gonzalez and Arango on another prospect, one the Cardinals ultimately didn't draft.

"Yeah, I love this kid," Gonzalez said. "He's one of these guys where—okay, let me break down his tools first. He's about five feet ten. He's a blond-headed Cuban kid from Key West. Talks with a Cajun accent. For some reason down in Key West, they do that. And this kid—he was around last year. He played at Key West High School. Was a tough, tough kid. Pitched. Closed games. Up to ninety-one. Played shortstop. He's not a shortstop. He played shortstop a lot this year, too. He's definitely not a shortstop. And he's good enough to hang at second base. And he might hang there for his whole career. He can definitely go out and play center field, too. He's got a plus arm. He's a plus runner. This guy's got some pop in his bat. He's got an approach like Pete Rose. You know, Pete Rose and the guy—[David] Eckstein. Kind of Eckstein-y. He kind of—he crowds the plate. Loves to get hit. He's just a dirtbag, and I love this kid, the way he plays the game. I don't really care where's he's going to play. I think he's got a chance to stay at second base. He is not as good a defender as Seferina at second base. He doesn't have as soft hands. However, I'm not saying he can't stay at second base his whole career. You talk to him and he says, 'Well, you know, I play at second base, but you're wasting my arm, you know? 'Cause I got such a—' You know? He hits. He hits on base. He runs. He's superaggressive.

"And let me tell you something. He can drive some balls out of the yard. I—he has a little bit of Lenny Dykstra, that tough kind of 'Let's brawl' kind of thing. I think our player development people will love him. He's an above-average runner. Let's see what he's got: 190 at bats. He hit .400. He hit three home runs. Twenty-six strikeouts. Fifteen walks. On base, .451. Slugging, .574. He stole twenty of twenty-three bags. He doesn't play the game to be passive. You know what I mean? And he wants to be the guy in the box with the bat in his hand to win the game."

Kantrovitz responded, "I want to point out, Charlie, those are not good numbers for—in the level of competition that he's facing—to suggest he's going to do well in pro ball."

"Well, that I can't argue, not with the numbers," Gonzalez said. "The numbers are what the numbers are. I'm telling you this much, Dan. You watch that kid play five games, you want him on our team. I do. We can sign him for a hundred grand. One twenty maybe. Dan, he's going to play center field or second base. He can spot you some third. He played short, third, second, and center field this year. Dan, let me tell you something. The strongest thing about this kid is his whole approach to the game. He hits. He hits balls hard. He's not pretty. You might laugh when you see him in the box tomorrow. To me, big league teams need a guy like this guy, you know? It's a no-brainer for me to want him to be in a Cardinals uniform."

Arango was clearly enamored by the guy as well:

"He hit a triple the first time up through center field. And he hit a home run off of a curveball."

"At a big park!" Gonzalez added.

"He run a four-two. He's got a hose for an arm," Arango continued. "And this guy comes to play. He's going to try to beat you any way he can, okay? That's all I got to say. Because this guy—the ball just jumps."

Kantrovitz remained skeptical. "Is carry tool just intangibles?"

"No, man," Gonzalez replied. "This guy hits, Dan. This guy hits. This guy hits. He runs and he's got a plus arm. And then you throw the intangibles in there with it and—look at Eckstein's tools. He used to hold the ball like a little trophy-case thing and frickin' launch it. I mean, you know?"

The problem with a David Eckstein comp is that almost all players with Eckstein's tools do not, ultimately, reach the major leagues, let alone have a long career.

"I'm trying to like him," Kantrovitz said. "I mean, guys that we overlook the numbers on typically have loud tools. And it doesn't sound like he's got loud tools."

Ultimately, he went to another team in the draft, but never hit minor league pitching.

"And don't think I didn't get the *look* from Charlie!" Kantrovitz e-mailed me shortly after it happened.

Gonzalez would not have much cause for complaint once the draft was complete, however.

Matt Pearce came up a few minutes later, and Gonzalez immediately declared Pearce would be "one of my gut feels."

"You only get one," both Almaraz and Arango called out. The other scouts needled Gonzalez throughout his presentation, but Gonzalez didn't engage, kept brushing them off and charging forward, starting to sweat through his Hawaiian shirt. These were max-effort scouting reports.

"That's the most frustrating thing every year for me," Gonzalez said. "I swear to God. No. We usually get three, I'll tell you. How do you do this? How do you do this? Okay. Listen. This guy here is a guy that—I knew him in high school and played for Frank Turco, Steve's brother over there. And he's got a really, really good delivery. He was a skinny kid, about six feet one, 180 pounds. He's now six feet three, about 215 pounds. He's got, in my opinion, I think [Cardinals minor league pitching coach] Paul [Davis] thinks the same way, one of the best deliveries on my list. He's six feet three, about 215 pounds. He's eighty-eight to ninety-three. I think he's got a little bit more in there, but that's not what this kid's about. He throws—pounds the strike zone. He's got a curveball, twelve to six, a slow roller. But it's a get-me-over pitch. Go through the order once or twice and you start getting me over early. Eighty-two innings, seventy-three strikeouts, nine walks. I love that. Two point six one ERA... I went out and saw him early. I always knew the kid. I saw him in the fall. God, I just love his mechanics. He just reminds me of one of those old, high, three-quarter classic delivery pitchers that doesn't blow you away with the velo, but it'll get you downhill. And you know what? Everyone tell me, he never shows you his changeup is his best pitch.... Talked to the coach. He said, 'Charlie, his changeup is his best pitch.' He had a slider for Fernando and I, I think up at seventy-nine, eighty-one. The curveball is twelve to six. But we got there late and I talked to a few friends of ours who were sitting right there. They tell me the truth. They said he had a couple ninety-threes. And he had several ninety-twos for us. He's always been eighty-seven to ninety-two for me and he's throwing harder. He's downhill.

"I love this kid. I love his delivery. There's nothing electric about him, but he's a starter and he's like flipping a switch. He's got one of the best deliveries I got here, and he's got his stuff. And he doesn't walk people. And he's the one with the number. I go to the family, I say, 'Listen, what's the deal?' And I'm sitting there with the parents and they say, 'Well, we have a number.' And I said, 'What's the number?' They said eighty thousand dollars, and I about shit. He goes to the Padres' workout the other day, and he throws for them and I heard he was lights-out at their workout in a bull pen. And they talked to him about the money and he said—he told them and he said—I told you the rest, Dan. They told him, 'We'll work something out. Tell people different. We're going to take you.'"

Arango, too, talked about Pearce's mechanics, and Kantrovitz reminded everyone that the mechanics grade is separate from the scouting grade.

"I want to make sure that we're liking him because you see his stuff now, and know that he's going to improve," Kantrovitz said. "So at what point in the draft do I need to start thinking about him?"

"Well, for me, I think kid's going to go," Gonzalez said. "Guys like the—like the Padres and people like that. I would say the sixth round. Get him by the sixth round. And if I find out, Dan, and I feel that it's later, I'll let you know. You know, you start throwing eighty grand."

"I'm hearing you," Kantrovitz said. "And I want to try and get him."

"This guy's a strike thrower and he's got four distinct pitches. I really—like I said, I would take a gut feel and slap it on this guy," Gonzalez concluded.

It would not be his only gut-feel guy. Not even close.

Another player Charlie Gonzalez liked, Austin Gomber, almost got devalued by a stray news article and his coach's preference for changeups over curveballs.

"Austin Gomber is a twenty-year-old, twenty-point-six junior. He's a year ahead. Six-feet-five, 210–pound, left-handed starter. Eighty-eight to ninety-five is his range," Gonzalez said. Then: "What happened?"

FERNANDO: Nothing.
CHARLIE: What?
DAN: Fernando just said Gomber got hurt?
FERNANDO: He was hurt for a week.
CHARLIE: Hurt?
FERNANDO: He was hurt.
CHARLIE: Oh, no.
FERNANDO: There was text by the coach that said his elbow has bothering him. And the way he hit the last time, he wasn't here. We'll talk about it later.

Gonzalez continued, painting the picture. "Yeah. No, no, no. He's here. He'll be here tomorrow. He's throwing tomorrow. I talked to [Florida Atlantic coach John McCormack] about it. He was—he missed one start because he was sore and flu-ish, and then they said, 'Do you want to miss the next start?' But then he said no and he threw.

"Okay. Austin Gomber. Six feet five, 210–15 pounds. He's a young kid. A year ahead. Eighty-eight—the range is eighty-eight to ninety-five. He probably pitches at around ninety. Well, used to pitch at a higher level—a higher velocity. He's got a curveball. It's turned into a pretty good curveball. I don't know, mid to higher seventies, and he's got a good changeup. I don't like the way this guy's been used. I don't like the pitches he's used this year. I don't like the way that they have groomed him. He had a good year last year. He was throwing the hell out of it this year in the fall. Ninety-threes, ninety-fours. And he's now—we saw him last week and he was eighty-eight, topped out at ninety-two. And the curveball was good. He only threw seven curveballs in six innings.

"I talked to Mack yesterday for about forty-five minutes about him. He says there's nothing there other than the fact that him and [Florida Atlantic pitching coach] Jason [Jackson] have come together with a game plan of what they think the way to attack people is. They thought they should throw more changeups than the curveball. He said have him throw as many curveballs as you want. He says curveball to death. Let it rip. Clean bill of health.

"Big young kid and he's got decent delivery. He's got a little bit of a leg jolt when he comes back. It's a little different, but he's clean from here throughout there. For me, he had a hard time keeping the ball down this year. He's not a real finesse kind of dude. He doesn't have a great feel for anything. But he's a six-foot-five lefty that's young and he throws hard and he throws strikes. I like Gomber. I'd like to get Gomber. He's a country boy. Wants no part of school. He's signing wherever the hell he is. He would take two grand.... But he's not going to get near there.

"This guy can hold 245 pounds. So, some things about him I like. I've got any medical that he's had. I talked to the people. I talked to Mack about him missing the start. They said, 'No. In fact, we asked him, 'Do you want to miss the next start? Are you feeling—' He said absolute not, and they threw him out there on six days' rest. I like this guy. We have to reinvent him and teach him how to pitch a little bit, but the package is there. But he's signable. And that's that. He's a blue-collar kid from Orlando."

But the concern had been planted—the FAU site had a story when he missed the start, "Gomber Lost for Season?" Now Gomber wasn't throwing his curveball much. They'd have to see what the curveball looked like at the following day's workout. Gomber's entire future with the Cardinals might rest on it.

He also had to overcome that when Arango saw him, he didn't pitch well.

"There's a couple of things that I want to bring up, and I want to leave the last one that happened the other day, because there's something that needs to be checked," Arango said of Gomber. "I might be a jinx for this guy. Every time I go see him, in the third and fourth inning he had troubles. You were there. Remember that? Matt Slater was there. The same thing happened. Now, he's got ability and he's a young guy and all that. But I find out—Charlie and I are driving together—that he came out that he was sore. So I checked in their Web site and all of that and the question was "FAU wins. Is Gomber lost for the season?"

Gonzalez objected as Arango continued, returning to the questions about Gomber's health, an emphasis of how the Cardinals project potential draft picks.

"And—that's what it was, Charlie. I got it on the text. And then, find out there's a text from the coach that says that he has sore body and a tender rib, okay? And they say okay. He's going to pitch there. So I went to see him pitch. He touched ninety-two once. He mostly pitched with his fastball and changeup. He was eighty-eight, eighty-nine with the fastball. He threw four curveballs. Only one was a strike. In three innings. Which makes you wonder, too. Why isn't he throwing his curveball more? And it wasn't the curveball that he's shown that's better than that. And what I put on the report, relied on his fastball and change. His use was struggling in the third inning. He did it again. And I said, 'Would have him checked by a trainer and doctor if possible.'"

After a discussion to drill down into precisely what the information was, how much credence to give the report, and precisely how to determine whether Gomber still had an issue, Gonzalez proposed the solution.

"Okay. Listen. I think the kid's perfectly healthy. He's going to be here tomorrow to throw. I spoke to Mack. I've known Mack for twenty-five years. He said, 'Charlie.' I said, "Shoot me straight. What's with the seven curveballs?' He says, 'Charlie, I'm going to get the numbers and see how many curveballs.' He said he's perfectly fine. He goes, 'Check him out. Bring him to any doctor.' He's throwing tomorrow at our workout. And he says clean bill of health as far as we know. He said check him out if you want."

Arango agreed. "And listen. I'm not trying to kill the guy. All I say is have him checked out. That's all I'm saying because that's something that needs to be addressed."

Gonzalez concluded, "I bet that writer got fired that put that on the Web site."

Gonzalez finished around five fifteen; or more accurately, Kantrovitz waved him off at that point.

DAN: Okay. Well, we went a little bit over, Charlie, because you've got a great area and you talk so, you know. It's great to hear you talk about your players.
JAMAL: You owe me a steak dinner.
DAN: Why? Because he's over time?
CHARLIE: We didn't go—we didn't stay under fifty-five minutes?
JAMAL: He said fifty-five minutes.
DAN: You broke your old record.
FERNANDO: Holy shit. He did. It's five fifteen. We started at noon.

After a five-minute break, it was Ty Boyles's turn to present. This was his first season as an area scout, but he clearly knew the business well. If his presentation lacked the voluminous details of Gonzalez's, he was ultraprepared and knew which questions needed answering on each of his players.

It started to get dark outside, and another player came up who looked good the previous summer, changed his approach with his high school coach, and saw his performance and projection suffer.

"We need to make a study of all the guys that we liked offensively in the summertime and then their performance in the [following] spring that changes our mind again," Almaraz said. "Because he's not the only player we talked about this [happening with], you know? We repeatedly talked about this. Then after that, to see how many guys go on to have success on the original mold that we had from the summer. Because this kid—I liked this kid."

A few minutes later, Boyles began his presentation on another arm who'd eventually become a Cardinal.

"Jordan DeLorenzo. Left-handed pitcher at University of West Florida. Fell in love with this guy early. Left-handed pitcher. Plus command, plus pitchability. Average fastball, eighty-seven to ninety-one. Curveball's a bit of a slurve pitch. Somewhere between a slider and a curveball. Seventy-six to eighty. Changeup, eighty to eighty-one. Just a guy that went out and pitched. I mean, he's absolutely pitched. The stuff was average for me across the board. I liked the way that he went about it. He went about it like a big leaguer. But I think at the end of the day, it's—he's not a big kid. There's not a lot of projection left in the body. He kind of is what he is, and I think that's what he's probably going to be. I think he's always going to have that kind of stuff. But I think he can go out and do well. And he's a competitor. Ultra-competitor. Keeps the ball down. Keeps the ball out of the middle. Knows how to pitch. Knows what he's doing. I mean, I think he's got a chance to go out and do well."

Arango agreed:

"Tell you what. I like this kid. He goes after it. He pitched with an average fastball. His curveball, I think, is going to get better. He has one of those sweeping curveballs that goes into the back foot of the right-handed hitter. And his makeup is off the charts. I mean, I really liked him. And he's a stocky—what, five-feet-ten, five-eleven guy?

"But I tell you what, he's got that face on the mound. The mound presence. And he just stands there and says, 'Let's go.' And I mean, he's stocky. Not big, but he's stocky and strong. So he's one of those guys—we might be able to get this guy in the fifteenth round. Around there. And if you want a lefty that can really come in here and win for you."

Kantrovitz recalled the excitement in Boyles's voice when they first discussed DeLorenzo on the phone and wondered what round the Cardinals would need to start thinking about drafting him.

"I think you got to take him in the top ten rounds," Boyles said. "I think there's been a lot of teams who have been there to see him. I know cross-checkers have been there to see him. The guys that have seen him, I think that's what they're asking for is top-ten-round slot money.... I mean, I would say seventh to ten, somewhere in there. But I don't think he'll slip after that." Arango's projection slipped a few rounds—all because of an inch of top height.

"I would wait until the eleventh or twelfth round. I think that's where he fits. If he were a six-footer or something like that, maybe, more potential for his fastball. But I think this kind of guy's usually taken after the tenth round."

The evening grew later. As Ty got near the top of his list, the conversation grew fuller, with most players seen not only by Boyles, but by Arango, the Southeast cross-checker, and often by Almaraz and Strong, the two national cross-checkers, as well.

That allowed for a deeper dive into not just what kind of player each prospect was, but what everybody thought about what kind of person each one was.

Take one player, who went on to be drafted in the first round, but not by the Cardinals:

"I mean, it's a tough one 'cause he's just dripping with tools that we like," Kantrovitz said. "I think Ty said earlier, in terms of what kind of kid he is. And I didn't talk to him, but I went down to the batting cage before he took it on the field, when he was in the cages, and there was another scout there that was just like grilling him. It was basically three of us and I'm just standing there listening. And I'll give the kid the benefit of the doubt and say that he was immature. Because if you're not saying he's immature, he has no aptitude, no ability to really carry on a coherent, intelligent conversation.

To give you any indication that he's going to, like, make some adjustment. I mean, it was very unimpressive.

"I know he's a baseball player, high school kid, and he doesn't have to be a rocket scientist, but you talk to the other guys we've drafted like Mercado and Carson Kelly, high school kids, and these guys are like mature adults almost. And, I mean, I think when we invest a lot in a high school kid, that that's the one thing we can certain of. We don't know if he's going to hit or not or all the other uncertainties, but we can know that he's this mature individual. I didn't get it from that. I mean, if you said otherwise 'cause you'd know better than I would, I would just go with that."

But Boyles agreed; the player had a strange lack of confidence in his own ability.

"And that's a strange combination, though, when you're that talented and it's a natural and you don't have confidence in it," Gonzalez added. "That's a bizarre coupling of stuff. There could be complications somewhere. 'Cause you don't have to be flamboyantly confident, but at least have some inner confidence."

Almaraz spoke up: "All players, I don't care where you play, all players have insecurities. Period."

"Even the big leaguers," Strong added, and he'd know—he was one.

"But the confidence of your tools that you have give you that confidence to play the game with some kind of confidence," Almaraz said.

"Yeah, I mean, when Mercado, Carson Kelly, Rob Kaminsky, came to Busch Stadium after we signed them, and as I'm sure you guys were, I'm proud of them," Kantrovitz said. "I might be afraid to leave this guy alone, with the media or front office."

Yet, everyone agreed, the tools were undeniable.

"We can laugh about this now, but two years from now we might not be laughing," Arango said.

Kantrovitz concluded, "I know. Yeah. Well, I don't think we're going to figure it out."

But it *was* Kantrovitz's job to figure it out—not just broadly, whether the kid would be a bust or mature, but precisely how much money to bet on whether he ever would. To determine whether even making that bet would be a good idea, or if the Cardinals should be placing their wager on another player altogether.

So the meeting continued until nearly 9:00 P.M., each scout getting full say on every player mentioned, Kantrovitz cross-referencing his data, speaking those two languages back and forth as he translated them in his mind.

"There was something with this guy," Kantrovitz said about a player the Cardinals didn't draft. "It wasn't a medical. I don't think he's liked very well by the video right now. One of our worst. I'll talk with those guys and see if there's a reason why he's—ends up being lower than you guys like him. That's a pretty good bet."

"So the video grade is incorporated into, like, an overall STOUT-type thing?" Gonzalez asked.

"No," Kantrovitz answered. "I just did it in my head, and I can estimate where he's going to come in relation to some other guys we're looking at." That meant Kantrovitz was capable of replicating the process created by the Cardinals over roughly a decade and apply it, balancing all the information—statistical, scouting, medical, and mechanical—in his own head.

It helps to have someone making the picks who can do that.

When Ty was finished, well after 8:00 P.M., Kantrovitz made sure to praise him for the presentation, as did the rest of the group. The other scouts also took the opportunity to needle Charlie Gonzalez.

DAN: Fair enough. Okay. Let's go get dinner. Ty, that was an excellent job.
JAMAL: Heck of a job.
DAN: That was one of the best we've had.
JOE: Two hours.
DAN: You were concise. You were to the point.

JAMAL: Good job, Ty.

DAN: You spent time on guys that you liked and you were prepared. That was outstanding.

JAMAL: Charlie, take some notes.

DAN: Thank you, Jamal.

JOE: You weren't elaborate, you know, unnecessarily.

May 27, Jupiter, Florida

Nearly fifty area players gathered on the main field at Roger Dean Stadium early Tuesday morning. This was the final chance for the Cardinals to ask questions and to observe, and for each player, it was the final chance to make an impression on the group of scouts and Kantrovitz, all of whom had been tracking the prospects for a year, often longer.

Charlie Gonzalez was utterly in his element. Gonzalez's red complexion, honed through years in Florida sunshine on surfboards and in the stands at baseball games, actually paled in comparison to his bright red, button-down shirt, Gonzalez protected from that sun by a tan panama hat.

He seemed to be moving in every direction at once, lining up the would-be shortstops to make the throws from various distances at the position, along with the few second basemen. (Generally, if the players weren't shortstops, they weren't getting drafted. You could always move a shortstop to second, but not the other way around.)

A name is called, a coach hits a grounder, the prospect fields and throws. Everybody watches, none closer than Kantrovitz, standing in a striped polo shirt and dark Cardinals hat, a few feet from the first baseman.

A few of the prospects were moved to second base—those the Cardinals thought might have to move there sooner rather than later if drafted.

"Okay, we're going two!" Gonzalez declared. "Game-time speed, fellas!"

Turco's Gulf Coast day had been canceled. It was all hands on deck at the combine. A group of the coaches saw one shortstop's throws that reminded them of Jeter's at that age, and they speculated about whether Jeter would have enjoyed the same success on another team.

"How do you know he's gonna be what he is?" Davis said. "Would he have wanted to be the shortstop for the Houston Astros?" Another intangible question they'd all gathered to answer.

A catching prospect, a switch-hitter and a *Baseball America* Top 100 amateur prospect who ultimately went to college, drew raves in the box. He wanted $2 million to forgo school. He wasn't drafted high, as his skills warranted, because teams chose not to give it to him. And yet...

"That's what you do," Arango cooed, as the hitter connected, the ball sailing over the wall in right-center field.

"That's a swing," echoed Gonzalez.

Players grouped in the outfield for fly balls, getting called in groups of about a half dozen to take their turn at BP. The pitchers warmed up along the first-base line, where a pair of mounds served as the bullpen during the season in the Florida State League, and the final stage on this day.

"This is where the final conversations take place," Kantrovitz said to me as we watched the batting practice. "We take final temps on how they feel, and we determine whether inquiries into signability prices are worth having."

The shortstop with the Jeter arm hit three over the wall. He ultimately got drafted late and didn't sign. Signability—so many kids lost chances to be professional baseball players in 2014 because of poor advice within an NCAA system designed to deny them basic info, and to force teams to guess.

Dash Winningham, a burly, left-handed high school kid from up in Ocala, Florida, knocked a few home runs into the right-field corner. Kantrovitz and Gonzalez pay particular attention—this was another Gonzalez gut feel.

"Can he go opposite field?" Kantrovitz asks.

Fortunately, the Cardinals have a coach who specializes in instructing young hitters right there. Steve Turco puts a hand on Winningham's shoulder when he steps out of the box.

After He's Gone

"You ever go oppo?" Turco asks him. "You want to be able to use the whole field. You can do it—you've got a lot of bat speed."

Winningham returned to the cage and hit everything to left center, as instructed. The Cardinals gathered two pieces of information from a quick exchange: he's coachable, and it wouldn't take long for him to be a more polished hitter than he is now.

By contrast, the kid with "Lenny Dykstra" in him, per Gonzalez, took some weak cuts in the box. Kantrovitz made a note of it.

Another lefty swinger entered the cage. The scouts perked up. He headed to college, though you could see why Charlie Gonzalez thought so highly of him. And I recognized his mom from the scouting report.

Up the first-base line, Arango was arranging the pitchers, instructing those who needed to show the Cardinals specific parts of their arsenal what to be ready to throw. Kantrovitz watched. Boyles took radar-gun readings, grabbing them from one pitcher, then the other, two throwing at a time. Davis recorded video to feed into the mechanics algorithm. Turco calmly talked them through the pen session—"Okay, third-place hitter up, what do you do?"

Then it's Gomber's turn. They know the fastball, they know the changeup. They want to see the curveball.

"I haven't thrown it in a while," Gomber cautions the group. Then in it comes, looping over the plate in textbook fashion at 75 miles per hour. Grunts of appreciation all around me. Another, just as good, 74. That's the stuff. Good curveballs are like shooting stars when you witness them up close.

I asked Gomber a few weeks later, after he'd been drafted by the Cardinals in the fourth round, if he knew what was at stake when he uncorked that pitch.

"Yeah. It was a good one," Gomber said, standing on the field in Williamsport, Pennsylvania, about to make his professional debut with the State College Spikes. "Actually, when I left, some people asked me how it went.

I told them they were the best curveballs I've thrown in my life. So—that was a plus. Those were some really good curveballs I threw that day." Gomber smiled. "A great time to do it. Good timing."

After Gomber, Gonzalez had brought over a pitcher he hadn't discussed the day before, but had been pushing Kantrovitz on since March, I learned later.

"This is Daniel Poncedeleon," Gonzalez said. "He's gonna throw for us."

Everything about the presentation was designed to get the maximum attention for a guy Gonzalez wanted to flag. "This is my favorite pitcher in the state of Florida," Gonzalez told me while Poncedeleon warmed up. A few hitters were kept around so he could pitch, off the mound, to live hitting.

Poncedeleon hit 93 with the fastball, impressed with the cutter. He hadn't pitched since the end of the college season, one he'd had at NAIA Embry-Riddle after a near deal with the Cubs following the 2013 draft led the NCAA to rule him ineligible. This typical NCAA nonsense meant fewer eyeballs on Poncedeleon as a senior sign.

"The best part about this? We're gonna get him for five thousand fucking dollars," Gonzalez said. "For the best pitcher in the state of Florida."

Gonzalez had a value of $1.75 million on Poncedeleon. A $1.75 million value for a $5,000 signing bonus: this is the mother lode, given the rules that govern the 2014 MLB draft.

When Poncedeleon finished, the combine winding down, Kantrovitz discussed his travel plans. He'd be getting on a plane that afternoon and going through this exact process at several other regional sites, then back to St. Louis for nonstop draft prep.

"What's the last time you saw your family, Dan?" Gonzalez inquired.

The question caught Kantrovitz off guard, and for a moment the baseball man thought of his wife, of his two girls back home. He shook it off—he couldn't afford to lose focus for a moment. Not right now.

"It's been tough," Kantrovitz said. "But this is also the most fun time of the year. It's crunch time."

June 5, St. Louis, Missouri

John Mozeliak sat at his desk, approximately four hours before the start of the 2014 MLB draft. An agent on the phone wanted to get Mozeliak to commit to paying $3 million to his client if he fell to twenty-seven.

"Yes, I'm saying that sounds good if it happens," Mozeliak said. "That sounds real good to me."

The agent brought up another player, and Mozeliak expressed some interest in him as well. Immediately, the agent steered the conversation to what it would cost for the pair as a package. The Cardinals had picks twenty-seven and thirty-four, but Mozeliak, who pounces on things cerebrally—sentences uttered as surely as opportunities—saw one here.

"We'd want some guidance from you about when we could expect each guy to go, so we know who we'd need to take first," Mozeliak said.

You might think he was ironing out his final draft scenario. He wasn't. Not even close. This was one of fifty calls he estimated he'd already had today. He expected that number to rise precipitously over the coming hours.

Draft day means your strategy is dependent on twenty-nine other teams, hundreds of high school and college players, and a budget that is unforgiving if you believe one player might cost one amount, only to discover, after picking him, he costs significantly more.

On the shelf were Cardinals player contracts going back a decade, *Bill James Handbook*s, along with *The Fielding Bible* and *Baseball Prospectus, 2014*. So, too, was a bottle of champagne from that World Series on-field celebration back in 2011. Mozeliak had a few more calls to make, so we reconvened later that afternoon in Bill DeWitt's office, DeWitt and Mozeliak calm as their seventh draft as owner/general manager approached.

"I've been to the draft every year since I've been involved with the club,"

DeWitt said, when I asked what his night would be like. "And it depends on the year, and as time has gone on, it's changed somewhat. It's more strategic. I get a rundown after they're all said and done with their scouting. I mean, along the way I'll hear about certain players. But there's nothing more to do at this point except wait and see.

"There have been times over the years when Mo is your primary point person on the agent to particulate in the top picks. Where there's a call to make on should we do this/should we do that, and we talk about that. More financially oriented."

I said it seemed as if there were fewer decisions to make on the financial side, given the caps, and Mozeliak said there were "different decisions."

"Before the pool system was in place, there was a system of slotting that if you wanted to go over a slot, you were required to check in with the [MLB Labor Relations Department]," DeWitt said. "And LRD would either talk to the commissioner or request that you talk to the commissioner. They couldn't tell you what to pay a player. But they would try to give you information about what the market was and their opinion of the player's value. So there was never a requirement to get permission, just a request that you get their opinion."

Permission no, but as Mozeliak put it, "speed bumps. Cautionary advice."

Realistically, though, the days ahead were going to be Dan Kantrovitz's show.

"But Bill and I, our roles have typically been more strategic, more financial, and more of a sounding board," Mozeliak said. "A lot of times it's very fluid and a lot of things are happening. And so, we're not that close to the players. We really don't know A is better than B, or B is better than C. We just know that they're highly thought of by our group. But, yes, we can be much more rational in thinking about the dollars and cents and, if we do X, will it allow us to do something else down the road and help think through that. That's what we do."

DeWitt echoed this: "Yeah, I mean, in the end the scouting director's the one who's managing the whole process all though the year, and when it comes time to draft, he's the one that we're looking to put the board together, make the decision on who the team should take. Unless there's something beyond just a pure player that [serves as] a reason to talk about it."

Having a system that, as Mozeliak put it, both "allows us to know how to value a player now... and knowing what we want to pay for" gives him a chance to focus on process instead, the way he was while talking to that agent on the phone earlier in the day. I mentioned that he had looked at his computer and come away with a skeptical expression.

"Actually I was trying to reverse engineer because he mentioned another team," Mozeliak said. "And he was telling me that they were willing to pay X for that player, and I was just trying to see if they could really afford it. And the answer is no. So, I don't think it was true."

This is how the rest of Mozeliak's draft day would go.

"My day today has been I met with you twice," Mozeliak said. "I met with Dan probably four times. I need to go back and talk to him shortly in his office. And I've talked to a lot of agents today and just trying to get an understanding of what may happen."

Then again, without any picks until number twenty-seven, Mozeliak was limited in how prepared he could be. Given the recent run of success by the Cardinals, he had gotten used to a late first-round pick.

"I've resolved myself in this particular draft to not overconcern myself with what may happen," Mozeliak said.

"Just let it unfold," DeWitt said.

"We have four picks tonight, though, so there's a pretty good chance you and I are in that room all night," Mozeliak said to DeWitt.

"I think in a way I would approach tonight, if I were in your shoes, one is, just understand it's very fluid," Mozeliak said to me. "But it's a slow fluidity tonight. And so, like, your takeaway might be very little. Tomorrow, pace picks up and you can watch the board interaction change a little bit quicker. And then our system will benefit from that. And tonight, Bill sitting in there, me sitting in there. That's just the nature of the beast. Because we have a seven-and-a-half-million [dollar] pool and we'll spend four of it tonight."

The largest conference room in the Busch Stadium offices had been prepared for the draft. Multiple televisions played, one with the MLB Network broadcast of the draft, another with the Cardinals game in Kansas City against the Royals. Red, white, and blue bunting had been placed on walls around the room wherever there weren't individual draft magnets, each representing a player who'd been scouted on the field, talked to off it, analyzed statistically, mechanically, and medically.

With all the scouts, front office members such as Gary LaRocque and Matt Slater, a table in the far corner for DeWitt, Mozeliak, Kantrovitz, Michael Girsch, and Chris Correa, forty people were in the draft room.

And there was no getting away from all the magnets, separated into these categories: 245 college pitchers, 185 college position players, 51 junior college pitchers, 22 junior college position players, 118 high school pitchers, 150 high school position players, those with signability issues, those with medical issues. Separate from these, within easy reach of Kantrovitz's seat, was a kind of "next up" grouping: RHP, LHP, C, SS, CF, 2B, 3B, and simply BAT.

I asked a pacing Joe Almaraz what was going through his mind, his year of nonstop travel and evaluation leading up to this.

"You can't think right now," he said. "The game's about to start. Just want to put some runs on the board."

Everyone's in jacket and ties—I feel underdressed in a polo. Mozeliak's wearing his bow tie, Kantrovitz has on a black suit, gray-checked tie. Even Charlie Gonzalez has a sports jacket and tie, though over jeans.

Before it's even started, Dan patrols the carpet back and forth directly in front of his board, wearing a path as the first magnetic strips, with full info on players, come off the board as they are picked. At pick seventeen, Kantrovitz and Mozeliak confer with Almaraz, and Mozeliak disappears from the room to make some calls about potential outcomes just ten picks away. Now Mozeliak is mirroring Kantrovitz's movements, in and out of the draft room.

After He's Gone

At pick twenty, Mozeliak counts the picks left, then leaves again, while Kantrovitz doesn't even sit down, tapping a rolled-up sheet of paper against his right hip as he walks.

By pick twenty-four, the strategy is set. Mozeliak sits down next to DeWitt. The Cardinals are about to draft someone they'll spend $1,843,000 on. But Mozeliak taps DeWitt on the shoulder, gestures at the television. The two men are transfixed instead by an Oscar Taveras at bat. A few days earlier, in his Cardinals debut, Taveras launched a long home run into the right-field seats at Busch Stadium. The crowd reacted disproportionately to a run that put the Cardinals ahead 1–0 in the fourth. Everybody there believed they were seeing the beginning of history, like watching Musial's first home run, or Pujols's. Taveras received a curtain call from the Busch crowd. I ask Gary LaRocque how he will place these about-to-be-drafted guys in the player-development ladder. He breaks it down simply:

"Wait till you get them, then you listen a lot, then you figure out where to put them."

The Cardinals' pick is Luke Weaver, a pitcher near the top of Ty Boyles's board. Mo gets off the phone and nods. The room erupts in congratulations, fist bumps from everyone given to Ty, who sees the Cardinals pick one of his players first in his very first Cardinals draft. The MLB Network has a draft board with twenty-six players on it. For three minutes, the Cardinals' draft board is ahead of the rest of the world.

The pick hasn't even been made public yet, but Slater and LaRocque are already combing through every bit of data they have on Weaver.

"It's not just about innings," Slater explains. "It's stress innings. It's pitch counts. It's more than just innings, whenever we can get it."

Slater loaded up video on his laptop, analyzing the workload for Weaver over the last three years. For the video of Weaver pitching, each pitch registered in a white number superimposed on a blue box—velocity out of the hand and at the plate.

When the pick is announced on MLB Network, Mozeliak is back out in the hall, preparing for pick thirty-four. Kantrovitz resumes his pacing. DeWitt is relaxed, taking it all in. Later he told me the experience now is fundamentally at odds with how he felt back in 2005, when Luhnow was just getting started and the future of his ball club rested on this new process's working.

Once the Red Sox take Michael Kopech thirty-third, the Cardinals are on the clock. Kantrovitz has a final discussion with Michael Garciaparra, an area scout out west, and Jeremy Schied, the West Coast cross-checker. Mozeliak, meanwhile, is talking it over with Correa. It's the final mingling of pure scouting and analytics into the team's process.

It produces the pick of Jack Flaherty, a big, right-handed pitcher out of Harvard-Westlake High School in California, and fist bumps all around for Garciaparra. Slater and LaRocque repeated their analysis of Flaherty's usage, trying to determine what schedule to set for him.

Then, a bit of a lull, with the Cardinals not picking again until sixty-eight. Of course, as LaRocque, who used to be the architect of drafts, said as he went to grab some food from the buffet just outside the draft room, "The second through seventh rounds: that's where you build your draft."

One shortstop who wanted too much money is ruled out by the Cardinals—too many other places to spend that money, and they'd eventually need it to sign Weaver at slot and Flaherty above slot.

By pick sixty-six, Kantrovitz and Gonzalez confer. DeWitt and Mozeliak are interested, but this is Kantrovitz's show now, his jacket off, sleeves rolled halfway up his arms.

"Two guys in the queue," Kantrovitz said to Gonzalez. "If one of those guys goes, your guy is next, but that has to happen first."

It did. Right-handed pitcher Ronnie Williams, one of Gonzalez's favorites, gets his magnet tossed onto the big board, as Kantrovitz says, "All right, Charlie, you got him."

No needling of Gonzalez here, all congratulations come his way instead.

Three picks later, the Cardinals choose Andrew Morales, a right-handed pitcher out of UC-Irvine. He'll ultimately sign for a bit below slot, but it doesn't quite balance out how far over slot the Cardinals had to go to draft and sign Flaherty.

John Hart on MLB Network suggests the Cardinals need to get creative, under slot, to get more cash freed up, now or later.

"Later!" Mozeliak says back at the television.

Shortly after, Day 1 was over. "Great job, boys!" Mozeliak said, dismissing everyone for the night. A group of scouts, exiting Busch Stadium, discussed where to go at 11:00 P.M. on a Thursday night in St. Louis. They'd all just participated in choosing the next four St. Louis Cardinals, and now they walked past the statues of Brock, Musial, Gibson, into the St. Louis night.

June 6

"They laughed at me for having Plan C and D," Dan Kantrovitz told me as we sat at the main table, about fifteen minutes before Day 2 of the draft began. "And then last year, one round, we needed D. So they don't laugh anymore."

It's more casual, but LaRocque is right: this is where you build out your draft.

Mozeliak is calmer—back in his chair, rather than leaning forward or up and out into the hall to talk with agents, as he was last night. He described his role today as "making sure everybody's getting along."

And Kantrovitz, too, isn't pacing with quite the same amount of consistent intensity. His march is more of a stroll. But even when he sits, Kantrovitz stares at his board when he thinks a team might steal one of his favorite picks, as if trying to keep it on there by force of will. Mozeliak stares, too, but his focus on the competition is for different players.

But for some teams, I notice Kantrovitz and Mozeliak barely look at their own board.

All over the country, final bluffs were getting called. Of one catcher, I heard a scout say, "He could've been taken in a better spot today if he'd been more realistic yesterday."

The Cardinals took Trevor Megill, a tall righty out of Loyola Marymount with injury history, in the third round. Kantrovitz would need to spend much of the next six weeks figuring out if he should go over slot to get Megill, or if another of his plans would carry the day. Ultimately, Kantrovitz decided after a trip to the Cape Cod League to see Megill for a single inning.

By pick 135, it was time to reward Austin Gomber for those fortuitous curveballs. Immediately, LaRocque and Slater open up the Gomber file, trying to determine where to place him in the system.

"To be determined, but he profiles as a New York–Penn League kid," LaRocque told me, even as he and Slater look over the data. "We have three different places to put kids, and I love them all for development. So much of it is also based on estimated workload, and determining where a kid is going to have some initial success. That first year and a half is so important." Gomber eventually signs for slot plus $800, and heads to State College. He pitched to a 2.30 ERA there over 11 starts, a strong debut, , then improved his peripherals while impressing at full-season Peoria in 2015, a 2.93 ERA through August 2015.

One round later, the Cardinals decide to take Darren Seferina in the first round Gonzalez said they'd have to consider him, the fifth round.

"Under two hundred, Charlie?" Kantrovitz verifies. They need to save money somewhere.

"Under two hundred," Gonzalez answers. Seferina heads to State College, where he'll be the regular second baseman and debut nicely, for a $100,000 bonus in a slot that recommends $280,100. Seferina steals 20 bases in a short season, posts a .724 OPS, a solid beginning, then an even better jump to full-season Peoria in 2015, with a .793 OPS through August 2015.

Andrew Sohn, a shortstop, is another senior sign in the sixth round, gets slot.

After He's Gone

"We've got a really advanced college catcher. Where do you think he fits?" Kantrovitz asks LaRocque as the seventh-round pick approaches.

"He fits really nicely at State College," LaRocque answers.

"Good, he's from up that way," Kantrovitz replies.

The magnet for Brian O'Keefe is grabbed the moment after the Red Sox pick. He's out of St. Joseph's University, Pennsylvania, at a slot of $163,200, and the Cardinals give him $150,000. Now the Cardinals are starting to get some maneuverability.

The Cardinals aren't getting everybody they want, of course. Charlie Gonzalez pushes back despairingly in his chair as Dash Winningham, the one Steve Turco taught to hit opposite-field home runs in a few sentences, is drafted by the Mets.

"He could have come home with us, but they absconded with him," Gonzalez tells me just outside the draft room, as he takes a small walk to recover from the disappointment. He'll be happier soon, though.

Meanwhile, Matt Blood, another area scout, is finding the Cardinals a hitter and some savings. The slot is $152,400. Blood makes eye contact with Kantrovitz and holds up fingers—1, 3, 5.

"Good work," Mozeliak says. And just like that, Nick Thompson, a college hitter out of William and Mary, is the team's eighth-round pick.

LaRocque is putting the rosters together, sees Thompson will profile as State College's designated hitter.

"There's no chance of expectations being a problem about where he'll be playing?" LaRocque asks Blood.

"No, he knows he's a hitter," Blood responds. LaRocque nods and places Thompson on his provisional roster sheet loaded up on his laptop.

When I spoke to Thompson about it a few weeks later, just before he made his professional debut with State College in Williamsport, Pennsylvania, he revealed his surprise that the Cardinals ended up drafting him, a sign that Blood hid his cards well.

"Well, actually, it was interesting because going into the draft, I felt that there were two teams—there was sort of a two-horse race of teams that were going to draft me, and the Cardinals weren't one of those teams," Thompson told me in June 2014, standing in his Spikes uniform in front of the door leading to the visitors' dugout at historic Bowman Field. "And so the Cardinals, as you know, pick last in every round. 'Cause they had the best record last year. And so after the two teams that I thought were going to pick me in that round had already picked, I was actually getting in the shower to go to a Luke Bryan concert. And as I was hopping in the shower, my phone rang and I saw 'Cardinals Matt Blood.' And I answered it and he said, 'Hey, we're going to take you here in three picks.'

"I was shell-shocked for a second and then I ran downstairs and pulled up the computer and was watching it with my parents down in the kitchen."

One round later, the Cardinals decided they could wait no longer to take Charlie Gonzalez's top gut-feel guy: Daniel Poncedeleon. This wasn't a system pick Kantrovitz knew if he selected Poncedeleon, he would have to answer to questions from higher-ups about being too subjective, but he had too much faith in Charlie to let that stand in his way. Adding to the drama, there were also red flags on the medical side.

"Frankly, Charlie sold me the first time he called me about him in March, and we could've stopped there," Kantrovitz said in a January 2015 e-mail.

Poncedeleon was at home in La Mirada, California, watching the draft with his family and his girlfriend, Jennifer Beatty, a volleyball player he'd met at Embry-Riddle. He was receiving constant updates via texts from Charlie.

"Dealing with Charlie is great," Poncedeleon told me a few weeks later, as he prepared for his first game with the State College Spikes. "You know, it felt like he wanted you on the team. You want to go to a team that wants you. You don't want a team that drafts you just because you have talent, you know? You want a team that wants you and builds you up. So Charlie was the guy. Like, he was always—he calls me every other day like my father. He was there, you know? And it felt great to talk to him all the time. And he told me things to help me out and stuff and what he thought and his point of view. It was great."

Charlie recalled for me in a December 2014 interview the moment in St. Louis, just ahead of the draft, when Kantrovitz decided to pick Poncedeleon: "He says, 'We've never taken a guy inside the tenth round without ever having been seen by anyone in our organization other than the area guy.' And I looked and I said, 'Dan, I'm not trying to be an ingrate, but is that supposed to make me feel good? Had we not taken him, I would have been on your ass.'

"Scouting started becoming a lot more fun when I could tell that my guys listen to me and they believed in me, expressly after the round six to ten to thirty. And that's when scouting really starts getting good. You know what I mean? The top dogs, taking the top guys, okay. That's pretty much—we can figure that out, you know? But you start going with the 'Take this guy and take him here. If you don't take him by there, he's going to be gone and he may be a big leaguer. I'll worry about time.' Tony Cruz, you know?"

Back in June, the Dash Winningham disappointment had disappeared for Charlie Gonzalez, Wearing a cream-colored, button-down shirt, he had his man, Poncedeleon.

"If I had to win one game in the state of Florida, going up against Wainwright, I'd pick this guy," Gonzalez told me. "I have one point seven five million dollars on him!"

The Cardinals would go on and get Matt Pearce, too—five Charlie Gonzalez players in the top thirteen rounds, and they signed them all, including Poncedeleon for "five thousand fucking dollars."

June 13, Williamsport, Pennsylvania

Just days after the scouts had spent hours just trying to watch a few innings or four at bats for a possible target, and analytics had completed a survey of what often amounted to a few hundred at bats, roughly three dozen players were now St. Louis Cardinals. A good number of them get sent here, to the

State College Spikes in the New York–Penn League, and manager Oliver Marmol. By opening night, they make up fully a third of Marmol's roster.

"The first thing we try to communicate is that you're part of the St. Louis Cardinals family, and with that comes certain responsibility, and certain accountability," Marmol told me as we sat in the visitors' dugout at Bowman Field. "And there are certain expectations, a certain level of professionalism.

"But also, they're here for a reason. A scout saw something in them that made him believe they can play at the big league level."

Marmol and LaRocque, since the draft, have been in contact nearly every day, by phone, by e-mail.

"Personality traits, anything that can be useful. Not a whole lot is communicated about what their tools are. It's about who they are as people. They couldn't care less what you know about baseball until they know you care about them as people."

The personality-based scouting reports allow Marmol to begin to build a bond with his players, something vital to help guys get through their first professional experience.

"I was just in here with Nick Thompson, and he kind of looked over at me and asked, 'How do you even know to ask these questions?'"

In Thompson, Marmol had a particularly perceptive new player. He'd graduated from East Carolina in two and a half years—while playing varsity baseball. It's a stunning academic accomplishment. He continued playing ball at William and Mary while going for a master's degree.

"And then eventually I would have gone to medical school. So I think the master's is kind of just a segue into professional baseball," he joked.

Thompson reinforced that there isn't one kind of Cardinals player, but the Cardinals are definitely among the teams who saw his intelligence as a virtue.

"I think there were absolutely some teams that fit both those criteria, that were kind of turned away because I was a good student and were afraid that I would go right back to school after a year or two of professional baseball,"

Thompson said. "And then I feel like some organizations, like the Cardinals, who really appreciate professionalism, they were teams that were really interested and kind of made that extra effort to make me a part of their club."

Thompson knew enough to know he couldn't yet set realistic goals for himself. "Obviously everybody wants to move up every year, you know? Hopefully a step or two every year. So I think my goal for next year would be to be in Peoria at the least. But as far as statistic goals, I don't think I can put my finger on one of those yet. I haven't really faced any of this caliber of player yet."

If Thompson was circumspect, Daniel Poncedeleon was ready to come out and dominate. He had the mentality Gonzalez described—it didn't seem to even occur to him that he might struggle out of the gate or need to learn more than some fine-tuning from the Cardinals en route to the major leagues.

"Oh, yeah. He means so much to me," Poncedeleon said of Gonzalez. "I'm glad there's a guy out there who could see my competitiveness. I just love competing. That's what I thrive on."

It was obvious why Gonzalez had made sure Poncedeleon was the one pitcher at the combine who faced live hitting.

"It's just so different pitching just a bull pen. It's like kissing your sister, you know? You're not really competing. Like, when I pitch, I like to face batters. I like someone in there that wants to hit the ball so I can strike 'em out."

The Blue Jays, among other teams, had been in contact with Poncedeleon, but he was hoping it would be the Cardinals, for one reason. I asked him whether any other scouts he'd talked to sounded like Gonzalez.

"No. No. Charlie Gonzalez is some other guy. He's awesome." Poncedeleon didn't seem to think his trip up the ladder would take all that long.

"I don't know much about the minor leagues. I tried to learn, but it's hard. And I got a few levels to go. You got to go to A-ball, then high-A, then Double-A, and then maybe to the bigs or Triple-A. I mean, it matters. So hopefully, within two years I'm guessing. Well, this year I'll hopefully move up and maybe move up again. Hopefully less than two."

Nor did Poncedeleon believe the Cardinals would be changing him much.

"No, no. Just throw and get your arm feeling good and get ready for the game. I mean, I don't imagine they have much to tell me anyways. I mean, it's hard to coach, you know, when you just get 'em. They might have a thing or two to tell me."

Poncedeleon was right about that. Mark DeJohn, the field coordinator, and Tim Leveque, the minor league pitching coordinator, were in the business of collecting information, not disseminating it.

"Just to kind of observe the new players," DeJohn said as we chatted in the cramped visiting coach's quarters at Bowman Field. "What you're basically trying to see is what the scouts saw in them. And you think back when you first signed yourself. Just how nervous these kids are. So sometimes you'll see some really great things the first few days. And then you might not see it again. You just try to look for those tools. Just things that would get you excited. Things that you can project that would be big league tools. Whatever the scout has said about him, we try to make it fit."

Even so, the level of familiarity DeJohn, Leveque, and Marmol develop for the players, on and off the field, quickly outstrips what even the best scout can gather.

"In these six days that I'm here watching the team, I'll see them more than that scout has seen them," DeJohn said. "In maybe two years or so, he might not have seen the kid six times. One of the things that you really kind of want to manage is to see the kid's passion. You know, his determination. How much passion he has—if he really wants to be a big leaguer. There's a difference between wanting it and really wanting it, you know? They want it—but sometimes you want something till it doesn't go over well."

DeJohn and Leveque echoed what Turco said—players need to come to the staff looking for help, especially early on.

"They're instructed to not to even touch hitters for a month, and only then, not unless the guy comes to somebody and says, 'Hey, I want help,'" DeJohn told me. "Then obviously we help. But we leave them alone to try.

"They got here doing what they did. There's a lot of guys that you don't need to touch. You just leave them alone. And he'll figure things out himself without changing. But if a guy's really struggling, you let them struggle through it. And then if he wants that help, then you're there. When a student is ready, a teacher will appear.

"If the kid hit .350 every year in college, and now he's hitting .210, and you go to him and tell him, 'You need to change,' he's not going to really believe that, you know? He just thinks that 'I'm just going through this period.' They're just going through a tough time. And he figures—'I'll be okay.' But they're coming into pro ball. Now you're going to face kids that, on a daily basis, the type of competition that you haven't seen day after day after day. And then you have to remember, I'm not sure of their schedule right now, but when I was managing this league, they played seventy-six games in eighty days. So they have to get used to a schedule."

For Leveque, the same held true on the pitching side, he told me:

"A lot of it is, like, what DJ said, a lot of it is to observe. Obviously, the scouts saw something in these guys, right? So my job is to just observe them and watch them, see how they go about it. Their pitches. Whatever I would look for in a pitcher. It's a blank slate. I don't know these guys. So I just kind of want to see them—I want to see them in a game. Now, for the guys coming from extended [spring training]—this is a different environment. They're out there under the lights. They're not in Florida pitching at noon anymore. So a lot of it, too, is just seeing them in a different environment."

Two of those guys from the back fields who made it to State College were Chris Rivera and Rowan Wick. Rivera would stay for just a few days, before heading to Johnson City to be the regular third baseman, another new position. Wick would have one of the great seasons in recent New York–Penn League memory.

"I think maybe just doing what I had to do in practice and in our extended games and not really trying to do too much," Rivera said. "I think they notice that and they were confident in bringing me up here, and I just want to thank them for giving me the opportunity, and I'm going to take advantage of the opportunity that I was given."

His first call was to Angelia, his girlfriend.

"I just told her, you know—she's always the first person I call for some reason. 'I'm going out to State College to start the year.' She was real happy. At the same time, she didn't know what to say, just because she was so happy."

To be clear, the hands-off approach to changing anyone didn't mean the coaches shied away from the constant communication that is the hallmark of this organization.

So it was with Rivera—his quick movements with the bat as he prepared in the on-deck circle, eyes always on the pitcher, working to be quick to the ball. But he fell behind 0-1 and popped up chasing a ball out of the zone. Smoky Ortiz talked him through the at bat immediately, as he handed Ortiz his batting gloves and got ready to take his position in the field.

Austin Gomber sat behind the plate, dressed in a blue polo, with another young Cardinals hurler, Ian McKinney, a fifth-rounder back in 2013, and Leveque. There, the instruction began as well. Leveque notes it when a pitcher throws a fastball to the third batter of the inning, after the first two make outs, each on the first pitch.

"Throw a fastball there," Leveque says, noting the unlikelihood the third batter will follow suit and swing at the first pitch. "It's a free strike."

Thompson, preparing for his first professional at bat, takes a strong, sweeping swing through the imagined strike zone from the on-deck circle. He stretches, holding the doughnutted bat over his head, feet spread wide. Thompson is meticulous, measured, sweeping some of the warning-track dirt with his feet from the circle before strolling to the plate.

He strikes out looking, and for Leveque, it's another teaching moment.

"I love left-on-left changeups, right-on-right changeups. You know why? Hitters don't see it," Leveque told his young pitchers. "Look at the numbers—same-side changeups get offered at like four percent of the time."

Wick, meanwhile, told me before the game he knew the decision makers were present. It was true—LaRocque brought cherry fruit snacks for the group. Wick fell behind on a 1-2 pitch, then crushed a nasty pitch—down and away, with movement—over the center-field fence.

Something similar happened in the ninth—Wick fell behind 0-1, hit the next pitch, a slider, well beyond the right-center-field fence. An audible "Whoa" came from LaRocque. Wick registered another 2-homer game in his first four with State College, then a third just over a week later. He set the State College record for most home runs in a month—and he didn't start playing until June 13.

It was the beginning of a championship season for Marmol, who'd won the 2013 George Kissell Award from the Cardinals. He'd made the decision, like LaRocque, to be a young coach, rather than an old player.

"That's a good way to put it," Marmol said when I brought up LaRocque's quote. "Sometimes you have to be realistic. I asked myself, was I going to be a big league player for five, ten years? And the answer was no. So I decided it was time to start my career on this side of the fence."

Corey Baker said that's as much a product of the organization's ethos as it is Marmol's own decision, citing Marmol as one of those who made the jump in 2010. He played under DeJohn. His first hitting coach was Mike Shildt.

"So that [process of] grooming people who [stay] in the organization and become part of the Cardinals is basically visible everywhere you go in the organization," Baker said.

After coaching under Turco in the GCL, Marmol managed in Johnson City, then came to State College. And he brought George Kissell with him.

"When you're around guys like DJ, and Gary, and Vuch, he comes up a lot," Marmol said. "It's making sure you are thinking more about the players around you than your own career. You're here for a reason, and that's to develop the next players who are going to help the major league team.

"One thing we try to stress is not only a certain attention to detail, but competitiveness and focus throughout these drills, making them as gamelike as possible. So when they do get in the game, that sense of pressure is familiar to them. Whenever we take an infield, there's a certain amount of pressure behind it."

Ollie's wife, Amber, arrived during the opening game. They met when they were sixteen and got married when Marmol was twenty-one. Amber travels with Ollie during the season, the way George and Virginia Kissell did for so many years. During the off-season, they live in Jupiter.

"We've been able to experience some pretty neat stuff in some different cities," Marmol said. "And this organization, there's none like it. I've been entrusted with about thirty men. They've trusted me to develop these guys, and I have a job to do, my staff has a job to do. And I intend to try and do it well."

The End of the Beginning

In July, Sam Tuivailala got the call to go to Double-A.

It was a surprise to no one. Over his last 28⅓ innings, he'd walked only 9 batters—he'd struck out 47. The last 102 plate appearances against him at High-A included just two extrabase hits, both doubles. It was time.

"Well, for many of the players including, in this case, Sam, the process actually starts right after spring training," LaRocque told me in a July 2014 phone interview. "The players are assigned—in this case, he was assigned to Palm Beach.... But if you domino back and you say, 'How did it happen?' It happened because the projection started to turn to performance. Most of these moves are—in the full-season levels, are designed because their project—player's projections start to turn into performance. They move themselves ahead of the level of the league he was at. In Sam's case, that started to occur in May and June.

"Sam experienced a few things in the Florida State League. He experienced for the first time where he pitched back-to-back, meaning two days in a row. He experienced where he pitched multiple innings. Now, as a conversion player coming from third base to the mound, these were all built-in benchmarks that we knew he had to reach for in order to move him up. So one of our goals back in April, a few of our goals, was to accomplish that. He did. He did and we felt very comfortable with how he was then producing. You look at his body of work over three months. Those benchmarks were reached. Clearly, his performance was reached. The combination of it—the combination of it led right into he needs the opportunity to be challenged at the next level.

"I mean, he was in that period of time with, like—if I'm correct—he was in sixteen games, as I see it, during that—from May tenth to July tenth. Let's say two months. He was in sixteen games. And what was interesting was, we have over that time set up a—really, a focus on, and he's focused on the idea of how to get ahead of hitters. How to throw to the glove and get the ball in the strike zone. Get outs in the strike zone. During that stretch of time, he hit the benchmarks we felt he needed to for throwing—and he's still learning. But for throwing and getting his fastball command in order. And that's a big thing for him and he understands that. So he improved at that. And as we saw that improvement, clearly along with the results, but as we saw the improvement on a variety of benchmarks, one being fastball command, we also recognize that in his performance. I mean, during that stretch of time, it's really something that he struck out forty-seven percent of the hitters. His walk rate was eight percent."

For Tuivailala, it was nothing less than reaching the goal he'd set for himself—to earn that promotion.

"In June and July, I definitely think it was in the back of my head, where you want to end this year," Tuivailala said in a July phone interview just after it happened. "I definitely wanted to be in Double-A. But in June and July, I tried not to think about the future. I kind of just take one day at time, like I told you. I wanted to make sure that when I did get the call, I was ready and I have all pitches and command where I wanted it to be."

Finally, on a rain-swept Florida night, Tuivailala's future merged with his present.

"One of our games got canceled and it was raining hard. And then I finally got called into the office and we had Gary LaRocque there and all of our coaching staff and my manager, Dann Bilardello. He told me that there's good news and that I was getting called up to Double-A. It was kind of a weird feeling. I had the goose bumps at the same time. I was superpumped. And they all told me they believed in me and they told me it's the same game. Just go out there and compete. So I just shook all their hands and I was ready to go."

Then Tuivailala got to make the call home.

"I think once [my mom] answered, she was at the store with my sister. And then I just said, 'Guess what?' And she said, 'What?' And I said, 'I'm getting the call up to Double-A. I'm leaving tomorrow morning.' And then I could just—I could hear my sister in the background. I think she heard it through the phone and she's just screaming and they're all so excited for me. So then after I hung up the phone with them, I instantly got a call from my dad maybe a minute later. And he's all excited. So it was definitely a good day."

The transition was also eased, said Tuivailala, by the continuity in the system. He'd known Shildt, his Double-A manager, for years.

"I definitely think it's an easier way," Tuivailala said. "Spring training, they definitely mixed it up a lot. And that's what makes it a little bit easier for the transition. They tend to have a Triple-A coach, he'll help out lower guys, and the Double-A will swap every now and then. I definitely think that was a lot easier so that we got to know a lot of the staff members even through we're not at their level yet. I think that was a pretty good idea of theirs."

I listened to Tuivailala's first game with Springfield on an Internet broadcast, coming back from an assignment in Fenway Park. The announcer struggled with Tuivailala's name. Then he marveled at the radar-gun readings. He'd once sat 95. Now he was frequently hitting 100, 101, 102, and sitting 99.

"After playing in front of attendance of maybe one hundred to two

After He's Gone

hundred, to, man, like three thousand to five thousand in the house," Tuivailala recalled of his Double-A debut, "it was definitely different. But I was definitely juiced and pumped. When I got out there, I tried to breathe and just think of one pitch at a time. It's the same game I've been pitching in. And then when I got my first strikeout, I think that's what really got me going, and I felt confident up there."

Tuivailala faced six Double-A batters in his debut. None of them reached base. Half of them struck out.

"I know that I'm throwing hard and everything. I made those typical pitches where I definitely feel like I threw a little bit harder. But after the game, I know a lot of the people—they tweeted me about the 102, and I'm not sure if the gun was a little bit juiced, but it was definitely good to get the attention of everyone after that."

Tuivailala mentioned tilt again and pointed out that his teammate Nick Petree had also helped him to incorporate it into his delivery. Petree, who tops out in the eighties, couldn't be more different from Tuivailala as a pitcher. But that constant communication, in this case, allowed Tuivailala to discover what worked for him.

For Baker, another voice in Tuivailala's development, the joy was tempered, naturally, by frustration, the kind of natural tug between collaboration and competition that is the Cardinals' minor league system.

"I'm really happy for him," Baker told me in September. "I was talking to Jenna about this last night, and I was, like, 'I'm so happy for him.' He's borderline uncomfortable with how good he is. He's so humble. So that's awesome. But I think it's both. I think it's inspiring and demoralizing."

The promotion still felt surreal for Tuivailala.

"At this level it's kind of crazy how fast this happened. Just going from spring training, back then I was just thinking, 'Man, I don't want to go back to Peoria.' And then the next thing you know, I'm looking at myself now that I'm in Double-A. It's crazy how things happen.

"I told my parents and all my friends and everyone. They're all juicing me, telling me, okay, I'm going to be in the big leagues this year and I'll be there by around this month, you know? I just tell them I want to end strong and just keep playing hard and then I'll just—I'll see how things end up. But I definitely just want to end strong."

It's fair to say he ended strong, and things got even crazier. His parents and friends were right. Tuivailala pitched through July and August for Springfield, notching a 2.57 ERA, a strikeout rate of 12.9 per 9 innings, and keeping his walks to just 3.9 per 9 innings. That got him a quick bump to Triple-A Memphis, where he struck out three of four Triple-A batters he faced, and then it was on to St. Louis.

"Sam hit all the benchmarks we set out for him," LaRocque said of Tuivailala in a September 2014 interview. "Our conversation a year ago focused on what he could be if he accomplished certain things. So this was within the realm of what we had for him in terms of goals."

In the realm, maybe. But was this the best-case scenario? "Absolutely."

By January 2015, Tuivailala, who'd been trying to locate his command and an off-speed pitch less than a year earlier, found himself among the Cardinals big leaguers in the team's winter caravan, preparing to come to big league camp and win himself a bull-pen job. He'd pitch intermittently in St. Louis in 2015, while spending the bulk of his time with Triple-A Memphis. And he'd catapulted all the way onto the team's Top 10 prospects, according to *Baseball America*. Derrick Goold, in his write-up of Tuivailala, talked up his curveball:

"With the frame of a power forward, Tuivailala is the Cardinals' latest converted power pitcher after Jason Motte and Trevor Rosenthal. Fine command is all he lacks with the heat. In the Arizona Fall League, Tuivailala's curve advanced. He throws [it] hard and with a sharp drop."[5]

As for Rowan Wick, he doubled and tripled on July 21 in support of Daniel Poncedeleon in a game in Troy, New York, against the Tri-City ValleyCats, the New York–Penn League entry from Jeff Luhnow and Sig Mejdal's Astros. Wick's demeanor couldn't have changed more since that May day in

Jupiter when he had to explain his decision to even keep playing the field, instead of leveraging that arm and giving pitching a try.

"I'd like to say we saw something different, but we didn't," Marmol told me in the dugout before that July 21 game in Troy. "I know when we were getting on the plane, leaving Jupiter [back in June], he came over, put his arm around me, and said, 'Don't worry, I'll hit at night.' Because he had a really tough extended.... The biggest thing we've seen with him is, he's gotten a taste of success, and it's brought him more confidence. There's a presence to him."

Wick talked about his goal of making the NY-P All-Star team, and I laughed, telling him I thought he was pretty safe, seeing as how he'd put up a 1.290 OPS, and nobody else in the circuit had cracked 1.000.

But Wick was right, and I was wrong. There'd be no New York–Penn League All-Star Game. The next day, he was off to Peoria, and full-season A-ball.

"You know, when we work with these players every single day, we constantly in our minds hope for their ceilings and hope that they reach their ceilings," LaRocque said of Wick. "And as players come through the system and do that, we're thankful that they're getting it, and he's clearly put himself in a position to be watched.

"But back in May three of our staff members came to me and said that Rowan had talked to them about stepping on the mound, meaning a bullpen type of thing. And when it got to me, I said, 'Turco, please sit with Rowan and find out what he's really thinking.' You know, the best way to communicate is, let's be transparent. Let's talk to the player.

"And it's just the way we do business. And Steve sat with him and said, 'Hey, listen. Is this something you're really thinking about?' He said, 'Oh, no. I said I want to hit.' And from that moment forward, there was never any other discussions from Rowan or anybody about him potentially even looking ahead into being on the mound. I mean, we're talking about eighteen- to twenty-three-year-old young men. And we're trying to help them through the grind of this. And he, Rowan, put the focus on 'I'm going to hit.' And the rest, in the last two months since that time in late May, it's been pretty well documented."

Wick struggled when he reached Peoria. His K-rate spiked, to nearly 40 percent of his plate appearances. His power remained, but the .220/.299/.433 line meant he'd probably need to go back and master Peoria before moving ahead. Wick headed to Instructional League this fall down in Jupiter, where George Kissell once ruled and where Steve Turco now presides.

The Cardinals didn't get a breakout from Rowan Wick in State College, whatever happens next, because they were certain he could hit. This wasn't scouting. This was listening. And so, too, was the two-way conversation that followed, when Rowan Wick decided to transition to the mound. Turco had him with the Gulf Coast League Cardinals by August 2015, Wick starting that process of climbing the ladder once again, in a new way.

Poncedeleon, too, got stronger as the year went along. In his first six starts, his ERA was 3.63, with a 20/9 K/BB rate in 17⅓ innings.

He revealed himself to be confident, but coachable.

"It's been fun," Poncedeleon told me before his July 21 start. "I'd say you get to see a lot of new places. I've been listening, picking the minds of the coaches, and they tell you things that I'm still kind of learning today, after twenty years of baseball. I've been around for a while. These guys always have something new to tell you. How to approach and stuff. So that's good."

In his last six starts, his ERA was 1.67, with a 32/5 K/BB rate in 27 innings. Then he threw six shutout innings on September 9. State College captured the league title. By August 2015, Poncedeleon had conquered Peoria, and posted a 1.17 ERA over his first six appearances with high-A Palm Beach.

Nick Thompson homered in that game. He'd struggled early on, and when I saw him on July 21, his season line was .236/.308/.358. He wasn't interested in waiting to seek out the coaches—the would-be premed student instead found Smoky Ortiz and got to work on remaking his swing.

"Smoky and I have been working a little bit in the cage," Thompson said that night, as we stood in front of the visitors' clubhouse in Troy. "I'm just trying to get a little more balance, a little more flex in my hips, and trying to get just a little lower so I can reach that lower pitch, the lower outside pitch, a little better than I had been in the past. So it's been working pretty well so far. But he said I was standing up a little too much, that he wants me to flex my hips a little more. So we'll see how that goes today."

Between Ortiz, and a reading regimen that featured C. S. Lewis and J. D. Salinger throughout August, something clicked.

"I think that was definitely the start of everything," Thompson told me in September, a week after he, Poncedeleon, and Marmol celebrated that New York–Penn League title. "And I think if I looked at my splits, I think in the month of June I hit like .170, and then the months of July and August I hit over .300. And that was about the time that we kind of changed it up a little bit. It was at the end of June. And so I think after that, having a little success at the plate, and I think that made everything else a lot easier. Just the adjustment, and I feel like my body was more used to playing six to seven games a week. And I had acclimated to the applicable competition. I feel like, yeah, that was definitely the start of things. I think the success brought on by that was definitely a big help and a big motivator.

"In August, Ollie talked to us all and he said, 'Hey, nobody's coming up. Nobody's going down. This is what we got and this is what we're going to win with.' And then we did. We put it together."

From the moment Thompson and I talked in late July through the end of the season, his line was .339/.469/.470. He was a big reason why the Spikes won. And Thompson believes that winning, even at that level, matters.

"I think that it's definitely significant. That's kind of something that they preach. The championship team. The championship club. And I know [DeJohn], he always talked about 'We're not breeding you guys to just become major league players. We're breeding you guys to be major league players on a championship-level team. And we expect our players to play through

September and our major league players to play in October. So that's what we breed you guys for and that's what I want to see out of you guys.' But it's definitely an awesome experience winning the championship my first year out. It's just a wonderful experience."

Down in the Appalachian League, Chris Rivera got off to a roaring start. His OPS in Johnson City in July was a blistering .860. But it dropped to .574 in July and .535 in August. He's still young—he didn't turn twenty until March 2015. And so the Cardinals moved him to catcher, where the cerebral Rivera not only excelled, throwing out 42 percent of would-be basestealers through August 2015, but posted an OPS of .778. Maybe he's the next Kissell and Turco, but maybe he's the next Yadier Molina, too.

As for Corey Baker, he finally earned that promotion back to Double-A. Baker looked at it as a reward, though it meant pitching on three days' rest. Bilardello and Leveque were there in Palm Beach to give him the good news.

"I mean, I would hope that's what it was," Baker told me when we talked about it a few days later. "I feel like I did earn it. It was described to me as I've kind of vocalized that I wanted this opportunity, and now I was going to get it and it was a chance to start, so it was guaranteed innings because one of my issues was if I was going up there for twenty games, I wasn't getting twenty games' worth of innings."

But Baker understood the moment he received: a chance not only to pitch at a higher level after a strong season with Palm Beach, but to Yadier Molina.

"I think it was—he's probably going to be a Hall of Famer. And this is something I want to be able to soak in and enjoy. As opposed to 'Hey, it's just another game. I'm going out there. It's the same thing as A-ball.' And it is. That's the approach that I spoke to you about and I wanted to take.

"But I wasn't throwing to a Double-A catcher. I'm throwing to the best catcher in the game. Probably a Hall of Famer. And so I think that changed a little bit. But I did think I did a good job with my approach.

"We went up there, last home stand of the season. Ten thousand people.

Yadi's there. Wacha [also rehabbing] was there. Just the environment was so much, and I think it was good for me to prove that, yeah, I can handle that. It was no big deal."

Baker pitched 4 innings, striking out 4, though he did allow 3 runs. A few days later, pitching in relief, he picked up his first Double-A win.

Baker knew if this is going to happen for him, needed to graduate permanently to Double-A in 2015.

"Yeah. I think twenty-five in A-ball would be—at least for me. I can't speak for anyone else. It's hard to make these statements because there's guys that are twenty-five in A-ball and have no problem with their timetable, their career path. For me, I don't think twenty-five in A-ball would be something that would be good for what I want to do. I'm not saying if I go camp in high-A, I would be, like, 'Okay. I'm done.'

"But I would have to think about it. I would have to talk to them and see where they see me and—yeah, it would be tough. I think at this point, not only have I earned it, I think it's time. I think they should want to know, too: 'Hey, can he do it or not?' And obviously they're probably not going to find that out with another go-around in the Florida State League. So, yeah, I would think that Double-A is where I need to be." In March 2015, Baker found out: he'd be getting his chance to prove himself at Double-A Springfield. Not only did he stay all season, he held his own, pitching in every role possible, to a respectable 3.86 ERA through August 2015, and with the best strikeout rate of his career, 8.8/9.

Baker is, at once, the embodiment of the positive and the negative that goes along with participation in the St. Louis Cardinals farm system. The consistent communication allows him to set goals, and coaching continuity allows him to pursue those goals wherever he's assigned.

But Baker is in a system overstuffed with young pitching. Through 2014, he's pitched 109⅓ innings at high-A ball. His ERA is 2.80, his strikeout rate is a reasonable 6.6/9, the walk rate is an excellent 2.1/9. Baker's worked hard at his craft, and his fastball is up to 92/93, the kind of velocity that can at least get him in the door at higher levels. He's working hard at improving his slider, that third pitch. He showed throughout his career that he can start, he can relieve, and now at his highest level, he even struck out some hitters.

It just all might not be enough.

"I think it's not something we talk about too much, because I don't think she would ever sit there and say, like, 'Hey, you're struggling. I don't think you're going to make it. I think it's time for you to stop,'" Baker said back in 2014 of his conversations with Jenna about his career. "But I think we haven't touched on it because I think she knows where I am in terms of being realistic and that I don't want to play in the minors until I'm thirty. You know, if I don't think I'm going to make it, if I'm doing terrible over an extended period of time at a level where I need to do well and I think the end is coming, I don't think I'll have any regrets at that time. We'll see and say, 'All right. I gave everything I had.' So we haven't talked about it too much.

"Like I said, I'll be twenty-five next season. I don't think she's, like, 'We're so old. I think you need to move on.' But I think it's something she thinks about. I think she thinks about more in terms of, like, 'You're not really starting your career until you're twenty-seven. How is that going to affect us, more so now than in ten years? Are you going to have enough money if we want to buy a house?'

"And things like that. But, for now, she is behind me. This season, she got really into it. She watched every game on her phone. She still, last night, she was looking up the Florida State League championships to see who won. So she's really into it, and I think if I quit now, she would disagree with that."

Every player, whether a prospect such as Taveras whom the Cardinals planned to make their right fielder in 2015, or Baker, who continues to fight against the odds a forty-ninth-round pick faces, understood precisely what he needed to do to take the next step in the Cardinals system.

That's particularly notable for Baker—Taveras received guidance from a face-to-face meeting with Mozeliak and Matheny at the end of the season. But Baker, too, heard from his manager, coaches, and LaRocque.

After He's Gone

Are the major leagues a long shot? Absolutely. No one believes otherwise, Baker included. But they also were for Nick Greenwood, a swingman who came up and pitched 36 innings for the Cardinals in 2014, debuting at age twenty-six.

"I think someone like Nick Greenwood getting called up this year did a lot for me," Baker said. "I think he was a guy that in my head, I would never vocalize to anyone, 'Man, he is really good and probably deserves a chance.' And to be honest, I was one hundred percent wrong. 'Cause in my head, I was, like, 'There's a zero percent chance he'll ever pitch in the big leagues with the Cardinals.' And then he got called up and it was, like, 'That's how I'm going to get to the big leagues.' It's force their hand. Get to Triple-A. Prove I can help, you know? And I think Nick Greenwood making it is the most inspiring."

LaRocque, too, had Greenwood in mind when he discussed Baker with me in September 2014: "Can Corey Baker be another Nick Greenwood for us? Absolutely, if he continues to grow and develop. Mo, our GPS, told me about a month before we called him up, 'We're going to need some relievers who can stretch, go long innings, maybe even spot start. So we discussed who we had at Triple-A, and soon enough Nick got the call.

"I tell the older guys, in the lower levels, it's about projection and talent. Once you get to Double-, Triple-A, it's about production, period. How your fastball moves in the zone. Once you get to Double-, Triple-A, it's time to get outs. We don't just plan a path for future stars. We have a plan, a way forward, for everybody in our system.

"We thought that Corey deserved it. We knew we had an opening for a start that week, and we wanted to make sure Corey got that chance."

So Baker continues on, battling the odds, with that vision of Busch Stadium in his mind. "I don't know if it'll happen with the Cardinals, but I hope it does," Baker said. "But I don't think I'd be playing if I didn't think I could see it anymore. Minor league baseball is an awesome job and a great experience, but I'm not playing minor league baseball to play minor league baseball. So I think if I couldn't see myself in St. Louis, I would probably end my career."

For Oscar Taveras, the results on the field in 2014 were mixed. His first call-up in May lasted just under two weeks before he returned to Memphis. He came up on July 1 for good, and on July 31, Mozeliak traded away Allen Craig to open up right field for Taveras. Still, though, Taveras wasn't hitting in St. Louis the way he had at each minor league level. Matheny would sit him at times (with Mozeliak's full support), infuriating the Cardinal fan base, with a long-term goal of trying to instill better habits into Taveras ahead of what everybody hoped would be a long career in St. Louis.

Yet, Taveras hit a game-tying home run in Game 2 of the NLCS against the Giants. After rounding the bases, he slapped hands with all of his teammates except for one: Carlos Martínez, his fellow Dominican, who gave him a half chest bump, half hug.

"My one takeaway for Oscar this year is I hope you learned a lot," Mozeliak told me on October 23, 2014. "I hope he saw how Matt Carpenter, Matt Holliday, work every day. And he realizes, well, if they have to do it, maybe I should. There is that cultural expectation of how we play the game up here. And if a young player does not quite understand that, it's not the end of the world. But they better learn it quick."

Mozeliak made it clear this wasn't some kind of Cardinals holier-than-thou attitude. Your starting right fielder should be a defensive asset for some pretty sound reasons. And the Cardinals have a clubhouse built around certain principles, making for a difficult fit should Taveras earn a regular spot in the lineup.

"I don't want to feel like that there's only one type of player that can play here," Mozeliak said, "because that's not true. But we do look for players that do carry high character or have regard for high character. But we also are looking for really good baseball players. Talented players. And one of the fundamental things that we try to do as we're developing players in the minor leagues or recruiting or scouting to bring into our system, we try to have common threads. But we make mistakes. It's not all perfect. And the moment we start acting like we have it perfect, it's probably going to blow up on us. So that's why we're hesitant to do that now. Some would say it's also one of those things that continually need to be nurtured or evolving. And we don't act internally as if we've got this thing figured out. We're always pushing the envelope just to figure out a way to do it a little better, a little more efficiently, a little more effectively."

The Cardinals have a standard they try to reach, and no one is more aware of the possibility of human error, that those standards won't always be reached by players or even the front office than the Cardinals.

The Cardinals planned to have Oscar Taveras return to Jupiter in November, begin a training regimen, and get in the kind of shape come spring training that would make it clear to Mozeliak on down that he was ready to be a Cardinal.

"I think the defining time for Oscar is going to be the next four months, frankly," Mozeliak said on October 23. "It's not to say that it's irreparable, where he couldn't, again, find a way to fix it. But I will say we've been pretty clear on what our expectations of him are when he shows up in spring training, so it would be quite defiant if he didn't do it."

As I listen back to this conversation, John Mozeliak sounds like a disappointed father. Just days later, he sounded like a grieving father.

Oscar Taveras was driving with his eighteen-year-old girlfriend, Edilia Arvelo, at home in the Dominican Republic. Edilia had just instagrammed a photo of the two of them, smiling, in the car. Taveras had been drinking. He lost control of the vehicle and crashed. Both Taveras and Arvelo were killed. Taveras was twenty-two.

"We were absolutely stunned to learn this last night," Mozeliak said from the Dominican Republic on October 27. "My first thought was 'Could this be true?' To see Oscar a week and a half ago, so full of life, and then to see this end so tragically in a car accident. I'm utterly shocked and saddened.

"When you think about how much has been written about him, how much has been spoken about him, and he never got to show it at the major league level."

By January 2015, Mozeliak had had a chance to think about Taveras, about what had happened, about what, if anything, he could have done to prevent the tragedy.

"I'm going to answer this in how I feel," Mozeliak said. "I have thought about it a lot. And my biggest takeaway from this is—and perhaps this is what we focus more on moving forward—is taking responsibility or ownership for yourself. Because we can certainly explain to you the risks. We can certainly try to position you to not make poor decisions. In the end, you decide what decisions you make.

"He could have had that same accident in Jupiter, Florida. And what did he do that day that was wrong? He drove too fast. May have been tired. Had alcohol. I mean, all these things factor into that outcome. And when you think about children or players or young players and you're trying to mitigate risk for them, it's all we can do. Is try to explain to them what these things can lead to.

"My saying to my kids all the time is 'Nothing good happens after midnight.' There's a reason for that statement. 'Cause nothing ever does. And isn't that a limit, though, of what a parent can do? Isn't that a limit of what an employer can do? Isn't that a limit of what a baseball team can do? I mean, I'm looking at this holistically in the sense of, how do you prevent these things? And frankly, it's about education and it's something that we do provide. And candidly, we understood who Oscar was. He was in the higher-risk category than others. That's why we wanted him to come to Jupiter in November. But when you look back at something like this, it still comes back down to the decisions people make."

An overwhelming sorrow blanketed everything Mozeliak said about Taveras. He wasn't talking about personal responsibility as a means of avoiding blame for what happened to Taveras—just the opposite. He'd spent the months since Taveras died searching for a way to prevent the next Taveras, or the next Josh Hancock, a Cardinals pitcher who'd killed himself while driving drunk back in 2007. Mozeliak's sadness was for Taveras, and for how little Mozeliak believed he could do to prevent the next tragedy.

"And on a personal level, I'm going to talk about it to the entire organization," Mozeliak said. "So we will continue to emphasize this. There needs to be a specific curriculum we develop for our Latin American players. Because it is a different environment there than it is here. It's not to say these things can't happen domestically. But just the way that their infrastructure's designed, we have to be a little more aggressive in how we teach it and how we talk about it for that program."

To lose a twenty-two-year-old man, no matter who he is, is heartbreaking enough. But it is impossible to be a baseball fan and not feel the loss of Oscar Taveras on a sporting level as well. A young man with talent like Taveras's simply doesn't come along often. Sometimes, not always, it is the precursor of someone transcendent. We'll never know whether Taveras could have done that, or if he would have fallen short while providing windows into what that talent might have been.

All there will be are memories of that vast, untapped potential that excited everyone who saw it, everyone who knew him. All else is lost, just as Taveras himself is lost to his family and friends forever.

The Cardinals Way is to communicate constantly, to express goals, in the hope that it will ultimately benefit a baseball team, but that process forges friendships that last for decades, and a family atmosphere that is palpable to everyone in the organization, and to millions who view it from the outside.

Not every family can save every member. The Cardinals know the fallibility of what they do. Oscar Taveras provided a particularly poignant reminder of this. And there'd be another reminder to come.

EPILOGUE: TRANSITION AND THE IRREPLACEABLE CARDINAL

There are no true counterfactuals.

We cannot go back in time and see what would have happened if Bill DeWitt hadn't hired Jeff Luhnow in September 2003 and given him broad powers that steadily increased. We cannot know what Walt Jocketty would have done had he continued the path he'd been using, successfully, to make the Cardinals into consistent winners. We cannot see how the Cardinals' path would have shifted if John Mozeliak, fed up with infighting, had left in 2005. We'll never know how the Cardinals, and baseball at large, would have responded to Jeff Luhnow, general manager, back in 2007, rather than in 2011, a huge time difference in the industry's embrace of analytics.

There are no true alternate histories. The definitive study of such things, Michael J. Fox's 1985 film *Back to the Future*, tells us so.

But as 2015 dawned, the dispersal of the principals in power during the great Cardinals' restoration of the past decade to the Branch Rickey ideal allows us to see, within limits such as revenue and ownership support, a number of those differing paths.

The John Mozeliak Cardinals entered their eighth season. Oscar Taveras

Epilogue

was gone. The team planned a uniform patch to memorialize him in 2015. They would build a baseball field in his hometown: Oscar Taveras Field. Carlos Martínez changed his uniform number to 18, in Taveras's honor, and said he planned to wear 18 for the rest of his career. Mozeliak went out and traded for another right fielder—Jason Heyward, from Atlanta. Mozeliak gave up Shelby Miller and Tyrell Jenkins, draft/development products surplus to needs. Heyward had one year left on his contract when the Cardinals acquired him, and they gave him the Matt Holliday treatment—let him spend some time with the Cardinals, see what it is to play in St. Louis, then decide on his future. Heyward joined the Cardinals Caravan, the traveling Cardinals who meet with fans all over the wide swatch of Midwestern territory where Cardinals fans were seeded thanks to the reach of KMOX.

It was a two-way mirror. The fans got to know Heyward. Heyward got to know the fans.

But Mozeliak declined to spend big money on a starting pitcher. Instead, international scouting's Carlos Martínez and draft product Marco Gonzales would do nicely for a fifth-starter battle, with Martínez earning the job out of spring training, and becoming the team's best pitcher by August 2015.

The Walt Jocketty Reds entered their eighth season. For Jocketty, the language on analytics had changed, though it would be impossible to fully document how much of that was reflected in the way the Reds do business, and how much of it reflects the changing baseball landscape between 2007 and 2015.

"Well, I think it was something that was part of [my thinking]," Jocketty told me in January 2015 of incorporating analytics into what the Reds do. "They were working on their own system at the time, but it was just very primitive. And we worked to advance it."

But while Jocketty himself had been a major impediment to the Cardinals' implementation of Luhnow's suggestions, Jocketty just five years later tried to bulk up the analytics side of the Reds operations. When asked whether the Reds had offered any resistance, Jocketty said, "Not really. There wasn't a lot of convincing to do to change people's mind-set. We were going to find a way to blend the two together. And I think everybody was okay with that."

Meanwhile, the Arizona Diamondbacks hired Tony La Russa in May 2014 to oversee baseball operations. La Russa, in case you had any doubts about how he felt on the Jocketty/Luhnow split, hired Dave Stewart as general manager. In January 2015, Stewart said, relative to his pursuit of free agent pitcher James Shields:

"I think James is a throwback guy by the way he goes about his business and the innings he pitches. I think the fact that Tony [La Russa] is here and that we have more baseball people—he probably sees us as a true baseball team versus some of the other teams out here that are geared more toward analytics and those type of things."[1]

Leaving aside the problematic notion inherent in the idea of "a true baseball team," nothing could more fully capture how much the ground had shifted since Bill DeWitt brought in Jeff Luhnow less than twelve years earlier. The Diamondbacks intended to make a case that they were unique, essentially, because they weren't embracing analytics. Forget what that might mean for the limitations the Diamondbacks would create for themselves. That's an astonishing statement on just how pervasive data had become, in a short time, within baseball.

The Houston Astros entered their fourth season with Jeff Luhnow as general manager and Sig Mejdal as director of decision sciences.

It was a rough 2014, at least publicly, for the Astros. They did improve 19 games over 2013, finishing at 70-92. A battle over television rights cost the franchise tens of millions of dollars.

In May 2014, Astros beat reporter Evan Drellich published a piece that described the view of the Astros around baseball this way:

> The Astros have become one of baseball's most progressive franchises as they try to rebuild and avoid a fourth consecutive 100-loss season.

Epilogue

But general manager Jeff Luhnow's radical approach to on-field changes and business decisions has created at least pockets of internal discontent and a potential reputation problem throughout baseball.

"They are definitely the outcast of Major League Baseball right now, and it's kind of frustrating for everyone else to have to watch it," said former Astros pitcher Bud Norris, now with Baltimore. "When you talk to agents, when you talk to other players and you talk amongst the league, yeah, there's going to be some opinions about it, and they're not always pretty."

The criticism, through interviews with more than 20 players, coaches, agents and others, comes in two parts:

On the field, the Astros shift their defenders into unusual positions to counteract hitter tendencies more than any other team, including in the minor leagues. They schedule minor league starting pitchers on altered and fluctuating rotation schedules, what they call a "modified tandem" system, a development strategy unique in baseball.

Off the field, the Astros are said to handle contract negotiations and the timing of player promotions with a dehumanizing, analytics-based approach detected by some across their operation.[2]

Drellich, an excellent reporter and anything but hostile to analytics, drilled down into what remained of the hostility toward Luhnow and his ideas within the industry. (Or so we thought, prior to June 2015.)

Then negotiations broke down with Astros top pick Brady Aiken, and Aiken ultimately went unsigned. The extent to which the pool links all negotiations with draft picks spilled over into public view as well: the reduced slot money after not signing Aiken meant that to sign Jacob Nix, the team's fifth-rounder, the Astros would have had to exceed their pool and forfeit a future draft pick.

There was plenty of positive press, too: a *Sports Illustrated* cover story called the Astros "Your 2017 World Series Champs," and *Bloomberg Businessweek* went long on Luhnow and Mejdal, though oddly focused exclusively on the data, essentially providing half the equation of a maturing organization steadily adding Luhnow people on the player-development and scouting sides.

So what's followed in 2015 looks awfully similar for Luhnow's Astros to what 2011 was for Luhnow's Cardinals—contending, the integration of young players Luhnow drafted like shortstop Carlos Correa, and a hasty retreat from critics unable to argue with the results. Vindication. Again.

"I do think that when you're in an organization, and you're doing things for the long-term, it often takes a long time for those things to manifest itself," Luhnow said to me in August 2015. "And in the meantime, it is difficult to be patient, and defend yourself. The longer it takes, the critics line up. We had a lot of that in St. Louis. And last year in Houston, we had a rough year, with the things that happened. It takes a lot not to react at the time, and believe you're doing the right thing. And ultimately, over time, you hope that things work out. I think there's an analogy, between the Cardinals players who began to filter in and help the team, same thing, a lot of the strategies we employed in Houston that people criticized are coming to fruition and helping the ballclub. So yeah, there's some satisfaction in that."

One fascinating aspect of this antipathy to Luhnow came from treating the Astros' doing things differently as an inherent weakness, not a strength. A rival executive said to me of the Aiken issue, "I mean, that wouldn't happen in twenty-nine other organizations."

The question is this: Should the Astros, should any team, *want* to do things like the other twenty-nine? Baseball is an industry where nearly the entire advantage Luhnow once brought to the Cardinals, with Luhnow and Mejdal shocking both themselves and Bill DeWitt by quantifying just how much analytics would give them an edge in the draft, has disappeared.

"To answer your question, the gap's almost gone," Mozeliak told me in October 2014. "And that's because twenty-nine other teams are aggressively trying to get smarter. And [compared to where] we were from an analytical standpoint, there's not too many teams that have an advantage in making

Epilogue

decisions than others. There might be a small one in how teams do that, but overall I think that the playing field is much more level. But that's where aggressive teams or teams willing to take risks have advantages now. And there's just far less fruit to grab than there was ten years ago."

Everybody I talked to echoed this—DeWitt, Luhnow, Mejdal.

"Part of it, I wonder, is—because Jeff is a modern manager so he revealed what we were doing to the scouts," Mejdal said. "To not only keep them inspired, but perhaps to encourage them to question convention. What they're doing. To make the system transparent. But you know how scouts go between organizations. So some of it may have come about because of that. I don't know. There's, perhaps, the press. I think when I got hired, there probably weren't but a few other teams that had analysts. And now, I think every team has analysts. So, I think it's just a case of it making it to the top of the list of the analysts, perhaps."

If anything, that the Cardinals—who in the eyes of so many old-school baseball people represented the platonic ideal of old ideas—succeeded by becoming data-driven limited how much the critics could go after Luhnow for doing it.

"I'm not sure this is the fault of anyone in the A's, but I mean, I think we've been pretty quiet about [our success]—I guess it's the whole boastful thing," Chris Correa said to me in January 2015. "A lot of people in the game viewed *Moneyball* as, for a lack of a better term, being boastful, right? That they had sort of outsmarted everyone. And I don't really feel like that's been the message that we've ever tried to promote."

It was true. From DeWitt on down, the concern throughout my time reporting this book was the polar opposite of what I'm used to experiencing in the midst of reporting. The Cardinals don't believe they've figured out anything, nothing permanent, nothing that won't require continual innovation to stay ahead of the competition. The pushback came not when anything negative came up—the principals themselves often brought up their failings along the way—but, rather, against the idea that the team had created anything like a bulletproof methodology for building a baseball team.

"I don't really feel like that's been the message that we've ever tried to promote," Correa continued back in January 2015. "I think, if anything, we've tried to be very quiet, close to the vest, about our decision-making processes and even what we're trying to accomplish here. In some ways it's too bad you're writing a book about it. I don't think that we should pretend that we have all the answers. We've been very fortunate to have some success. I think that a lot of our core decision-making processes are pretty sound, but at the same time, there are a lot of smart people all over the game trying to get better, and we'll see. We're going to do our best to make sure that we're the best that we possibly can be over the next decade."

They've done it without Luhnow and Mejdal since 2011. A cursory look at the team's top ten prospects as of January 2015 reveals that of the ten, only two—outfielder Charlie Tilson and pitcher Sam Tuivailala—had been acquired before Luhnow left for Houston. The other eight came during the Dan Kantrovitz era of drafting, five of them through that draft (Marco Gonzales, Stephen Piscotty, Rob Kaminsky, Jack Flaherty, Tim Cooney), two via amateur international signings (Alex Reyes, Magneuris Sierra) and one via trade (Randal Grichuk).

Accordingly, Correa assured me that if there was one thing he and his staff weren't worried about, it was the Houston Astros.

"Nothing is the same as it was three or four years ago when Jeff left or Sig left," Correa said in January 2015. "I mean, it's all an updated and new—and we hope it's all better. I mean, I'm sure they're making improvements, too, to the point that they want to be, you know, better than all the other teams. But I really don't think it's all that productive for me to be worrying about what other teams are doing."

So. About that. In June 2015, Michael S. Schmidt of *The New York Times* revealed that "Front-office personnel for the St. Louis Cardinals, one of the most successful teams in baseball over the past two decades, are under in-

Epilogue

vestigation by the F.B.I. and Justice Department prosecutors, accused of hacking into an internal network of the Houston Astros to steal closely guarded information about players."[3]

Correa had said this to me in January 2015: "I've had a lot of people ask me and frankly I was a little afraid you were going to ask me, 'cause I'm a little tired of this. How are we going to survive now that Sig and Jeff left for Houston? How are we going to survive now that Dan's left? We have a great group of people here. We have a great group of people here, and frankly I'm not even interested in recreating whatever success we've had from past years because I think we can do better."

In July 2015, the Cardinals dismissed Correa after a team-imposed leave of absence. Further comments on it were neither forthcoming nor legally permissable: the investigation was ongoing. Suddenly, the intellectual throughline from that three-man group, Jeff, Sig, and Dan, had a significant rupture. And exactly how fully the Cardinals needed to rebuild it, or even start it anew, remained a great unknown to even the Cardinals themselves as this book went to press. Correa was to be the replacement for Kantrovitz, the hometown front office star who left for Oakland back in November 2014.

Here's how Dan's departure went down. The Los Angeles Dodgers, another customer for analytics, lured Andrew Friedman away from the Tampa Bay Rays.

Friedman needed a GM, and hired Farhan Zaidi, previously the assistant GM in Oakland.

That meant Billy Beane needed an assistant GM, something Mozeliak realized at the GM meetings out in Phoenix in November.

"And so I was walking back, late afternoon, with Billy and David [Forst] and I kind of joked, 'Are you guys going to come after Dan now?'" Mozeliak recalled. "And Billy candidly said that, yeah, he's someone that he's thinking about, but hasn't made any decisions yet."

But the fit was obvious. Kantrovitz had excelled as scouting director, but he'd also been Oakland's head of international. Mozeliak had him involved in other areas, too, making him a generalist as well as a specialist.

"The transition was so quick, but it was not without emotion," Kantrovitz told me in January 2015. "St. Louis will always be my home and where I grew up. But the truth is Oakland feels more like my baseball home. I had just completed a three-year extension with Bill and Mo and was not planning to leave. But when Billy calls, it's tough to say no."

The man at the other end of the table back in June at the regional scouting meetings moved on as well. Charlie Gonzalez, who'd never imagined a career in baseball, was hired by Jeff Luhnow as a special assistant. Suddenly, his trips weren't just around Florida—his dress shirt hanging in the back window of his car to keep it unwrinkled—but in planes flying all over Latin America.

Back in September 2014, Luhnow said, "There are people that really don't like Charlie Gonzalez."

Oz Ocampo, Luhnow's director of international, responded, "I love Charlie!"

Luhnow nodded, indicating that he did as well, saying, "I think that he's an acquired taste. For sure. Because he can be a little overbearing. I'll put it this way: if he weren't able to produce the number of big leaguers that he's been able to produce, he would have been fired a long time ago. Because he's a high-maintenance guy. He is the definition of high maintenance."

Two months later, Luhnow brought the definition of high maintenance to the Astros.

"He and I didn't really keep in touch very much after I left," Luhnow told me in January 2015. "Would see him at a game here or there. But after we lost two of our senior scouts—Marc Russo to run Atlanta's international, and David Post went to become a special assistant in San Diego—we felt we needed some heft in our scouting department and wanted to maybe find someone who was ready to be a national cross-checker.

"I thought through all the scouts that I've known throughout my career.

Epilogue

And Charlie clearly has the passion for it, the track record. So we requested permission. It was not an easy conversation because several Cardinals have come over, as you know. They were reluctant to lose him. But we were able to interview him and bring him over here, and he really is playing a pretty important role for us."

Luhnow is right—there's certainly annoyance in some corners back in St. Louis about the number of Cardinals he's taken to Houston. Gonzalez is merely the latest. Ace Adams, too, joined the Astros, working under Brent Strom, another Cardinals coach turned Astros coach. Mike Elias, Houston's scouting director, Ocampo also worked for Luhnow in St. Louis.

"All the people who came over to Houston from St. Louis are people that I'd hired originally in St. Louis," Luhnow pointed out in August 2015. "Mike Elias and Brent Strom and so on. And not all of them were so welcome the whole time they were in St. Louis, either. To a certain extent, I felt like—not that I was abandoning them by leaving, but a lot of the promises I'd made to them about what we'd be doing over there—now I was leaving them to fend for themselves.

"For example, in the case of Brent Strom, I really felt as if he should be a major league pitching coach. And I didn't feel like that was going to happen in St. Louis. And I had hired him originally, and he had gone through a lot of resistance, some of the things he teaches and how he teaches. I did feel somewhat responsible, and probably appreciated his value more than others do because I'm the one who originally hired him. And the same thing applies to Sig, and Mike Elias. The Cardinals could have made Mike Elias scouting director instead of Dan and I wouldn't have had a shot at him. But they didn't, and so I felt partially responsible for his career, appreciate his value, and I brought him over."

But what Charlie Gonzalez in specific also represents, both in St. Louis and now in Houston, is the greatest possible rebuke to the idea that there isn't room for a significant human element within a data-driven organization.

The Cardinals have every scout in their draft room. But ultimately, the ideal is that the scouting reports are incorporated into STOUT, not overriding it. A scout pounding the table, to use the old baseball cliché for a scout advocating forcefully for his player, is nothing more than double-counting what the scout is saying. If Charlie Gonzalez or any other Cardinals scout submitted a report high on a player, that information was already part of the team's complete evaluation of a player, just like his statistical history, his mechanics, his medical history.

And saying that Charlie Gonzalez would pound the table for his players doesn't even begin to describe it. Charlie Gonzalez's existence is pounding the table for whatever he believes in. Plenty of people, even in St. Louis, where he'd seen success, didn't like it.

Perhaps the Luhnow-Gonzalez reunion makes sense: a pair of baseball men going about things differently from those who came before them, missing the typical baseball pedigree and path.

Baseball traditionalists might still object to the Astros, even with Gonzalez. But it became impossible to claim the Astros were somehow immune to human subjectivity. Luhnow faced this issue, actually, with his analytics team—making some draft picks that the scouts loved, but his emerging system didn't, to help keep the peace. Even Kantrovitz would do this from time to time—an accommodation for his scouts, who were spending an obscene amount of time on the road, traveling great distances to procure, ultimately, the tiny sliver of information that would give the Cardinals an edge when that draft started.

"You sometimes allow things into your decision making that when we're actually talking about the fundamental principles of the draft, you'd be steadfast on them," Mozeliak said in January 2015. "This is how we make decisions. But we saw some leakage [of subjectivity] in how we were picking players the last couple of years. And I would imagine even with someone like Correa, who's probably a little more disciplined to the process, you're going to see a little there, too. And that's just human nature. There's that human element that I don't think any system could ignore unless you don't have them in the room."

Then came Correa's firing. And suddenly, Mozeliak needed to rethink a fundamental challenge to how the Cardinals would move forward in a position that made most of the final calls as gatekeeper for the players entering the Cardinals' development system. The hiring of Correa, as Mozeliak acknowledged, was a huge bet on analytics over pure scouting, since Correa had no such experience. Would his replacement have a similar résumé? Could Mozeliak continue to empower the analytics department, when the greatest public embarrassment the Cardinals had faced, perhaps ever, originated out of that very department?

"No it has not but finding the right person may be difficult," Mozeliak told me when asked if his willingness to empower the analytics team had changed following the scandal in August 2015. "Finding someone with a more balanced background may make the transition easier when trying to move forward.

For Mozeliak, it is time to build a coalition once again. FDR's broke apart, let's not forget. The South left the Democrats behind eventually. Civil Rights tore the party apart. By 1948, four major candidates for president included three who were once FDR Democrats: Harry Truman, Henry Wallace, and Strom Thurmond. Truman won, however. Mozeliak has excelled at this kind of team-building for his entire career. Now he needs to do it again, at a time few expected it. Mozeliak said he wouldn't consider changing that basic setup, with scouts and analysts together in the draft room on draft night—it helps with quick answers to signability questions, and more significantly, it is vital for morale, which was clear back in June when Almaraz pointed it out. Don't underestimate the loss of Chris Correa when evaluating how the Cardinals have operated over the past few seasons. So much of Correa's background, from analytics to psychology, have been key drivers in how the Cardinals operate. And now, with many of those who trained Correa and Correa himself gone, how the Cardinals move forward becomes more complicated than simply promoting the next person in line.

"It's our job to continue building our baseball operations department," DeWitt told me in August 2015. "It has been diluted to a degree but you can be sure that it will be replenished and as robust as ever."

Added Mozeliak: "Loss of quality employees is always a concern and like all companies we face challenges with retention. Creating a rewarding working environment [so] that individuals can grow within is our goal."

So what happened? It's something the key figures in this drama that's played out over the past dozen years, leading to some of the greatest success of any baseball organization in baseball history, profess to still be in the dark about.

Luhnow remembers the shock he experienced as he gradually discovered that not only was someone with his former employer responsible for the hacking, but within the very group that he'd founded, like Frankenstein's Monster turning on its creator (though Frankenstein's Monster never had nearly this much success in the draft).

"It's a fair point," Luhnow said in August 2015. "It's the last thing I expected. When I found out that someone had illegally accessed our information, I didn't know what I thought it was, but the last thing I expected was it would be a Major League Baseball team, especially one I had worked with. It was shocking and disappointing."

And yet, it is important to distinguish this schism from the one Luhnow faced early in his Cardinals' tenure. The people who served as his biggest impediments upon his arrival simply wouldn't have thought to hack a database. Many of them wouldn't be caught dead in front of a computer. So something else, something beyond divergent worldviews, drove this hacking.

"I think there may be some resentment/jealousy/some other unhealthy stuff that led to this happening," Luhnow said. "I don't think it had anything to do with a philosophical approach on how to make good decisions. I think

Epilogue

they're all on the same page about that—get good information, and make decisions based off of that."

Mozeliak said he was in spring training in Jupiter in February 2015 when he was informed of the investigation and all that came with it: "Needless to say, I was shocked and had many questions."

For DeWitt, the moment had to be especially painful. It was his relationship with Luhnow that drove so much of what's resulted in the past dozen years for the St. Louis Cardinals. The two men hold each other in the highest esteem, even after all that's transpired.

"My first thought was total disbelief," DeWitt recalled in August 2015. "I thought that the alleged activity, if true, goes against everything I believe in. I have always tried to surround myself with smart people who do things the right way. I had and still have a great relationship with Jeff. I know that he knows I would never allow this type of activity."

And Luhnow said of DeWitt, unprompted, in August 2015: "I have a tremendous amount of respect for Bill DeWitt, and I think he's a class act. He would never condone, or be involved in anything like this. I think he's a great man, and he's done great things for this organization."

Still, Luhnow did not underestimate the challenge facing his former club: "They've got some big decisions to make—who's going to be scouting director, is there any more fallout from this. I don't know [what will happen], but I do believe Bill is very concerned about the Cardinals doing the right thing at all times. So I do have high confidence that he's going to do the right thing."

So it is left to DeWitt and Mozeliak to continue building the way they always have. Each of them expressed the belief that this hacking will not, ultimately, impact their legacies, or the long-term view of the ballclub. Whatever the ultimate changes that come from the FBI investigation, any action Major League Baseball takes, and any further alterations to the Cardinals made by Mozeliak and DeWitt themselves, the continuity at the very top of the organization remains in place.

"I would say just from a very high level that this organization is built for the future" Mozeliak said in January 2015. "And obviously pulling me out of the equation here, I would say that from a baseball standpoint, I feel really confident about the leadership we have in place for many years to come. And when I think about having that sustained success, the one thing that you think about with the St. Louis Cardinals over the last twenty years is one owner, two general managers, and two managers."

That one owner, Bill DeWitt, now enters his twentieth year in charge of the Cardinals. He's at the top of his profession in every measurable way. The Cardinals are the model organization for the rest of baseball, something the scandal hasn't changed. (Though don't sleep on the Astros, especially if they win in October, as the new paradigm. That's just how baseball works.) He led the search committee to find the new commissioner, and the person they chose, Rob Manfred, quickly replaced seven of the eight members of the powerful owners' Executive Council.

The member remaining? Bill DeWitt.

A full accounting of the Cardinals' success since he arrived reinforces that there's ultimately a single constant. The Cardinals, since 1996, won with the twentieth-century model, under Walt Jocketty, and the twenty-first-century model, under John Mozeliak. They won with an older, experienced field manager in Tony La Russa, and a young manager in Mike Matheny. They won under collective bargaining agreements that emphasized free agency, and those that emphasized player development and leveled the financial playing field. They won in the old Busch Stadium and they won the new Busch Stadium. They won before and during a hacking scandal that put the organization in an unfamiliar, notorious light, and the smart money says they'll keep on winning after the investigations and headlines from it all have faded.

Bill DeWitt has been the constant.

DeWitt turned seventy-four in August 2015. His son, Bill DeWitt III, has been learning under him just as DeWitt Jr. once learned the baseball business from DeWitt Sr., the Branch Rickey protégé.

Epilogue

DeWitt Sr., near the end of his life, joined Bill Veeck as an investor in Veeck's purchase of the Chicago White Sox. Longtime St. Louis baseball writer Bob Broeg said of the return of DeWitt Sr., then seventy-four, to the game: "In recent times, DeWitt has served as a member of the baseball Hall of Fame's Committee on Veterans. But, like Veeck, he has been like a kid outside the candy store with his nose pressed against the window. Not now, though."[4]

Just as his father stayed in baseball through the end of his life, DeWitt Jr. can't conceive of doing anything else. Reflecting on his tenure in September 2014, he said:

"I can't say what I really expected twenty years would look like, but I feel good about how it's all occurred and where we are. I will say this: I did feel back in 1996, when we bought the team, that we could build an organization that had every opportunity to be successful. You have to have a lot of good fortune to go along with it. That's for sure. But I felt confident that, given our fan base and given the Cardinals franchise and brand, it was incumbent upon us to build on it, enhance it, and maintain it as best we could. And we have made every effort to do that."

When it comes to succession, both DeWitts look at the future in the same way.

"I would think he would," DeWitt Jr. said of DeWitt III succeeding him someday. "I think he views himself at this point as an all-in baseball guy for his career. You never know when things could change, but that's clearly his view today." Mozeliak, with his office right next to DeWitt III's, has noticed this as well:

"Big Bill is still very active. But I will say my relationship with Billy continues to grow. And I make sure that I share with him on how we think about decisions because obviously his energy is more on the business side. But in a way, it's like a minitutorial for him from time to time. I have talked to Big Bill about this and I certainly understand the long-term planning."

I asked Mozeliak if the succession plan is similar to what he's tried to build in every department throughout the organization.

"I would say that's comparable. I mean, obviously he's been working for this club for some time now, and his exposure to all the different areas is acutely high. From a day-to-day baseball standpoint, I mostly speak with his father. But that's not to say we don't grab lunch or stop by one another's office from time to time and chat. I mean, we're only separated by a wall, so we do see each other."

That future comes with expectations unlike those for virtually any other baseball team, thanks to all the consistent success. It also comes, with the disruption of the hacking scandal, with some of the biggest challenges DeWitt has faced since he altered the underlying structure of the Cardinals back in 2003. It comes back to precisely what DeWitt was betting when, back in 2003, he hired Luhnow to, as his memo put it, "take advantage of the inefficient market." And as Mozeliak pointed out, the success on the field cannot flag while they weather it all.

"The St. Louis Cardinals can't blow something up," Mozeliak said. "Our expectations here, I mean, I would get run up a flagpole. Bill would get sent down the Mississippi. It's just not practical. This is more of a cultural level of expectation. I've always said that the one thing about working in St. Louis is they demand winning.

"And that's the one thing that—like, my peers always make fun of me. They're, like, 'Ah, it's an easy job here in St. Louis.' But it's really not."

So now, even as the St. Louis Cardinals battle a changed, more intelligent competitive atmosphere that they helped create, they have a hundred years of success to live up to as well. DeWitt knows it's up to his team to find the next innovation, the next logical extension of Branch Rickey's work, to make sure that the next George Kissell is managing in the minor league system, that the next Stan Musial, Albert Pujols, or Oscar Taveras is progressing through that system, that the money is there to sign that next great Cardinals hero long-term, after drafting him or trading for him.

A new TV deal with Fox Sports Midwest, reported by Derrick Goold in

Epilogue

July 2015[5] to have a value of more than $1 billion over the next 15 years, should help with the latter, and DeWitt acknowledged to Goold that spending would go up accordingly, a frightening thought for the rest of baseball, who struggled to keep up with the Cardinals when funded by a below-market TV deal.

As long as the Cardinals keep progressing, every team trying to chase and catch them—and there are many smart organizations—aren't just keeping even. Twenty-nine other teams have hundred years of foundation to build before they can surpass what Branch Rickey passed on through Bill DeWitt Sr. and George Kissell to Bill DeWitt Jr., Jeff Luhnow, and John Mozeliak in St. Louis.

"We're going to continue to make every effort to keep the Cardinals a top-tier franchise in every way," DeWitt said, "whether it's the best facilities for a minor league player, or a state-of-the-art ballpark in St. Louis. Clearly, on the field is where it all ends up mattering. We will keep striving to do the best possible job. That's the goal. Whether we can maintain the level of success we have had remains to be seen. We stress over every ball game but always look three to five years out as well. The first thing I do every morning is check the minor league game reports from the day before, to find out how our prospects are performing and developing."

DeWitt leaned back in his chair as we sat and talked in a New York restaurant in September 2014. As Mozeliak said to me, "It's good to be Bill DeWitt." A play-off-filled October beckoned, the fourth in a row. So, too, was the difficult calendar year to come, filled with the Taveras tragedy, the hacking scandal, but all set against the backdrop of one of the finest runs any baseball team has ever enjoyed. In retrospect, it's not surprising that a visionary like Bill DeWitt, who saw 2015 as a graduate student in 1965, issued a note of caution at that moment.

He's also the best reason to bet on the St. Louis Cardinals in the years to come. "Well, I always say enjoy the moment because baseball can be cyclical, and we all know what can happen if you get injuries to key players, or prospects who are coming up are not as good as you thought. I do think our decision-making process, which continually evolves, has been good, and it has enabled us to have success. But it doesn't necessarily mean that success will continue, and that's the beauty of baseball."

Acknowledgments

A book such as this one cannot happen without the help of so many people along the way. I felt a great responsibility to tell this story properly, and that only increased as I had the privilege of seeing this organization up close across the country, from the very beginning of the player-development system right through to Busch Stadium.

The extent to which the Cardinals opened their organization to me was remarkable at the time, and even now as I reflect upon it. This came from a desire to allow me to fully tell the story of how the Cardinals remade themselves, but from ownership on down, the Cardinals didn't shy away from any question or any period. If anything, their reluctance came during discussions about the team's greatest advances.

This starts with Bill DeWitt, who was so generous with his time, his memories, and his careful documentation of a life spent within baseball. That he could spend so many hours in interviews with me in person, on the phone, and via e-mail while simultaneously running a major league ball club and leading the search for a new commissioner of baseball simply amazed me. It was a pleasure to get to know him as I worked on this book.

The same is true of the executives for the Cardinals during this time. Dan Kantrovitz found answers to the most obscure questions I had, ranging from

Acknowledgments

his initial impressions of long-before-drafted players to his experience in high school with Jon Hamm. John Mozeliak didn't shy away from any premise I presented to him and applied the macro thinking he uses as general manager to larger themes within the book.

I'm also thankful to all those with the Cardinals who not only let me observe them working, but would stop and answer questions I had, including Gary LaRocque, Matt Slater, Tim Leveque, Mark DeJohn, Oliver Marmol, Steve Turco, Ramon "Smoky" Ortiz, Ace Adams, Tony Ferreira, Chris Correa, John Mabry, Derek Lilliquist. and Mike Matheny.

This book also owes a great deal to the help and memories of Jeff Luhnow, Sig Mejdal, and Charlie Gonzalez, all of whom work for the Astros now, all of whom are fascinating in dramatically different ways.

Thank you also to Walt Jocketty, Terry Collins, Tony La Russa, Willie McGee, Whitey Herzog, and many others who shed light on the Cardinals in ways large and small.

A huge thank-you to the players who helped me tell this story: Corey Baker, Chris Rivera, Sam Tuivailala, Rowan Wick, Nick Thompson, and Daniel Poncedeleon. Thank you to many other players who shared details or their personal stories with me as well, on or off the record.

I'm hugely grateful to all those who talked to me about George Kissell, particularly Tommy Kidwell, George's grandson, who simply opened his home to me and allowed me an incredible opportunity: unlimited time with George Kissell's papers, which had been sealed since George's death back in 2008. Huge thanks to Joe McEwing, Mike Shannon, Todd Steverson, Robin Ventura, and many others throughout baseball who provided story after story about the impact George had on them.

A special thank-you to Red Schoendienst, who somehow remembers every single moment from his seventy-three years in professional baseball and took me through as many of them as I asked. If this book project had merely given me the chance to get to know Red, it would have been more than satisfying.

Acknowledgments

For insight through both their previous work and conversations during the writing of this book, thank you to Derrick Goold, Evan Drellich, and Bernie Miklasz, excellent baseball scribes.

Thank you to Hilary and Jason Schwartz, my in-laws, for their enthusiastic caretaking of my children during so much of this book process. The book in your hands couldn't have happened without you.

Thank you to the St. Louis Symphony Orchestra radio broadcasts, with hosts Adam Crane and Robert Peterson, and David Robertson's great orchestra, for providing the sound track to so many writing sessions, including the final one for this manuscript.

Thank you to St. Martin's Press: Rob Kirkpatrick, for believing in the project; Emma Stein, for sheperding the project to completion against the clock; Peter Wolverton, for making certain an unexpected man tied to the tracks didn't derail our progress; and Joe Rinaldi, for helping me tell the world about this remarkable story.

To my parents, Myrna and Ira Megdal, I am grateful for giving me the unwavering belief in myself and my judgment and to pursue what matters most to me in life. I am thrilled to have this model to pass on to my children, and that you are both here to show them the way toward that life as well.

To Mirabelle and Juliet, my two young prospects, thank you for an endless supply of happiness, adorable pictures to help get me through my writing, and for all the thrills still to come.

And to Rachel, who never hesitated when I started talking about writing this book, only thought about how to help me make this happen: more today than yesterday. Not as much as tomorrow. It's been lovely, since completing the book, to see you again. You haven't aged a bit.

Notes

Prologue

1. "Matheny Weary of 'Cardinal Way' Slogan," *St. Louis Post-Dispatch,* April 4, 2014.
2. Lee Lowenfish, *Branch Rickey: Baseball's Ferocious Gentleman* (Lincoln: University of Nebraska Press, 2007).

1: The Cardinal Idea

1. Russell A. Carleton, "Why the Cardinal Way Is the Most Important Book in Baseball," *Baseball Prospectus,* March 4, 2014.
2. Donald Ray Andersen, *Branch Rickey and the St. Louis Cardinal Farm System: The Growth of an Idea* (Madison: University of Wisconsin Press, 1976).
3. Steve Steinberg, "Robert Hedges," SABR bio, http://sabr.org/bioproj/person/b91246d7.
4. Andersen, *Branch Rickey and the St. Louis Cardinal Farm System.*
5. Lowenfish, *Branch Rickey.*
6. Andersen, *Branch Rickey and the St. Louis Cardinal Farm System.*
7. William O. DeWitt, interview by William J. Marshall, September 29 and October 1, 1980, A. B. Chandler Oral History Project, University of Kentucky Library.
8. Lowenfish, *Branch Rickey.*
9. DeWitt, interview by Marshall.

2: The Language of George Kissell

1. Mike Wilson, "The Professor of Baseball," *St. Petersburg Times,* March 16, 1997.
2. Joe Strauss, "Cardinals' Kissell Is Honored for Contributions to Baseball," *St. Louis Post-Dispatch,* December 14, 2003.
3. Letter to George Kissell from Randy Voorhees, Mountain Lion Press, December 6, 1994.

Notes

4. Marty Noble, "As Carpenter Trains at Third, Kissell's Legacy Remains," *MLB.com*, March 16, 2014.
5. Warren Corbett, "Earl Weaver," SABR bio, http://sabr.org/bioproj/person/0cfc37e3.
6. Wilson, "Professor of Baseball."

3: Bill DeWitt Jr.

1. Memo from Bill DeWitt Jr. to Francis L. Dale, January 19, 1967.
2. Murray Chass, "Going, Going, Sold: Orioles Auctioned for $173 million," *New York Times*, August 3, 1993.
3. Via the Associated Press.

4: Luhnow Enters

1. Alan Schwarz, *The Numbers Game: Baseball's Lifelong Fascination with Statistics* (St. Martin's Press, 2004).
2. Derrick Goold, "Top Ten Prospects: St. Louis Cardinals," *Baseball America*, November 30, 2007.
3. Woody Allen, *Stand Up Comic, 1964–1968*, Rhino Records, 1999.
4. "UPI 8 Named for Swim Hall of Fame," *Chicago Tribune*, December 9, 1967.
5. Bill Madden, "Walt Jocketty Gets Axed from Cards Because of Numbers Crunch," *New York Daily News*, October 7, 2007.

5: Happy Days Are Here Again

1. Bernie Miklasz, "Check Your Jocketty Conspiracy Theory at the Door," *St. Louis Post-Dispatch*, October 5, 2007.
2. Girsch Michael bio, http://stlouis.cardinals.mlb.com/stl/team/frontoffice_bios/michael_girsch.jsp.
3. Kevin Goldstein, "Future Shock: Organizational Rankings, Part 1," *Baseball Prospectus*, March 8, 2010.
4. Derrick Goold, "Draft Analysis, St. Louis Cardinals," in *Baseball America Prospect Handbook, 2010*, ed. the Editors of *Baseball America* (Baseball America, 2010).
5. Murray Chass, "A Jocketty Jeer for Cardinals," *MurrayChass.com*, September 26, 2010.

6: After He's Gone

1. Derrick Goold, "Cardinals Top Ten Prospects," *Baseball America*, January 14, 2015.
2. Derrick Goold, "Cardinals' Taveras Will Sell Tickets in the Future," *St. Louis Post-Dispatch*, March 18, 2012.
3. B. J. Rains, "Mozeliak Discusses the Future of the Cardinals," *Fox Sports Midwest*, October 25, 2012.
4. Alex Halsted, "Cardinals Calling Up Top Prospect Taveras," *MLB.com*, May 31, 2014.
5. Goold, "Cardinals Top Ten Prospects."

Epilogue: Transition and the Irreplaceable Cardinal

1. Nick Piecoro, "Diamondbacks Still Interested in James Shields, Despite Tight Budget," *Arizona Republic*, January 13, 2015.
2. Evan Drellich, "Radical Methods Paint Astros as 'Outcast,'" *Houston Chronicle*, May 23, 2014.
3. Michael S. Schmidt, "Cardinals Investigated for Hacking Into Astros' Database," *New York Times*, June 16, 2015.
4. Bob Broeg, "Candy-Store Complexes Gone," *Sporting News*, January 3, 1976.
5. Derrick Goold, "Cards, Fox Sports Midwest Reach Lucrative TV Deal," *St. Louis Post-Dispatch*, July 30, 2015.

Index

A-B. *See* Anheuser-Busch
Abreu, José, 184
Adams, Ace, 180–81, 191–92
Adams, Matt, 144–45, 187
advisory board, Luhnow creating, 68
Aiken, Brady, 259–60
Albert, Jeff, 114
Alicea, Luis, 39
Allen, Woody, 97
Almaraz, Joe, 200, 214–15, 226
analytics. *See also* STOUT system
   Chass' disdain for, 160
   free agency strategy incorporating, 153
   hacking scandal and Mozeliak's unwavering approach to, 267–68
   Jocketty finally incorporating, 257–58
   Jocketty's hesitations with, 59, 67–68, 117
   Kantrovitz on Craig and, 96–97
   Luhnow's mandate with, 66–67
   Mejdal on methodologies for, 96
   Mejdal preparing for draft with player evaluation and, 87–88
   organizational inefficiencies highlighted by, 65
   Pujols' decline shown with, 171
   rapid acceptance of, 64
   shrinking advantage of, 260–61
   St. Louis Cardinals' gradual implementation of, 89, 96
   St. Louis Cardinals history with, 8
   St. Louis Cardinals marrying scouts with, 97–99, 111
   St. Louis Cardinals revamped with, 6
   Tendu analysis and, 81
   Vuch's expertise in, 156
Anderson, Sparky, 28
Angelos, Peter, 48
Anheuser-Busch (A-B), 49–50
Ankiel, Rick, 51–52, 79
Antinoja, Ron, 81
Antonetti, Chris, 130–31
Arango, Fernando, 198, 205, 208, 210–16, 221
arbitration, salary, 54
Arizona Diamondbacks, 258

Bacon, Francis, 55
Baker, Corey
   on Cardinals farm system continuity, 192
   on Cardinals farm system grooming personnel, 239
   Cardinals farm system's competitiveness and, 249–50
   Double-A promotion of, 248
   draft of, 178–80
   family supporting, 193, 250
   goals and aspirations of, 251–52
   on Greenwood's improbable success, 251
   LaRocque on potential of, 251
   Molina catching, 248–49
   skills and challenges facing, 191

Index

Baker (*continued*)
   Tuivailala helped by, 194
   on Tuivailala's promotion, 243
   on working through struggles, 192–93, 250
Ball, Phil, 13
Baltimore Orioles, 8, 28, 48–49
Bando, Sal, 116
Barrett, Charlie, 13–16
Baseball America Prospect Handbook, 150
Baseball Prospectus, 11, 149–50
Beane, Billy, 55, 142, 263
Bench, Johnny, 46
Big Red Machine, 8
Bilardello, Dann, 180, 192–93
Blades, Ray, 16
Blood, Matt, 231–32
Bogard, Dick, 157
Boggs, Mitchell, 162
Boras, Scott, 52
Bottomley, Jim, 16
Bower, Joseph L., 41
Bowman, Bob, 81
Boyer, Ken, 21–22
Boyles, Ty, 198–200, 214–17, 221, 227
Breadon, Sam, 14, 49
Broeg, Bob, 271
Brush, John T., 12
Bush, George H. W., 48
Bush, George W., 47–48
Butler, Keith, 145

Carbo, Bernie, 46
"Cardinal Idea," 13
Cardinals fans, 2–3, 64, 185–88
Cardinals farm system
   Baker and competitiveness of, 249–50
   Baker on continuity in, 192
   Baker on personnel groomed in, 239
   clear expectations in, 176–77
   continuity within, 192, 242
   depth and talent of, 190
   DeWitt, Bill, Sr., as director of, 14–15
   early success of, 16
   innovation of, 7
   Kissell signed into, 19–20
   longevity of initial, 17
   new players and introduction to, 234
   optimism within, 251
   players learning from each other in, 177–78, 194
   Poncedeleon's expectations and goals with, 235–36
   position shifts in, 182
   Rickey and creation of, 12–17
   success of, 3
   Wacha's ascension in, 171–72
Cardinals Way
   communication and benefits of, 255
   disdain for, 2–3, 11
   Kissell's impact on, 39–40
   Matheny on meaning of, 2
   modesty of, 4, 261–62
   origin of, 3
   Rickey's importance to, 7
   tradition and building of, 7–9
Carleton, Russell, 11
Carpenter, Matt, 144–46, 187
CBA. *See* collective bargaining agreement
Chass, Murray, 159–60
Chicago Cubs, 57
Chicago White Sox, 104, 271
Cincinnati Reds, 8, 28, 46–48, 159–60, 257–58
collective bargaining agreement (CBA), 53–54
college players, drafting high school players or, 75–76
Colorado Rockies, 127
Correa, Chris, 4, 7, 111, 142–43, 228
   hacking scandal and firing of, 263, 267
   Houston Astros not focus of, 262–63
   on *Moneyball* being boastful, 261
Craig, Allen, 96–97, 113, 159, 162–63, 187
Crane, Jim, 164
Cressey, Eric, 95
Cruz, Tony, 140
Cunningham, Joe, 155–56

Dale, Francis, 46
Davis, Paul, 177, 220–21
Dean, Dizzy, 19
DeJohn, Mark, 36, 94, 114, 236–37
DeLorenzo, Jordan, 215–16
DePodesta, Paul, 84
Descalso, Daniel, 159, 162, 186
Devine, Bing, 27
DeWitt, Bill, III, 50, 185, 270–71
DeWitt, Bill, Jr., 4, 7–8, 14, 69–70
   Baltimore Orioles ownership pursuit of, 48–49
   baseball acumen of, 86
   childhood of, 42–44
   Cincinnati Reds job and responsibilities of, 46–47
   Cincinnati Reds ownership pursued by, 47–48
   college degrees of, 44
   college policy paper of, 41, 44–46
   draft experience of, 223–25
   draft of 2004 mistakes and, 74–76

Index

draft strategy of, 45, 51–53
financial recommendations of, 45–46
on free agency valuations, 151–52
on future of franchise, 273–74
on hacking scandal, 269
hiring strategies of, 60–61
on Holliday acquisition, 151
investment business success of, 47
Jocketty's firing and criticism on, 121–22
Kantrovitz on vision of, 85–86
on legacy, 60, 271
on losing Luhnow, 166
Luhnow discussing general manager position with, 131
Luhnow supported by, 72, 85–86
on Luhnow's role, 60–63
minority ownership positions of, 48
Mozeliak strengthening relationship with, 136–37
on Mozeliak's appointment as, 134
on need for outside perspective, 57
on opening day, 185
on organizational unity, 120–21
on player development, 6, 41, 44–46, 51, 61
process trusted over results by, 76–77
on rebuilding baseball operations department, 268
Rickey's influence on, 42
salary arbitration strategy of, 54
St. Louis Browns uniform of, 42–43
St. Louis Cardinals ownership acquired by, 50–51
St. Louis Cardinals success and new direction from, 59–62
Texas Rangers and financial role of, 48–49
2011 World Series victory validating, 161–63
DeWitt, Bill, Sr., 5, 7, 13, 41–42, 271
as Cardinals farm system director, 14–15
draft success of, 46
as New York Yankees assistant general manager, 43
nomadic career of, 44
Rickey supporting education of, 16–17
Rickey's model followed by, 43–44
Rickey's relationship with, 14–15
as treasurer, 17
Diggins, Ben, 53
DiMaggio, Joe, 20
DiPuglia, Johnny, 109
Douthit, Taylor, 16
draft
 of Ankiel by DeWitt, Bill, Jr., 51–52
 of Baker, 178–80

Boyles' success in 2014, 227
college players compared to high school players in, 75–76
delay in benefits from, 143
DeWitt, Bill, Jr., and mistakes of 2004, 74–76
DeWitt, Bill, Jr.'s, experience with, 223–25
DeWitt, Bill, Jr.'s, strategy for, 45, 51–53
DeWitt, Bill, Sr.'s, success with, 46
of Gomber, 230
Gonzalez's disappointments with, 231
Gonzalez's preparation for, 198
of Kantrovitz, 79
Kantrovitz feeling pressure on, 169–70
Kantrovitz on Gonzales as target for, 173–74
Kantrovitz's activities and behavior during 2014, 226–28
Kantrovitz's philosophy and goals for, 199–200
Kantrovitz's preparation for 2014, 197–200, 229
LaRocque on second through seventh rounds of, 228, 229
LaRocque's philosophy following, 227
Luhnow and mistakes of 2004, 74–76
Luhnow's responsibilities with, 88
Luhnow's strategies for, 90
Luhnow's success with 2009, 143–45
Mejdal preparing analytics for player evaluation for, 87–88
Mejdal's confidence and insecurities with, 88
Mejdal's philosophy on, 100
Moneyball and assumptions with, 75
Mozeliak and mistakes of 2004, 74–76
Mozeliak comparing approaches to 2004 and 2005, 88–89
Mozeliak's preparation for 2014, 223–24
Mozeliak's schedule and activities during 2014, 225–28
psychological considerations for, 202–3
regulations for signing bonuses in, 201
scouts and strategies for, 90
scouts evaluated by "shadow draft," 98
of Siegrist, 139
St. Louis Cardinals value system for, 201–2
STOUT system utilized for, 120, 138, 198–99
of Thompson, 231–32
of Tuivailala, 181
of Turco, 30
Turco confused by Luhnow's philosophy for, 99–100
of Wacha, 171, 173
Drellich, Evan, 258–59
Drew, J. D., 52–53, 69–70

Index

Duncan, Dave, 85–86, 117
Dykstra, Lenny, 207

Eckstein, David, 207–8
Edmonds, Dave, 155
Edmonds, Jim, 53
Elias, Mike, 265
Ellenbogen, Mark, 198
Epstein, Theo, 64

fantasy baseball, Luhnow and, 57, 68, 107
farm systems, 15, 99, 180–81. *See also* Cardinals farm system; player development
Fick, Chuck, 101
Flaherty, Jack, 228
Forst, David, 84
Fox Sports Midwest, 272–73
free agency, 151–53, 156, 170–71
Frey, Nick, 177
fundamentals, 28–29, 114–15

Gaedel, Eddie, 42–43
García, Jaime, 162
Garciaparra, Michael, 189, 228
Gebhard, Bob, 70
Gibson, Bob, 155, 186
Giles, Warren, 42
Girsch, Michael, 8, 137–38
Gomber, Austin, 211–14, 221–22, 230, 238
Gonzales, Marco, 145, 173–74, 178
Gonzalez, Charlie, 6, 102
  Arango debating Gomber with, 211–14
  on background as strength, 110
  background of, 103–4
  business ventures of, 109
  as coach, 107, 110
  DiPuglia working with, 109
  on draft disappointments, 231
  draft preparation of, 198
  on finding his career path, 106–7
  "gut feels" of, 209–11
  on importance of player confidence, 217
  Kantrovitz on personality skills of, 104
  Kantrovitz on scouting attributes of, 111–12
  Luhnow hiring, 264–66
  Luhnow on hiring, 103, 111
  Pearce evaluated by, 209–10
  physical appearance of, 219
  player list presentation of, 202–14
  Poncedeleon evaluated by, 222, 233
  scout training and personal education of, 108–9
  on scouting of any sport, 110–11
  Seferina evaluated by, 204–6
  on Siegrist draft, 139
  surfing passion and trips of, 105–6
  teased by colleagues, 214, 218–19
  travel experience of, 110
Goold, Derrick, 175, 244, 272–73
Greene, Tyler, 89
Greenwood, Nick, 251

hacking scandal, 4
  accusations of, 262–63
  Correa's firing and, 263, 267
  DeWitt, Bill, Jr., on, 269
  Luhnow on, 268–69
  Mozeliak's unwavering analytics approach in face of, 267–68
Hafey, Chick, 16
Hahn, Rick, 84, 130–31
Hancock, Josh, 255
Hart, John, 229
Hedges, Robert Lee, 12–13
Hernandez, Keith, 29
Herzog, Whitey, 186
Heyward, Jason, 257
high school players, drafting college players or, 75–76
Hoke, Travis, 8
Holliday, Matt, 150–53
House, Tom, 94
Houston Astros, 164–66, 169, 177. *See also* hacking scandal
  Correa not focused on, 262–63
  Luhnow and new success of, 258–60
  St. Louis Cardinals' personnel poached by, 264–65
Hughes, Phil, 75–76
Hutchinson, Chad, 52–53

injury prevention, pitching mechanics and, 92, 94
internal book, St. Louis Cardinals creating, 11–12
international scouting, 72–73, 115, 138. *See also* scouts

James, Bill, 82, 156
Jay, John, 159, 162, 186
Jocketty, Walt, 53, 58, 64–65, 256
  analytics finally incorporated by, 257–58
  analytics hesitations of, 59, 67–68, 117
  Chass defending, 160
  with Cincinnati Reds, 159–60, 257–58
  firing of, 121–23
  Luhnow complaints expressed by, 112–13
  Luhnow undermining, 70–71

on Luhnow's new methods, 66
Luhnow's style conflicting with, 118–20
Mozeliak mentored by, 129
Mozeliak recommend for general manager by, 133–34
Mozeliak recruited by, 127–28
success of, 118
John, Tommy, 91
Jorgensen, Mike, 51

Kaminsky, Rob, 173–74, 178
Kantrovitz, Dan, 4, 6, 60, 87, 208–9, 229
on analytics and Craig, 96–97
college injury of, 78–79
on DeWitt, Bill, Jr.'s, vision, 85–86
draft day 2014 activities and behavior of, 226–28
draft expectations and pressure on, 169–70
draft of 2014 preparation of, 197–200, 229
draft philosophy and goals of, 199–200
drafting of, 79
end of on-field career of, 79–80
on excitement of organization's new direction, 85
front office ascension of, 80–81
on Garciaparra's exclusive information, 189
on Gonzales as draft target, 173–74
on Gonzalez's personality skills, 104
on Gonzalez's scouting attributes, 111–12
Harvard education of, 140–41
on importance of player confidence, 216–17
on leaving St. Louis Cardinals, 264
Lehman Brothers job of, 80
Luhnow on continuing education of, 141
Luhnow pursuing, 168
Luhnow training, 81–82
Luhnow's departure and success of, 262
Mejdal's personality and goals compared to, 83
Mozeliak hiring, 81
Oakland Athletics hiring, 142, 263–64
Poncedeleon and confidence of, 232
on pre-draft combine, 220, 223
Redbirdog system created by, 140
signing strategies of, 230
St. Louis Cardinals and childhood of, 77–78
on St. Louis Cardinals culture, 142
St. Louis Cardinals return of, 167–69
Taveras and expectations of, 196–97
on Wacha draft, 171, 173
on Wick's potential, 190–91
Kelly, Carson, 173
Kennedy, Adam, 51
Kennedy, Terry, 32

Kerlan, Robert, 92
Kern, Jay, 55–57, 62–64
Kershaw, Clayton, 145
Kidwell, Tommy, 29, 38–39
Kissell, George, 3, 5, 7, 17, 115
Boyer instructed by, 21–22
Cardinals farm system signing, 19–20
Cardinals Way and impact of, 39–40
childhood and upbringing of, 19
consistency of, 25
family's importance to, 34–35
fundamentals mastery of, 28–29
imitations of, 31
on La Russa's staff, 35, 37
language of, 38, 40
legacy of, 18–19, 28–29, 32, 39–40
Leyland fishing with, 33
Luhnow on new ideas and openness of, 86–87
major league playing opportunity declined by, 21
in major leagues, 28–29
managers' syllabus of, 25
McEwing instructed and influenced by, 37–39
minor league player career of, 20
Pendleton trained by, 32
perfection of, 37
player development beliefs of, 34
as player-manager, 20–21
praise for, 22, 24–25, 28–29, 32, 35–36
religion's importance to, 34
Rickey impressed by, 23
on Rickey's presence and approach, 24
Schoendienst collaborating with, 27
Shannon instructed by, 25–27
St. Louis Cardinals and loyalty of, 29–30
switch-hitter drill of, 35
Turco and impact of, 36–37
Turco instructed and supported by, 30–32
work ethic of, 31
Kittle, Hub, 115
Kopech, Michael, 228
Koufax, Sandy, 96

La Russa, Tony, 2, 85–86, 117, 186
Arizona Diamondbacks hiring, 258
Kissell on staff of, 35, 37
Luhnow complimented by, 162
Luhnow's first meeting with, 58–59
Mozeliak's style conflicting with, 135–36
Rasmus conflict with, 143
Labor Relations Department (LRD), 224
Lacy, Devante, 177–78
Lambert, Chris, 75–76

Index

LaRocque, Gary, 4
- on Baker's potential, 251
- player and coach background of, 156–58
- on player development and league placement, 230
- player development benchmarks of, 178
- post-draft philosophy of, 227
- as scouting director, 158–59
- on second through seventh rounds of draft, 228, 229
- on Tuivailala reaching benchmarks, 240–41, 244
- Vuch paired with, 154–55

Lee, Travis, 52

Leveque, Tim, 95, 114, 181, 236, 238
- on player development goals, 183
- player development observation strategies of, 237

Leyland, Jim, 33

Lichtman, Mitchel, 68

Loria, Jeff, 48

Los Angeles Dodgers, 115–16, 157–58

Lowrie, Jed, 89, 96

LRD. *See* Labor Relations Department

Luhnow, Jeff, 4–6, 176, 256
- advisory board created by, 68
- analytics mandate of, 66–67
- business consultant background of, 55–56, 61–62
- Chicago Cubs studied by, 57
- on commitments to former colleagues, 265
- DeWitt, Bill, Jr., discussing general manager potential of, 131
- DeWitt, Bill, Jr., on losing, 166
- DeWitt, Bill, Jr., on role of, 60–63
- DeWitt, Bill, Jr., supporting, 72, 85–86
- as director of player development, 114
- draft of 2004 mistakes and, 74–76
- draft of 2009 success of, 143–45
- draft responsibilities of, 88
- draft strategies of, 90
- Drew trade evaluated by, 69–70
- early baseball interest of, 56–57
- evaluating success of, 149–50
- expectations and criticism with hire of, 64
- fantasy baseball and, 57, 68, 107
- Florida focus of, 102–3
- on fundamentals consistency, 114–15
- Gonzalez hired by, 264–66
- on Gonzalez hiring, 103, 111
- on hacking scandal, 268–69
- hiring of, 7–8, 60
- as Houston Astros general manager, 164–65, 169
- Houston Astros' new success with, 258–60
- on importance of good instructors, 114–15
- on importance of on-field immersion, 165
- innovations of, 165
- international scouting overhauled by, 72–73, 115
- Jocketty and complaints with, 112–13
- Jocketty on new methods of, 66
- Jocketty undermined by, 70–71
- Jocketty's style conflicting with, 118–20
- Kantrovitz pursued by, 168
- Kantrovitz trained by, 81–82
- on Kantrovitz's continuing education, 141
- Kantrovitz's success after departure of, 262
- Kern recruiting, 55–57
- on Kissell's openness to new ideas, 86–87
- La Russa complimenting, 162
- La Russa's first meeting with, 58–59
- at McKinsey and Co., 61
- Mejdal on collaboration with, 166–67
- *Moneyball* read by, 56
- Mozeliak on new system of, 67
- Mozeliak on office tensions and, 71
- Mozeliak on skepticism with hire of, 64–65, 67
- Mozeliak supported for general manager by, 132–34
- Mozeliak's views and responsibilities aligning with, 136–37
- new scouts found by process of, 101–2
- organizational inefficiencies highlighted by, 65
- on patience and success, 260
- player development challenges of, 113
- scout review philosophy of, 98–99
- scouting director promotion of, 76
- scouting lists expanded by, 99–100
- scouts accommodated by, 266
- on Siegrist draft, 139
- St. Louis Cardinals and early resentment of, 66–67
- St. Louis Cardinals presentation of, 58
- Strom supporting, 95–96
- Suppan signing and influence of, 69
- thick skin of, 63–64
- on Tuivailala and position choices, 181–82
- Turco confused by draft philosophy of, 99–100
- 2011 World Series victory validating, 161–63
- unorthodox personnel hired by, 77
- vice president of baseball development responsibilities of, 62–63

Lynn, Lance, 54, 138, 162, 186

288

Index

Mabry, John, 31, 35
MacPhail, Larry, 17
MacPhail, Lee, 42
Madden, Bill, 121–22, 132
Maness, Seth, 145
Manfred, Rob, 270
Manno, Bruce, 113–14, 117
Marmol, Oliver, 38, 120, 189
   on coaching decision, 239
   family of, 240
   in-game pressure taught by, 239–40
   new players welcomed by, 234
   on Wick's development, 245
Maroth, Mike, 76
Martin, Pepper, 19
Martínez, Carlos, 186, 257
   concerns with, 149
   major league success of, 148
   name discrepancy problems with, 146–47
   Slater evaluating, 147–49
   Slater on signing, 146–47
Martínez, Pedro, 99, 147–48
Martinez, Tino, 156
Matheny, Mike, 8–9, 38
   on Cardinals Way meaning, 2
   personality and charm of, 1
   physical appearance of, 1
   Taveras and expectations of, 196
   on Taveras' minor league success, 175
McCormack, John, 211
McCourt, Frank, 115–16
McEwing, Joe, 37–39
McGraw, John, 15
McGraw, Tug, 87, 126
McKinney, Ian, 238
McKinsey and Co., 61, 63–64
McLaughlin, Jim, 45
McRae, Hal, 46
Medwick, Joe, 19
Megill, Trevor, 230
Meier, J. Dale, 22
Mejdal, Sig, 4, 77, 111, 258
   on analytics methodologies, 96
   baseball and education of, 82
   draft confidence and insecurities of, 88
   draft philosophy of, 100
   draft preparation with analytics for player evaluation of, 87–88
   employment in baseball efforts of, 84
   with Houston Astros, 166
   innovations of, 165
   Kantrovitz's personality and goals compared to, 83
   on leaving St. Louis Cardinals, 167
   Lowrie favored in model of, 89, 96
   on Luhnow collaboration, 166–67
   on Mozeliak's capabilities as general manager, 133
   on organizational conflict, 121
   organizational inefficiencies highlighted by, 65
   on press interactions, 83
   scout lists combined by, 100
   scouts evaluated by "shadow draft" of, 98
   St. Louis Cardinals hiring, 84
   on system transparency, 261
   2011 World Series victory validating, 161–63
   work enjoyed by, 82–83
Mejia, Alex, 196
Melvin, Bob, 81
Mercado, Oscar, 139–40
Miklasz, Bernie, 132
Miller, Dyar, 95, 117, 147
Miller, Shelby, 145, 186
Mize, Johnny, 19
Molina, Yadier, 79, 112, 162, 187, 248–49
Moneyball (Lewis), 55, 142
   Correa on boastful attitude of, 261
   draft assumptions based on, 75
   Luhnow reading, 56
   myths on scouts and misreading of, 97
Moore, Terry, 19
Morales, Andrew, 228–29
Moran, Sean, 174
Morris, Matt, 69
Motte, Jason, 162, 244
Mozeliak, John, 1, 4–5, 52, 78
   as assistant general manager, 76, 90–91
   childhood baseball memories of, 125–27
   with Colorado Rockies, 127
   DeWitt, Bill, Jr., on general manager appointment of, 134
   DeWitt, Bill, Jr.'s, relationship strengthened with, 136–37
   draft day 2014 schedule and activities of, 225–28
   on draft of 2004 and 2005 comparisons, 88–89
   draft of 2004 mistakes and, 74–76
   draft of 2014 preparation of, 223–24
   on future of St. Louis Cardinals, 269–70
   general manager competition facing, 130–31
   grandfather influencing, 126
   hacking scandal and unwavering analytics approach of, 267–68
   on human element in system, 266–67
   Jocketty mentoring, 129
   Jocketty recommending, for general manager, 133–34

Index

Mozeliak (*continued*)
  Jocketty recruiting, 127–28
  on Jocketty's firing, 123
  Kantrovitz hired by, 81
  La Russa's style conflicting with, 135–36
  on Latin American player development changes, 255
  on Luhnow and office tensions, 71
  Luhnow supporting general manager bid of, 132–34
  on Luhnow's hire and skepticism, 64–65, 67
  on Luhnow's new system, 67
  Luhnow's views and responsibilities aligning with, 136
  Mejdal on general manager capabilities of, 133
  negotiation skills learned by, 129
  on organizational change and 2007 on-field results, 121
  organizational support for, 131–32, 135
  political skills of, 129–30, 133
  press supporting, 132
  on replacing employees, 268
  Roosevelt as uniter compared to, 124–25
  scouting and player development separated by, 154
  as scouting director, 128–29
  on shrinking advantage of analytics, 260–61
  St. Louis Cardinals unified under, 125
  on standards for players, 252–53
  on Taveras' death, 253–55
  2011 World Series victory validating, 161–63
Musial, Stan, 170

New York Mets, 126, 158–59
New York Yankees, 4, 43
Nix, Jacob, 259
Norris, Bud, 259
Nyman, Paul, 92–94

Oakland Athletics, 142, 169, 263–64
Ocampo, Oz, 115, 264
O'Keefe, Brian, 231
Oriole Way, 8
Ortiz, Ramon ("Smoky"), 188, 246–47

Pearce, Matt, 209–10, 233
Pendleton, Terry, 32
Percival, Troy, 54
Pérez, Audry, 138
Pérez, Chris, 120, 143
personality-based scouting, 234
Pham, Tommy, 96, 190
Philadelphia A's, 8

Piazza, Mike, 159–60
Piscotty, Stephen, 173
pitching mechanics, 85
  Strom on injury prevention and, 92, 94
  Strom on Wainwright and, 118
  Strom's philosophy shift on, 93
  Strom's principles for, 95
  of Tuivailala, 195–96, 243
  Witte assisting new system for, 87
player development. *See also* Cardinals farm system; farm systems
  Barrett's tactics with, 15–16
  DeJohn's observations on, 236
  DeJohn's strategies for assistance and, 236–37
  DeWitt, Bill, Jr., on, 6, 41, 44–46, 51, 61
  international, 72–73, 115, 138
  Kissell's belief in, 34
  LaRocque on league placement and, 230
  LaRocque's benchmarks for, 178
  Leveque's observation strategies with, 237
  Luhnow as director of, 114
  Luhnow's challenges with, 113
  Mozeliak on new design for Latin American, 255
  Mozeliak separating scouting from, 154
  psychological considerations for, 202–3
  St. Louis Cardinals inventing, 11–12
  Vuch as assistant in, 156
Poncedeleon, Daniel
  Cardinals farm system expectations and goals of, 235–36
  confidence and competitiveness of, 235
  development and improvements of, 246
  Gonzalez evaluating, 222, 233
  Kantrovitz's confidence in, 232
  signing of, 233
pre-draft combine, 219–23
professionalism, St. Louis Cardinals and, 234–35
psychological considerations, for draft, 202–3
Pujols, Albert, 99, 162
  analytics showing decline of, 171
  free agency departure of, 170–71
  Musial compared to, 170
  payoff in letting go of, 170–71
  success of, 169–70
  2013 struggles of, 172

Ramsey, James, 183–85
Rapp, Vernon, 29
Rasmus, Colby, 135, 143, 159
Redbirdog system, 140
Rehm, Flint, 16
religion, Kissell and importance of, 34

Index

Reynolds, DeWitt and Co., 47
Reynolds, Mercer, 47
Richards, Paul, 29
Rickey, Branch, 3, 5
  Cardinals farm system created by, 12–17
  Cardinals Way importance of, 7
  DeWitt, Bill, Jr., and influence of, 42
  DeWitt, Bill, Sr., following model of, 43–44
  DeWitt, Bill, Sr.'s, education supported by, 16–17
  DeWitt, Bill, Sr.'s, relationship with, 14–15
  firing of, 9
  Kissell impressing, 23
  Kissell on presence and approach of, 24
  legacy of, 12, 41
  organizational foundation built by, 7–8
  Schoendienst on system established by, 23
Riggleman, Jim, 33
Ritter, Jerry, 50
Rivera, Chris, 180–81, 188–89, 237–38, 248
Rivera, Mariano, 4
Robinson, Shane, 113
Rodriguez, Moises, 146
Roosevelt, Franklin Delano, 124–25
Rose, Pete, 207
Rosenthal, Trevor, 144–45, 186, 244

sabermetrics, 82
Saigh, Fred, 49
salary arbitration, 54
Salas, Fernando, 162
Sandberg, Ryne, 32
Scanio, 176–77
Schied, Jeremy, 228
Schlueter, Dick, 21
Schmidt, Michael S., 262–63
Schoendienst, Red, 7, 18, 23, 26–27, 184
Schott, Marge, 47–48
Schweppe, Bill, 157–58
scouts. *See also* international scouting
  challenges and mistakes of, 148
  criteria for hiring, 102
  draft strategies with, 90
  farm systems and importance of, 99
  Gonzalez on any sport and, 110–11
  Gonzalez personally learning and training to be, 108–9
  Internet for finding, 101–2
  Kantrovitz on Gonzalez's attributes for, 111–12
  Luhnow accommodating, 266
  Luhnow expanding lists of, 99–100
  Luhnow overhauling program of international, 72–73, 115
  Luhnow's philosophy in reviewing, 98–99
  Luhnow's process for finding new, 101–2
  Mejdal combining lists from, 100
  Moneyball misreadings and myths on, 97
  Mozeliak separating player development from, 154
  personalities evaluated by, 203–4
  personality-based methods for, 234
  "shadow draft" evaluating, 98
  Slater on hybrid approach of, 115–16
  St. Louis Cardinals marrying analytics with, 97–99, 111
  STOUT system incorporating reports from, 266
  talent and signing factors investigated by, 200–201
Scully, Vin, 145
Seferina, Darren, 204–6, 230
"shadow draft," of Mejdal, 98
Shandler, Ron, 68
Shannon, Mike, 11, 18, 25–27, 185
Sheridan, John B., 15
Shields, James, 258
Shildt, Mike, 36, 159, 242
Siegrist, Kevin, 139–40
signing bonuses, draft regulations for, 201
Slater, Matt, 213, 227
  Holliday evaluated by, 152–53
  hybrid scouting approach of, 115–16
  international scouting success of, 138
  Martínez, Carlos, evaluated by, 147–49
  on Martínez, Carlos, signing, 146–47
  St. Louis Cardinals supporting education of, 116–17
Smith, Al, 124–25
Smith, Bud, 99
Smith, Roger, 173
Society for American Baseball Research, 82
Sohn, Andrew, 230
Spence, Wally, 105
St. Louis Browns, 12–13, 42–43, 186
St. Louis Cardinals. *See also* Cardinals fans; Cardinals Way
  analytics and scouts utilized together by, 97–99, 111
  analytics gradually implemented by, 89, 96
  analytics history of, 8
  analytics revamping, 6
  Baseball Prospectus ranking organization of, 149–50
  continued success of, 2–4
  DeWitt, Bill, Jr.'s, acquiring ownership of, 50–51

Index

St. Louis Cardinals (*continued*)
- DeWitt, Bill, Jr.'s, new direction despite success of, 59–62
- draft value system of, 201–2
- dual strategies of, 117, 120
- Fox Sports Midwest television deal with, 272–73
- free agency and retention success of, 151, 153
- future of, 271–74
- hacking scandal and, 4
- Houston Astros poaching personnel from, 264–65
- innovation of, 5, 87
- intelligence in organization of, 6
- internal book created by, 11–12
- Kantrovitz on culture of, 142
- Kantrovitz on leaving, 264
- Kantrovitz return to, 167–69
- Kantrovitz's childhood love of, 77–78
- Kissell's loyalty to, 29–30
- Luhnow and early resentment of most in, 66–67
- Luhnow's presentation to, 58
- Mejdal hired by, 84
- Mejdal on leaving, 167
- modesty of, 4, 261–62
- Mozeliak on future of, 269–70
- Mozeliak unifying, 125
- opening day excitement for, 185–87
- ownership changes of, 49
- ownership succession plan for, 271–72
- player development created by, 11–12
- Slater's education supported by, 116–17
- standards of, 252–53
- Strom hired by, 94
- Thompson on professionalism and, 234–35
- tradition and expectations for success of, 64

State College Spikes, 234
Steverson, Todd, 39
Stewart, Dave, 258
STOUT system, 120, 138, 143, 198–99, 266
Strom, Brent, 114, 117, 265
- family responsibilities of, 93
- with Houston Astros, 177
- Luhnow supporting, 95–96
- Nyman influencing, 92–94
- as pitching coach and instructor, 92
- on pitching mechanics and injury prevention, 92, 94
- pitching mechanics and training principles of, 95
- pitching mechanics philosophy shift of, 93
- resistance to methods of, 94–95
- St. Louis Cardinals hiring, 94
- Tommy John surgery of, 91–92
- on tradition in baseball, 91, 95
- on Wainwright's pitching mechanics, 118

Strong, Jamal, 171, 198
Suppan, Jeff, 69
Swanson, Matt, 173
switch-hitter drill, of Kissell, 35

Taveras, Oscar, 138
- batting practice audience of, 183–84
- big league call up of, 196–97
- confidence of, 184–85
- death of, 253–54
- expectations for, 176
- Kantrovitz's expectations with, 196–97
- Matheny's expectations for, 196
- memorials to, 257
- minor league success of, 175, 196
- organization focusing on, 183
- rookie struggles of, 252
- work ethic and injuries of, 175–76

television, baseball revenue from, 44, 272–73
Tendu analysis, 81
Texas Rangers, 48–49
Theriot, Ryan, 161–62
Thomas, Darren, 33
Thomas, Lee, 33, 156
Thompson, Nick
- college career of, 234
- draft of, 231–32
- first at bat of, 238
- goals of, 235
- improvement and development of, 247
- re-tooling swing of, 246–47
- on St. Louis Cardinals and professionalism, 234–35
- on success at all levels, 247–48

Tommy John surgery, 91–92, 118, 145
Toronto Blue Jays, 235
Torre, Joe, 28, 39
tradition, 7–9, 64, 91, 95
Tuivailala, Sam
- Baker helping, 194
- Baker on promotion of, 243
- big league promotion of, 244
- on Double-A promotion, 241–42
- draft of, 181
- family excitement with promotion of, 242
- on getting comfortable pitching, 182–83, 196
- improvements made by, 194–95

Index

LaRocque on benchmarks reached by, 240–41, 244
Luhnow on position choices with, 181–82
minor league challenges of, 182
pitch speeds of, 242
on pitching in front of Double-A crowds, 243
pitching mechanics of, 195–96, 243
Triple-A promotion of, 244
Turco, Steve, 39, 102–3, 114, 172, 231
  career longevity of, 188
  coaching career of, 36
  coaching opportunity for, 33–34
  drafting of, 30
  Kissell instructing and supporting, 30–32
  Kissell's impact on, 36–37
  Luhnow's draft philosophy confusing, 99–100
  on player flaws, 182
  Winningham evaluated by, 220–21

Valentine, Bobby, 35
Van Slyke, Andy, 32
Veeck, Bill, 42, 271
Verducci, Tom, 2
Villa Mella academy, 138, 147
Viña, Fernando, 38
Vuch, John, 67, 117, 133, 175–76
  analytics expertise of, 156
  childhood baseball memories of, 155
  LaRocque paired with, 154–55

Martinez, Tino, and free agency evaluation of, 156
  as player development assistant, 156

Wacha, Michael
  on Cardinals fans' enthusiasm, 187
  Cardinals farm system ascension of, 171–72
  draft of, 171, 173
  success in first season of, 172
Wainwright, Adam, 70, 118, 187
Warner, Ron ("Pop"), 36
Weaver, Earl, 22, 28–29
Weaver, Luke, 227–28
Weiss, George, 43
Whiten, Mark, 99
Wick, Rowan, 182
  confidence gained by, 244–45
  hitting focus of, 245–46
  Kantrovitz on potential of, 190–91
  Marmol on development of, 245
  minor league success of, 237–39
  pitching transition of, 246
  struggles of, 190
Williams, Ronnie, 228
Williams, Ted, 20
Winningham, Dash, 220–21, 231
Witte, Mike, 77, 87, 91
World War II, 20

Zeller, Bart, 24–25

THE COMPELLING STORY OF THE SUCCESS OF THE CARDINALS' HISTORY OF ACHIEVEMENT

The St. Louis Cardinals have experienced the kind of success that is rare in baseball. Regarded by many as the premier organization in Major League Baseball, they not only win but do so with an apparently bottomless pool of talent, one that is mostly homegrown.

Despite years of phenomenal achievements, including going to the World Series in 2004 and again in 2006, the Cardinals reinvented themselves using the "Cardinal Way," a term that has come to represent many things to fans, media, and other organizations, from an ironclad code of conduct to the team's cutting-edge use of statistics, and analytics, and a farm system that has transformed baseball.

Baseball journalist Howard Megdal takes fans behind the scenes and off the field, interviewing dozens of key players within the Cardinals organization, including owner Bill DeWitt and the general manager, John Mozeliak. Megdal reveals how the players are assessed and groomed using an unrivaled player development system that has created a franchise that is the envy of the baseball world.

In the spirit of *Moneyball*, *The Cardinals Way* tells an in-depth, fascinating story about a consistently excellent franchise, the business of sports in the twenty-first century, and a team that has learned how to level the playing field, turning in season after successful season.

RACHEL MEGDAL

HOWARD MEGDAL writes for *Politico, New York* magazine, *USA Today, VICE Sports,* and many other publications. He lives in Rockland County, New York, with his wife, Rachel, and his two daughters, Mirabelle and Juliet.

JACKET DESIGN BY JAMES IACOBELLI

JACKET PHOTOGRAPHS:
FIELD © BLEND IMAGES / ALAMY STOCK PHOTO;
BASEBALL © RANPLETT / GETTY IMAGES;
BIRD © SHUTTERSTOCK

WWW.THOMASDUNNEBOOKS.COM
WWW.STMARTINS.COM

ST. MARTIN'S PRESS
175 FIFTH AVENUE, NEW YORK, N.Y. 10010

www.ingramcontent.com/pod-product-compliance
Lightning Source LLC
LaVergne TN
LVHW091709140525
811257LV00005B/24